Popular Culture in Everyday Life

An accessible and engaging introduction to the critical study of popular culture, which provides students with the tools they need to make sense of the popular culture that inundates their everyday lives.

This textbook centers on media ecology and equipment for living to introduce students to important theories and debates in the field. Each chapter engages an important facet of popular culture, ranging from the business of popular culture to communities, stories, and identities, to the simulation and sensation of pop culture. The text explains key terms and features contemporary case studies throughout, examining aspects such as memes and trends on social media, cancel culture, celebrities as influencers, gamification, "meta" pop culture, and personalized on-demand music. The book enables students to understand the complexity of power and influence, providing a better understanding of the ways pop culture is embedded in a wide range of everyday activities. Students are encouraged to reflect on how they consume and produce popular culture and understand how that shapes their sense of self and connections to others.

Essential reading for undergraduate and postgraduate students of media studies, communication studies, cultural studies, popular culture, and other related subjects.

Charles Soukup is Professor of Communication Studies at the University of Northern Colorado, where his work engages the social impacts of communication technology and media ecology. Soukup is the author of *Exploring Screen Culture via Apple's Mobile Devices: Life through the Looking Glass* (2016), and has published work on digital ethnography, representations of technology and pleasure in film, television and conspiracy, video games and masculinity, and fandom.

Christina R. Foust is Professor of Communication Studies at Metropolitan State University of Denver, where her work engages rhetoric, power, and social change in a variety of contexts, including social movements and popular culture. She is lead editor of *What Democracy Looks Like: The Rhetoric of Social Movements and Counterpublics* (2017), and author of *Transgression as a Mode of Resistance* (2010). Her recent work considers media ecology and memes in social movement.

Popular Culture in Everyday Life

A Critical Introduction

Charles Soukup and Christina R. Foust

Routledge
Taylor & Francis Group

NEW YORK AND LONDON

Designed cover image: © Getty Images

First published 2024
by Routledge
605 Third Avenue, New York, NY 10158

and by Routledge
4 Park Square, Milton Park, Abingdon, Oxon, OX14 4RN

Routledge is an imprint of the Taylor & Francis Group, an informa business

© 2024 Charles Soukup and Christina R. Foust

Library of Congress Cataloging-in-Publication Data
Names: Soukup, Charles, author. | Foust, Christina R., author.
Title: Popular culture in everyday life : a critical introduction /
Charles Soukup and Christina R. Foust.
Description: New York, NY : Routledge, 2024. | Includes bibliographical references and index.
Identifiers: LCCN 2023008672 (print) | LCCN 2023008673 (ebook) |
ISBN 9781032445939 (hardback) | ISBN 9781032430287 (paperback) |
ISBN 9781003372943 (ebook)
Subjects: LCSH: Popular culture. | Civilization, Modern—21st century.
Classification: LCC HM621 .S6455 2024 (print) | LCC HM621 (ebook) |
DDC 306—dc23/eng/20230413
LC record available at https://lccn.loc.gov/2023008672
LC ebook record available at https://lccn.loc.gov/2023008673

ISBN: 978-1-032-44593-9 (hbk)
ISBN: 978-1-032-43028-7 (pbk)
ISBN: 978-1-003-37294-3 (ebk)

DOI: 10.4324/9781003372943

Typeset in Sabon
by codeMantra

For R. and H.

Contents

Acknowledgments

We're grateful to our teachers and our students, who, over the years, have inspired us to check out new artists, albums, shows, films, memes, places, video games, etc., and who helped us work through the different perspectives that comprise this book. We're also grateful to our families, especially our parents and our kids, who have shown us encouragement and patience, who have shared the joy of popular culture with us. Special thanks to the College of Humanities and Social Sciences and Department of Communication Studies, at the University of Northern Colorado, which granted Charles a sabbatical leave in Fall of 2022 to support the writing of this book. Thanks to our research assistant, Rose, and our colleagues for offering their support throughout the process (with special thanks to Drs. John Rief and Raisa Alvarado for feedback on draft chapters).

1 Introducing popular culture in everyday life

Introduction

In the summer of 2022, *Stranger Things*, season four, seemed to dwarf all other popular culture events (including the new *Top Gun* and *Jurassic World* movies). While *Stranger Things* has been criticized as a pastiche of old movies, the new season leaned into the psychology of its characters, especially experiences with anxiety and depression. If you are unfamiliar with *Stranger Things*, the story centers around a group of tweens and teenagers in the town of Hawkins, Indiana, in the mid-1980s. The adolescent characters encounter supernatural forces that appear related to a mysterious government conspiracy. In season four, a monstrous force they name Vecna appears to target vulnerable characters struggling with anxiety and/or some form of trauma. In particular, Max, who is mourning her brother's death and expressing possible suicidal impulses, is attacked by Vecna, only to escape with the help of her favorite song by Kate Bush (see Figure 1.1), played by her friends on her Walkman.

Vecna is the antagonist in season four's storylines; but at a deeper level, the "monster" is adolescent experiences with mental illness and even traumatic memories or grieving. As one fan on Reddit expressed, "Yeah I really loved the way they tied Max's guarded-nature and her fear of her own angry and big feelings that arise in response to crappiness of the world around her into the way her depression and grief manifested this season" (iwritealright, 2022).

For the core audience of the show, season four was a home run. *Stranger Things*, already the centerpiece of Netflix's streaming catalogue, reached new heights of popularity, single-handedly reviving Netflix's lagging subscription numbers. Kate Bush, in a strange twist of fate, earned a Billboard Number One hit for a song that she had recorded 37 years ago, as "Running Up that Hill" was inescapable in the summer of 2022. It was as though Netflix, *Stranger Things*, and even Kate Bush had created lightning in a bottle, and for good reason. For fans of the show, watching

DOI: 10.4324/9781003372943-1

Figure 1.1 Scene from *Stranger Things*, season four.

characters overcome their struggles with their friends helped some viewers make sense of their own everyday life (in this case, mental health challenges), something we describe in this chapter as **equipment for living**. Another main character, Eleven, was severely bullied, mourned the disappearance of her adopted father, and struggled with angry outbursts. In simple terms, if Max or Eleven can find strength through the support of friends and family, I can too. If young characters of *Stranger Things* can reach some sort of stability amid chaos, then perhaps we can persevere in our own chaotic world.

To be sure, popular culture like *Stranger Things* is, well, popular, because it provides us with resources to make sense of, and navigate, collective challenges (and individual trauma). But that doesn't explain the whole story for why tens of millions of fans binged *Stranger Things*. Or why they stayed glued to their radio to sing along with a British indie rocker from the 1980s for the fifth time in one day. Disparate cultural forces intersected to create the unique sensation of *Stranger Things*, some of which have as much to do with economics and media, as they do with characters and song lyrics. Would *Stranger Things* season four have "blown up" were it not digitally streamed content? If somehow the Public Broadcasting System (PBS) had acquired rights to broadcast season four over the span of nine weeks, would it have been the same sensation of 2022? Would it have even been the same story with the same actors, etc.? As this thought experiment introduces, the business and media context in which popular culture emerges shapes it in important ways, a point which is clear through what we elaborate below is a **media ecology** perspective.

Popular Culture in Everyday Life introduces readers to tools to help them sort out the more just and mindful uses of pop culture from the more harmful ones. Popular culture, as we note in this chapter's first section, seems to be *everywhere*, all the time, whether it's a viral sensation (like

"Running Up that Hill"), a topic of text exchanges with friends (like *Stranger Things* perhaps was for you), or simply an easy diversion while waiting in line (seeing a magazine cover with Winona Ryder and Sadie Sink). But this ubiquitous presence is not merely entertainment. As we see below, in the second section, it both represents and creates reality: images of who "young people" are, like Max or Eleven, provide points of identification for who "young people" are and can be. We then return to elaborate on two important concepts in the study of popular culture, which help explain how people use it in everyday life: equipment for living and media ecology.

Popular culture: Defining a ubiquitous presence in our lives

Popular culture is now everywhere, all the time. Think about your typical day. Like most of us, you probably touch your phone when you wake up to see any social media posts, notifications, or "headlines" (usually associated with celebrities, sports, and pop culture "news") from overnight. Next, you might flip on Spotify or Netflix while you eat breakfast, shower, or work out. Then you likely turn on the radio or a podcast on your drive or bus ride to work or school. While at school and work, you likely fill any downtime with YouTube or TikTok videos and play background music while completing routine tasks. You probably unwind at the end of your day with a favorite TV show, some relaxing music, or a fantasy novel. Public spaces such as grocery stores, college campuses, restaurants, and airports are now filled with TV screens and pop music. This wasn't always the case. Before the 20th century, relatively little time was spent with popular culture. In the 20th century people would unwind with TV, radio, or popular novels at the end of the day, but this was largely confined to the home and a couple hours of "free time."

Popular culture is so ever-present that it becomes a kind of white noise, always there but hidden in plain sight. Only when the machinery of popular culture is disrupted do we even notice it all around us. In March 2022, for instance, the Academy Awards was just another routine event with scripted comments from celebrities, red carpet photo ops, etc. When Will Smith slapped host Chris Rock, his action suddenly interrupted the enormous machinery of film and celebrity self-promotion with something completely unexpected. The world almost seemed to stop spinning. *The Guardian* reported that there were 70 million views of "the slap" videos in a 24-hour period, breaking the YouTube record for views of any video on a single day (Ichimura, 2022). Netizens immediately unleashed memes, with social media and Internet commentary about the memes also pervasive for the few days following the Oscars. In a sense, the "natural order" was unsettled, because popular culture is now so much the natural order of things.

There are many academic definitions of popular culture, and most of them distinguish popular culture as a kind of middle ground between elitist (or "highbrow") art and smaller-scale folk traditions (see Storey, 2012). Reflecting on these sometimes competing approaches, we define **popular culture** as widely available products and experiences that regular people engage. Popular culture products and experiences are produced for the purpose of entertainment, though, as we will see, the intentions and consequences of engaging popular culture far exceed recreation and diversion. Popular culture is a kind of "Goldilocks" zone between highly distinctive art forms (such as opera and ballet) that first developed so that they could only be accessed by the wealthy and powerful; and folk traditions enjoyed by people who lived in the same geographic area, many of whom may have shared similar social identities. Such folk traditions weren't originally intended to earn a profit, or to be consumed on a large scale beyond the town or perhaps regional boundaries.

In sum, popular culture is *populist* rather than *elitist*, and *populist* rather than *folk culture*. To better appreciate the middle zone between folk and elite, let's consider food. The food many people eat is mass produced such as fast-food burgers or pre-packaged soups and frozen food. While we might not think of it as such, food advertising encourages us to think of eating as an entertainment experience representing consuming pizzas or soft drinks as "fun." Now, think about the foods that are not popular culture. Most obviously, the fine cuisine of fancy restaurants would be outside of popular culture—each meal is uniquely prepared for an elite consumer.

But also the traditional, homemade foods of your family (if you are lucky enough to have sustained these traditions) are, while for regular people, also uniquely prepared by each person (e.g., our grandmothers carefully guarded their secret pastry recipes from others in their small towns). These folk traditions, such as unique forms of dance, quilting, music, and food, are usually uniquely performed in each family or community. Of course, once your Italian or Mexican (or, in our cases, Czech or Dutch) traditions turn into canned tomato sauce or fast food tacos, you have crossed into the realm of popular culture. Similarly, when the "great" work of art, such as the *Mona Lisa*, is mass produced and printed on t-shirts or postcards, it is transformed into popular culture. In short, popular culture is mass produced, everyday forms of expression created for regular people, not elites. In this book, "popular" is best understood as populist (for an everyday person) not just hugely successful stuff like blockbuster movies or chart-topping pop songs. While not nearly as widely consumed as movies and TV, something like comic books or romance novels are still very much popular culture.

Distinguishing popular culture as populist (an expressive form designed for regular people, mass produced for economic gain) has a wide range of implications. Foremost, the idea that popular culture is populist also allows us to separate it from other forms of entertainment media, like "movies" or "music." Though many people use "pop culture" and entertainment media interchangeably, we do not consider them to be synonymous. Not all media are produced for the purposes of widespread consumption. As we elaborate in Chapter 2, popular culture has become widely available through the principles of mass production, where businesses create identical products (in large amounts) for the purposes of profit. Though many films can be considered popular culture, some are made exclusively for arthouse theaters, or to be screened in a museum for an elite audience. Likewise, some music is only performed in ornate concert halls for upper-class clientele. Additionally, not all popular culture arrives in the form of traditional entertainment media. Toys and food, for instance, are *material artifacts*, experienced immediately, in one's hands or enlisting one's body (see Chapter 8). Other pop culture **artifacts** (or distinct units of popular culture that can be sorted out from other units) are mediated, experienced via entertainment channels like television or the Internet.

For most of us, our everyday lives have become increasingly dominated by popular culture. Most of us, we assume, don't spend our free time like Frasier Crane at the opera or expensive restaurants; and for so many families, folk traditions have eroded or even vanished, replaced by popular culture. Consider holiday experiences now dominated by inescapable Mariah Carey songs, watching *Love Actually* or *Rudolph the Red-Nosed Reindeer*, shopping at Target, and the commodified, mass-produced "tradition" of Elf on the Shelf. We should study popular culture not only because it's everywhere around us, all the time; but also because it is a consequential presence in our lives.

The consequential presence of popular culture: Representing and creating reality

Popular culture, like other forms of communication, represents and creates reality. It does so in often subtle ways. And since we're often taught to simply "enjoy" (consume, uncritically) pop culture, we don't often see its effects or its potential to make life better or worse—not only for individuals or communities, but also for larger social groups (and perhaps even our culture as a whole). To offer another example of the power of popular culture to represent and create reality, let's look at the transformation of "the family" over the years. If we look at the TV family sitcom from the dawn of television to the present, it's clear that content creators have been responsive to the voices and experiences of viewers to some extent; but there is some distance to go in order for television families to represent a truly accurate (and just) reality.

Look at images from popular sitcoms in the 1950s and 1960s. The iconic *Leave It to Beaver* represents an "ideal" nuclear family in the US (see Figure 1.2), with a White man and woman, married, raising two boys. Young Theodore (aka "The Beaver") gets into mild trouble (particularly instigated by neighbor Eddie Haskell), while his doting mother and older brother keep him safe through "teachable" moments. *The Brady Bunch* introduced the potential of remarriage into the mix, with the well-known image of three girls and their mother blending with three boys and their father (see Figure 1.3). The kids face "typical" teen problems, and the show is a vehicle for pop culture stars like Davy Jones, who guest stars (in season three, episode 12), as oldest daughter Marcia promises to land The Monkees' lead singer for the junior prom—without having actually confirmed him.

In 1974, *Good Times* became the first spin-off of a spin-off (Florida Evans was Maude's housekeeper on *Maude*, and Maude was Edith Bunker's favorite cousin in *All in the Family*), as well as the first family sitcom featuring a Black mother and father. As blogger/producer Jam Donaldson (2008) reflects on the show, Florida and James Evans "had real life or death, how-we-gonna-eat problems. They faced poverty, VD [venereal disease, or sexually transmitted infections], unemployment, discrimination, gangs, suicide, child abuse, drugs, alcohol, teen pregnancy, hypertension,

Figure 1.2 Scene from *Leave It to Beaver*.

Figure 1.3 Opening credits from *The Brady Bunch*.

illiteracy, and the like." Though some criticized the show for its stereotyping (with oldest son, J.J., famous for his jive-talking performance), Donaldson continues that the show's characters offered models of perseverance, creativity, and love that defy the norms of most family sitcoms, White families included (see Figure 1.4).

Roseanne, which aired first in 1988, represented a lower-income family (headed by Dan and Roseanne Conner) facing troubles more consistent with their class status than the problems experienced by the Brady or Cleaver children. *Roseanne* creator Matt Williams describes in an interview how he developed the show from his life experience with a factory-working father and waitress mother, representing "hardworking people who worry about paying their bills and taking care of their kids" (Bennett, 2013).

Both *Good Times* and *Roseanne* have been (or soon will be) rebooted (with *Roseanne* cancelled in 2018 to be replaced by *The Conners*; and an animated *Netflix* run of *Good Times* planned by Seth MacFarlane and Steph Curry). This speaks to the power of better representation, which has grown to include openly gay characters (Mitchell Prichett and Cameron Tucker) in *Modern Family* (see Figure 1.5) and immigrant characters (the Huangs, a family migrating from Taiwan to Florida) in *Fresh Off the Boat*.

Figure 1.4 Scene from *Good Times*.

Figure 1.5 Opening credits of *Modern Family*.

Though shows like these are fictional or loosely based on real life, they demonstrate the need for popular culture to adapt to reflect reality. The Brookings Institute estimates that Whites will be a racial minority by 2045 if trends in increased Hispanic/Latina/o populations hold (Frey, 2018).

So as the US continues to diversify in terms of race and ethnicity, having families that represent what our communities look and sound like keeps popular culture relevant and interesting. Indeed, for the Disney Channel, family sitcoms continue to thrive as a genre, as they actively feature Black and Latina/o families.

Perhaps more importantly, though, as Rogers, Mastro, Robb, and Peebles (2021) remind us, avoiding negative portrayals of different identities has positive impacts for both individuals and groups. For young people of color, stereotypes and other negative representations of people of color can "lower self-esteem, satisfaction with one's appearance, confidence in one's own ability, feelings about one's ethnic-racial group, and academic performance" (p. 1). Rapper-turned-actor Common stated, for instance, "We got to see ourselves in *Good Times*. And every person of color didn't grow up poor, but these characters were real to us" (Orie, 2016). Seeing positive representations of minority characters also improves perceptions of groups, while chipping away at antiquated norms and expectations concerning gender and race, among other social identities (Chapter 4). There is still much work to be done to ensure quality representations, and a translation of representations into a better quality of life—a point we'll reinforce throughout the subsequent chapters.

This quick tour through family sitcom history demonstrates that popular culture should reflect reality, but also that its representations of reality matter for individuals, groups, and society as a whole. Popular culture creates reality for enjoyable consumption. It reflects identities and meanings "in the land of" pop culture, but it also has become so ubiquitous that pop culture now regularly shapes realities outside itself, including politics and religion.

For a number of years, scholars, such as Postman (1985), have argued that all aspects of American culture is a kind of popular entertainment media. Politics has turned into sensationalistic theatre dominated by the candidate who appears most charismatic on screens. Of course, we've elected multiple actors, reality TV stars, and even professional wrestlers as governors, senators, and presidents. We receive health information, such as facts and assumptions about COVID-19, from social media influencers, athletes, podcasters, and TV shows. Our small talk with coworkers is dominated by the latest reality TV shows and local sports teams. Our kids rush home to watch YouTube and play their favorite video games after a public school curriculum now gamified with the structure of video games (Chapter 12). Religion is experienced via spectacular "mega church" services that closely resemble pop music concerts. Advertising constructs meaning for our food, prescription drugs, and the toys for our children's play. Truly, no facet of everyday life is outside the influence of popular culture.

How do you understand and study something that is everything and everywhere? We turn next to two important resources which frame our approach in the next 12 chapters: equipment for living and media ecology.

Popular culture and equipment for living

Family sitcoms across television history demonstrate in one way how popular culture reflects meanings and identities, while also shaping them, for viewers and users. But popular culture, like other art forms, provide "equipment for living," what Brian Ott and Eric Aoki (2002) summarize as "the symbolic resources and strategies for addressing and resolving the given historical and personal problems [individuals and collectives] face" (p. 221). To understand equipment for living, think of a proverb or "old timey" saying that adults in your family may have said to you when you were a child: "The early bird gets the worm," "Don't count your chickens before they hatch," and "A bird in the hand is worth two in the bush" are three of our favorite bird-related nuggets of wisdom that grandparents and uncles used to say to us. Within each of these examples, we see advice on how to get through tough moments and overcome obstacles: have the self-discipline to arrive early in order to succeed. Be conservative in your planning, and only count on what you have in front of you, not what you *could* have. What you possess now is at least twice as valuable as what you desire.

For rhetorical theorist Kenneth Burke (1974), sayings like these aren't the only equipment for living. He focused on literature forms, like comedy and tragedy, as they provided tools to make life easier to live (see Chapter 6). Scholars of popular culture also see in the many artifacts that surround us a guidebook, individual and collective. Interestingly, rhetoric and organizational communication scholar Dan Lair (2011) wrote about how *The Apprentice* is equipment for living in contemporary capitalism (and the success of a closely related show, *Shark Tank*, demonstrates its continuing value as equipment for living). The 15-season reality television show (originally starring Donald Trump) saw contestants compete to earn a six-figure salary (in the original, to promote a Trump property for a year). Lair argued that *The Apprentice*, on its surface, endorsed the morals that traditional business culture promotes for success, including hard work and perseverance. But a "savvy" read of the show demonstrates how incessant self-branding and self-promotion, detachment and even cynicism toward work as a game are the strategies necessary to succeed in contemporary business. The wild popularity of *The Apprentice*, and perhaps even Trump's own self-brand, demonstrate the power of this show's equipment for living—and the need for a humanistic critique (like the scholarship you read in such fields as our home discipline of Communication Studies, but also Critical Race and Ethnic Studies, Media Studies, etc.).

Equipment for living comes from the humanities tradition of research, which promotes vivid descriptions of life as it has been, is, and should be lived. Particularly since the 1960s, many humanities scholars are also deeply concerned with the study of power; that is, the ability to influence or move someone. In our "always on" reality, power is more complex than ever. Humanities approaches help hold people accountable to shared values, providing a valuable check on power. But they also encourage us to consider power not only as a form of control or a "power over." Led by women of color and others in marginalized identities, the humanities impulse encourages communities, students, businesses, and governments to recognize power as an empowering force, a "power to" or a "power with." Further, such work considers our identities, experiences, and communities valuable to the work we do. So while other academics in the sciences seek to "bracket" their subjective perceptions and experiences by using the scientific method, the humanities offers critical insight and argument as part of knowledge production. Critical work recognizes that all perspectives are partial, and provide a view from some embodied vantage or standpoint. And though humanistic work does not provide scientifically verified knowledge (through which people can make predictions and generalizations), it does offer an important perspective through which people can imagine, rehearse, and experiment in more just ways in their everyday lives.

Back to *The Apprentice*, we may question whether or not this show offers a desirable construction of what is needed to get ahead in today's workplace culture. Other humanities scholars may look at *The Apprentice* and criticize it for its celebration of masculine directness and control (as in Trump's catchphrase, "You're fired!"). Or, they may look at the show's uptake in other countries, and see how the values from *The Apprentice* influence other cultures. The point is not to find the end-all, be-all truth of this popular TV show, but rather to continue a conversation, enrich others' perspectives, hold others accountable to shared values, and/or promote others' abilities to make judgments for themselves.

This side trip into the humanities prepares you to read the chapters ahead, where we do not offer prescriptions on what to watch or play. We share what we have found to be the best ideas for navigating popular culture, illustrating them with contemporary episodes, memes, games, trends, and material artifacts. We also offer evaluations of what we consider to be better or worse through the perspectives we turn to; but we don't intend for our **critique** (an informed analysis, evaluation, conclusions) to be scientific. Rather, it is an informed and useful perspective (seasoned with some decades—ahem—of experience, as our kids will tell you). We invite you to consider ours and others' perspectives as you make your way through popular culture.

Thus far in our Introduction we've seen how popular culture is a bit like the natural environment around us, such as air and water that surrounds us everywhere we go, every day. Marshall McLuhan famously likened humans' relationship to media to a fish swimming in water. Along these lines, ecological perspectives that explore media as embedded in the fundamental structures and practices of a culture are extremely helpful, and join equipment for living as a kind of compass to guide our book's exploration of popular culture.

Media ecology: A compass for reflexive experiencing of pop culture

Media ecology is a term that grew from the interdisciplinary study of media in the mid-20th century and developed alongside debates about the effects (usually the harms) of a medium's day-to-day presence in our lives. Through the 1960s and 1970s, for instance, politicians pointed fingers at television and film for spreading "communist" values, and questionable morality. In the 1980s and 1990s, critics blamed violent imagery in song lyrics, comic books, music videos, and video games for rises in murders and assaults. The debates about media effects do include arguments to the contrary, especially in terms of how media can expand democratic values. For instance, the Internet and social media are often touted as making it easier for ordinary people to get information (as opposed to having to trust elites in authority to be transparent with information).

Amid these public questions about the effects and value of media, media ecologists argued that media *shape*, but do not *dictate*, reality. Marshall McLuhan (1964), who is a well-known figure in media ecology, believed that a medium is "any extension of ourselves," including such objects as cars or light bulbs, though most media ecologists are concerned with *channels* of communication that *mediate* ideas and identities. Put differently, **channels** connect, stand between, and/or convey symbols. Media ecologists are especially concerned with technologies such as the printing press, telecommunications (telegraph and telephone), broadcast (radio and television), narrowcast (cable and satellite enabled content) and digital (Internet, social media like Facebook, Twitter, Instagram, and TikTok) media.

Media ecology underscores the organic qualities of people's relationships to media and communication technologies. If you've ever had strep throat, you may remember getting a bacterial "ecology" or throat culture test. A nurse likely took a sample from your throat by swabbing it, and put it into a Petri dish. Lab personnel may have spotted the streptococcus bacteria growing there, among other things. The Petri dish is a medium in which the culture of streptococcus grows. Media ecology scholars suggest that media like print, radio, television, and the Internet were the Petri dishes in which human culture grew. More specifically, media nourish and support expectations, attention, experiences, identities, and meanings—the stuff of human cultures. Media ecology is a vantage point that tries to capture this same organic quality, allowing us to look at the *many moving pieces* in how people experience and use popular culture, while also being able to speak about a *community* of users, media, and ideas within the ecology.

For instance, new technologies have often radically changed people's expectations for pop music. In the 1970s, a time when FM radio and home stereo systems flourished, albums by what seemed like faceless musicians (they often didn't even appear on their vinyl album covers), such as Pink Floyd and Led Zeppelin, sold millions of copies. These artists were defined by their enigmatic qualities, including music that seemed darkly complex. In the 1980s, MTV emerged and, almost overnight, the images on television drove music sales with visually striking, larger than life artists, such as Cyndi Lauper and Michael Jackson, dominating the album charts (this continued through the 1990s with larger-than-life hip-hop stars such as the Notorious B.I.G. and Jay-Z).

In recent years, social media has redefined the public's relationship to pop stars. Now, artists who are skilled at generating attention on social media dominate the music industry. To get or keep attention, artists are expected to share deep private experiences and feelings (e.g., anxiety or depression, substance abuse, romantic breakups, body image issues, etc.). Posts on Instagram or TikTok make artists seem relatable to fans, or "down to earth" (not enigmatic or larger-than-life). As pop star Halsey stated, artists are expected by their recording companies to manufacture some personal crisis (in her words, "fake a viral moment") on social media when releasing new music (Garcia, 2022). In each era, the pervasive technology seemed to encourage some types of pop artists to flourish while discouraging the styles of a previous era. Of course, the norms that social media bring to pop music don't *determine* (or dictate) what people listen to, or how everyone listens to music. Many people still listen to Zeppelin, Cyndi Lauper, and Biggie, as original fans or/and as an act of nostalgia for the 1970s, 1980s, or 1990s (see Chapters 6 and 7). Rather, changes in communication technology seem to feed the growth of specific pop culture styles and forms more than others, like some trees flourishing in a forest, while others struggle or maintain. Media ecology helps us see such subtle influences as the ways social media shifts the expectations and experience of pop music.

Media ecology has a number of advantages to other lenses (Foust & Drazner Hoyt, 2018). First, media ecology focuses on relationships between elements in an ecology, rather than the uses of a specific medium in isolation, or the effects of one piece of popular culture in isolation. The metaphor of ecology draws our attention to an environment of organic growth, a product-in-process or process-in-product that works as an interconnected, organic system. So while a single popular culture event, like the Super Bowl, is an important solo occurrence, it would not emerge without a network of relationships, between the National Football League, television networks, the distribution of televisions in people's homes, advertisers, musicians, and so forth. Media ecology allows us to see the many moving pieces in a community of users, media, and ideas, while still distinguishing it from similar forms of popular culture (like the Stanley Cup playoffs or World Cup soccer).

Second, media ecology identifies and often seeks to combat simplistic understandings of media. As noted above, media ecology emerged in a political environment which seemed quick to blame media like television, video games, and the Internet for social ills; and a corporate environment which often gains from utopian visions of technologies as bettering humanity. Media ecology typically recognizes that one medium is not inherently better or worse than other media, nor is any one medium predestined for good or evil. During the Trump administration, some argued that Twitter fanned political division, because its 140–280 character limit did not allow for nuanced opinion formation. The simple "like" button on Facebook (which has been supplemented by additional "reaction" symbols since), similarly, was blamed for promoting dehumanization. Just six to seven years before, people around the world celebrated the ability of Facebook to "bring down dictators" in places like Egypt. Media ecology, as mentioned above, provides a different view, which recognizes the power of **affordances** (to oversimplify, features in technologies that shape interactions with them, like the character limit, share, hashtag capacity, and reaction buttons). Media ecology situates the power of affordances in context, in human uses and relationships. Media ecology is often suspicious of techno-utopian and techno-dystopian views, which quickly and loudly celebrate or denigrate new communication technology.[1]

Third, media ecology tends to take a telescopic (rather than microscopic) view of media, allowing users to map broad terrain and relationships over time. This "long view" of media overcomes dichotomies between new and old media, online and offline media, and even the "immediate" (or face-to-face) and mediated, which tend to proliferate our thinking (Treré & Mattoni, 2015). Distinctions between new and old media seem to matter more to marketers and trend followers than everyday users of media, where technologies like vinyl records, newspapers, or DVDs still bring joy, in spite of being "outdated." We invite you to keep a log of media you use in a week to explore the ways that "immediate" arts (like painting, storytelling, conversation, or live music), telecommunication, print, broadcast, and digital media blend together for different uses. You might listen to FM radio while driving to work, talk to coworkers about the basketball game you attended the night before and a text you received from your sister, wind down after work with dinner and three episodes of your favorite Netflix show, scroll photos and headlines on Instagram as you drift off to sleep. You have likely gathered around a friend's phone to watch a video or see a social media post completely unconcerned about your effortless integration of your "virtual" life with your physical experiences. Your day moves seamlessly through different uses of media, based on the technologies you have access to, your cultural values and personal relationships, your mood and needs.

The affordances of different media do matter, though, and media ecology encourages us to get to know their history, as the conditions which brought them into existence continue to affect them today. In 1704, about 250 years after the printing press arrived in Europe, the first newspaper in the US (Boston, Massachusetts) emerged. By 1830–1860, the penny press became popular, and professional standards for journalism (accuracy and impartiality) emerged. Live theater (vaudeville) grew in popularity from the 1860s through 1910 in the US, shaping popular tastes for content that would proliferate on the next major communication technology in the US: radio. The National Broadcasting Company and Columbia Broadcasting System (known by their acronyms as NBC and CBS) began programming in the 1920s. By 1940, 83% of US households had a radio (Smith, 2014).

Television technology first appeared the 1939 World's Fair in New York, and became widespread through the 1950s, as prices dropped. Cable television spread in the 1980s, with the transition from broadcast to narrowcast media established. Cell phones, similarly, began development in the 1970s, and technology developed to the first iPhone release in 2007. Then, in the late 1990s to early 2000s, digital communication technologies proliferated with the Internet. Social media platforms Facebook and Twitter launched in 2005–2006, and TikTok joined the scene in 2016.

As we've already established, media ecology concerns itself not only with the *content* of popular culture, but also the actual production of devices in which popular culture appears, is made, or is delivered. For media ecologists, the adoption of each of these mediums in people's everyday lives had a ripple effect across the culture, changing aspects of political discourse, economic processes, educational practices, family life, religious faith, etc., in often unexpected and subtle ways.

Media ecology also points out that we abandon one technology for another based upon new uses and institutional forces. For instance, in the 1980s, Sony introduced the Walkman which allowed consumers to listen to cassette tapes anywhere, anytime over personal headphones (recall Max from *Stranger Things*). Emerging alongside MTV, pop music exploded in popularity, particularly among teens wanting a sense of independence. In the early 2000s, cheap mp3 players emerged on the market with little success until the iPod (advertising "a thousand songs in your pocket") allowed consumers to find free music via the Internet (on sites such as Napster) and later purchase music for 99 cents per song on iTunes. In this era, music bloggers exploded in popularity, simplifying music discovery for consumers now overwhelmed by choices. Quickly, compact discs and cassette tapes became obsolete, replaced by digital downloads. As smartphones emerged, consumers preferred to stream music via mobile apps (rather than fill their phones with digital downloads) and Pandora and Spotify emerged, radically altering pop music consumption, particularly via algorithm-created playlists. In each of these cases, many forces influenced the adoption of the technology: the cost of the mobile device and music, access to music content, support by institutions, etc. When a new technology (Walkman, iPod, and smartphone) was widely adopted, the ripple effect spread across the culture changed the revenue of the music industry and artists, the viability of local record stores, intellectual property law, the communication practices within communities of music fans, the required speed of mobile cellular networks, the power of broadcast radio stations and MTV, the emergent influence of tech companies in entertainment media, the need for wireless Internet in homes, parent–child communication, and how listeners chose their music, and so on. Much like a new species being introduced into a forest or ocean, a new media technology has innumerable effects across a culture.

Media logic suggests that the features and values of technology travel as media develop, but in a given moment of time, one medium can gain power to shape the mediated experiences of others. Digital media offer the dominant logic of today. So though newspapers and magazines can still be delivered to your doorstep, their aesthetic has changed through digital logics. You may notice a lot more photographs, colorful text, etc. If you visit a newspaper website, it likely looks more like other websites than archived newspaper articles from the 1950s. Similarly, most American homes still have a television; but the television is probably now a "smart TV" designed for Internet streaming services such as Netflix, YouTube, and Hulu. Further, these TV screens grow larger and larger, ready-made for media spectacle such as football games and superhero movies—the most popular content in the present culture. As TVs get bigger, movie attendance declines, as more people prefer to watch movies on their big screen TVs at home. In response, movie producers create giant screen CGI (computer-generated image) spectacles like *Avatar: The Way of Water* that are designed attract people back to movie theaters. In the process, these technologies have encouraged bigger and bigger movie spectacles with giant budgets now in the hundreds of millions. The expense of these digital effects-dominated movies compels studios to only produce well-established franchises such as Marvel, Disney animated remakes, *Harry Potter*, and *Star Wars* with especially devoted fans—fans who gather via social media and other digital channels (more about this in Chapter 2). In this regard, a "media logic" extends across all aspects of popular culture production, distribution, and consumption.

We can't predict what new communication technologies or media will emerge in the next ten or more years. Thus, rather than offer prescriptions for how to study media, media ecologists encourage us to ask questions: How does a technology encourage or discourage certain types of popular culture content? How does technology change the experiences of consumption, especially fandom? How does a technology integrate, change, or eliminate previous mediums? How do seemingly "new" forms of media relate to technologies or forms considered "obsolete"?

As an interesting exercise, consider the proliferation of news personalities and media. Though it is true that the dominance of the digital logic has changed journalism (through much of the convergence economy trends discussed in detail in Chapter 2, though also in shifting from physical newspapers to websites), it would be difficult to say that "print is dead" or "journalism is dead." Journalism and other forms of news have certainly changed with the digital economy. Compare, for instance, *Meet the Press with Chuck Todd*, which drew 2.8 million video views and 183,000 viewers on YouTube in November, 2022—Nielsen Market Research data that Todd's parent network, NBC, touted as "impressive" numbers (Butcher-Nesbitt, 2022). In contrast, Joe Rogan has 11 million listeners per podcast (Sienkiewicz & Marx, 2022), and reportedly earned $200 million for exclusive streaming rights in early 2022 (Towey, 2022). Would you consider a personality like Joe Rogan a journalist? How do you make that determination? Media ecology would encourage us to ask such questions. Instead of using "old" versus "new" media to defend our positions, we would see how media from the past grew into these uses today; and ask whether such forms of popular media are serving us today.

A fourth and final advantage we see in media ecology is its often humanistic and critical approach to media. Media ecology recognizes that powerful entities own popular culture and media, and their primary purpose is to profit/make money. But we also know that people make use of popular culture and media to suit their needs. The use of affordances do not have to conform to what designers have chosen. Rather, uses evolve based on how affordances are actually used. Hashtags are a perfect example. In 2007, an individual Twitter user, Chris Messina, suggested using a pound sign (#) to group similar tweets together (Panko, 2017). For years, Twitter's management largely ignored hashtags, viewing them as only for obsessive social media users or nerds. But, over time, events such as natural disasters and political protests made hashtags invaluable for mobilizing interest and support, binding people together around a common phrase such as #Me-Too and #BlackLivesMatter. Today, hashtags have evolved further, emerging as effective marketing and generating interest in content or brands such as #ShareACoke or #OreoHorrorStories.

The critical approach to media leaves us to articulate a persistent tension you may see throughout the forthcoming chapters: How much power do we, as individual users and members of communities, have when it comes to pop culture? The answer to this question will vary chapter by chapter. At times, we see people mindlessly consuming pop culture as producers intend it to be consumed. At other times, we will see people using or experiencing pop culture in active, creative, even subversive ways. In the critical tradition, we seek to arm readers of this book with a vocabulary and perspective to challenge power, and to protect themselves and others against oppression, exploitation, and marginalization. We want to inspire readers to see themselves as active, self-reflexive users, rather than consumers alone.

Conclusion

This book's focus on everyday experiences with popular culture is not without some peril. If you are under 30 years old, you have likely been critiquing popular culture on social media since you were quite young. You have described your latest pop song obsession, "stanned" a trendy young actor, and quoted or shared your preferred influencers. These judgments are immediate, visceral, and in many regards quite valid. Further, we've all talked about a movie or TV show with such insights as "that sucked" or "that was awesome" or said something like, "she's a great actor." If pressed, most of us likely repeat the talking points from critics we've encountered online about what "good song writing" or "great acting" are, having never really interrogated where these assumptions are derived.

In this book, we'll push you a step further, through a variety of perspectives. We're not especially interested in whether or not a movie or pop song is "good" or "bad." Such subjective criticism can be fun to discuss with friends but usually simply returns to a matter of personal taste (often informed by your identities and experiences). Instead, we are more interested in questions such as: *Why* do these pop songs, reality shows, sports teams, etc. bring me (and others) such pleasure, or such disdain? Further, how is this artifact improving the quality of my life? How might this artifact diminish the quality of my life? Does the content and production of this popular culture promote the values I feel are most important to my community (e.g., equality, compassion, faith, self-determinacy, etc.)?

Today, we have an astonishing assortment of popular culture to choose from. In the touch of our finger, we can choose from *millions* of songs, movies, TV shows, sporting events, YouTube videos, social media posts, books, etc. Never before has this truly infinite menu of popular culture options been available to people (as Gen Xers, just a few decades ago, we grew up with three TV networks and a handful of local radio stations). Perhaps in response to the ubiquity of popular culture, a growing appreciation of mass culture such as blockbuster movies and pop music has emerged. A few decades ago, such artifacts were derided as both formulaic and infantile, designed only to attract a large audience. Among pop music critics, this is referred to as **poptimism**—a serious appreciation of the most popular forms of music of an era that had once been ridiculed as meaningless or mindless such as disco, early rap music, boy bands, etc. Though people see pop culture as trivial, mindless, and silly, the scale and ubiquity of it demands serious attention, returning us to the summer of 2022 and *Stranger Things*.

Stranger Things is a good show, yes. But why is it a phenomenon? Building on the introduction, for a TV show to reach these levels of cultural consciousness (like *Breaking Bad* or *Friends* in previous cultural moments), a kind of perfect storm of forces has to converge (and we have to have radar sensitive enough to see these forces converging). First, *Stranger Things* is heavily marketed by Netflix, with an advertising campaign comparable to a Hollywood blockbuster film. The show features incredibly likable actors who are adept at connecting directly with fans via social media. *Stranger Things* playfully references 1980s nostalgia and a wide range of filmmaking styles from directors like Steven Spielberg. The show is perfectly constructed for binging, with episodes ending on cliff-hangers keeping the audience desiring more. Further, *Stranger Things* provides a fantastic escape (especially desirable in the current political climate and constant apocalyptic news cycle) with the sensational emotions of horror and action filmmaking. Finally, the show is well suited to the psychological experiences of its core fans, offering opportunities for self-reflection and conversation. To account for the popularity of *Stranger Things*, all of these factors (and probably several more) should be considered. Similarly, this book is designed to explore popular culture from many perspectives in order to fully understand its place in everyday life, and to help you evaluate the choices you make in consuming and producing pop culture.

In closing, we defined in Chapter 1 the concept of popular culture, describing its unique significance in contemporary everyday life. Further, via equipment for living and media ecology, we offered tools for exploring the scope and importance of popular culture in your everyday experiences. In Chapter 2, we examine one of the central forces in the complex media ecology of popular culture: business.

Reflecting on popular culture in your everyday life

- What types of popular culture do you engage in your everyday life? How do access (e.g., devices you own, streaming services you subscribe to) and media affect what you choose to engage? How does content or style affect what you choose to engage?
- In this chapter, we looked at how television family sitcoms reflect and create reality. What family sitcom (discussed in this chapter, or not) best reflects who you and your family are? What does that family sitcom get right about your family, and what does it miss? Think back to episodes that seemed to really misrepresent your family and/or your identities. If you could rewrite that episode, how would it go? Think back to episodes that seemed to really "get" you and your family? If you could share this episode with a friend, what might you say about it?
- Think of a treasured pop culture artifact (or piece of pop culture), one that you have viewed or experienced multiple times. What keeps you coming back to this artifact, for repeat viewing or playing? What makes it enjoyable and valuable, where do you typically experience it, and who do you experience it with?
- What forms of popular culture provide equipment for living in your everyday life, especially as a member of a community?

Note

1 This is not to say that media ecology is a monolithic field—scholars take different approaches, sometimes focusing more on the channel than content or vice versa, sometimes sounding almost deterministic about the media (as in Marshall McLuhan's famous declaration "the medium is the message" and should be given primacy over the meanings traveling on airwaves). Media ecology scholars typically share attention to media as it is *used*, not media as it is traded in ideological debates.

Suggested readings

Cali D. D. (2017). *Mapping media ecology: Introduction to the field*. Peter Lang Publishing.

Deuze, M. (2011). Media life. *Media, Culture, & Society, 33*(1), 137–148. DOI: 10.1177/0163443710386518

du Gay, P., Hall, S., Janes, L., Mackay, H., & Negus, K. (1997). *Doing cultural studies: The story of the Sony Walkman*. Sage Publications.

Livingstone, S. (2009). On the mediation of everything. *Journal of Communication, 59*(1), 1–18. DOI: 10.1111/j.1460-2466.2008.01401.x

Towns, A. (2022). *On black media philosophy*. University of California Press.

References

Bennett, T. (2013, October 18). 25 years later, *Roseanne* creator reflects on working class inspiration. *Today*. https://www.today.com/popculture/25-years-later-roseanne-creator-reflects-working-class-inspiration-8C11405474.

Burke, K. (1974). *The philosophy of literary form*. University of California Press.

Butcher-Nesbitt, A. (2022, November 22). "Meet the Press" wins in the key demo for the fifth straight week. *NBC News*. https://press.nbcnews.com/2022/11/22/meet-the-press-wins-in-the-key-demo-for-the-fifth-straight-week/

Donaldson, J. (2008, May 30). *Good Times*: Ain't we lucky we got em. *The Root*. https://www.theroot.com/good-times-aint-we-lucky-we-got-em-1790899878.

Foust, C. R., & Drazner Hoyt, K. (2018). Social movement 2.0: Integrating and assessing scholarship on social media and movement. *Review of Communication*, *18*(1), 37–55. DOI: 10.1080/15358593.2017.1411970

Frey, W. (2018, March 14). The US will become minority White in 2045. *Brookings*. https://www.brookings.edu/blog/the-avenue/2018/03/14/the-us-will-become-minority-white-in-2045-census-projects/

Garcia, T. (2022, May 22). Halsey claims label "won't let me" release new song "unless they can fake a viral moment on Tik Tok." *Variety*. https://variety.com/2022/music/news/halsey-label-new-song-viral-tiktok-1235274753/

Ichimura, A. (2022, March 29). Will Smith slapping Chris Rock is so notorious, it just broke a YouTube record. *Esquire*. https://www.esquiremag.ph/culture/movies-and-tv/will-smith-chris-rock-youtube-record-a00304-20220329

Irightalright. (2022). Max Mayfield in season 4 character analysis. *Reddit*. https://www.reddit.com/r/StrangerThings/comments/w3uwau/max_mayfield_in_season_4_character_analysis/

Lair, D. J. (2011). Surviving the corporate jungle: *The Apprentice* as equipment for living in the contemporary work world. *Western Journal of Communication*, *75*(1), 75–94. 10.1080/10570314.2010.536966.

McLuhan, M. (1964). *Understanding media: The extensions of man* (1st ed.). McGraw-Hill.

Orie, M. (2016). Common speaks on the impact of *Good Times* and *Jeffersons*. *Curly Nikki*. https://www.curlynikki.com/2016/10/common-speaks-on-impact-of-good-times.html

Ott, B. L., & Aoki, E. (2002). The politics of negotiating public tragedy: Media framing of the Matthew Shepherd murder. *Rhetoric & Public Affairs*, *5*(3), 483–505.

Panko, B. (2017, August 23). A decade ago, the hashtag reshaped the Internet. *Smithsonian Magazine*. https://www.smithsonianmag.com/smart-news/decade-ago-hashtag-reshaped-internet-180964605/

Postman, N. (1985). *Amusing ourselves to death: Public discourse in the age of show business*. Viking.

Rogers, O., Mastro, D., Robb, M. B., & Peebles, A. (2021). *The inclusion imperative: Why media representation matters for kids' ethnic-racial development*. Common Sense Media. https://www.commonsensemedia.org/sites/default/files/research/report/2021-inclusion-imperative-report_final-release_for-web.pdf

Sienkiewicz, M. & Marx, N. (2022, February 10). How Joe Rogan became podcasting's Goliath. *The Conversation*. https://theconversation.com/how-joe-rogan-became-podcastings-goliath-176124

Smith, S. (2014, November 10). Radio: The Internet of the 1930s. *APM Reports*. https://www.apmreports.org/episode/2014/11/10/radio-the-internet-of-the-1930s

Storey J. (2012). *Cultural theory and popular culture: An introduction* (6th ed.). Pearson.

Towey, H. (2022, February 17). Spotify reportedly paid $200 million for Joe Rogan's podcast. *Business Insider*. https://www.businessinsider.com/spotify-paid-200-million-for-joe-rogan-experience-podcast-report-2022-2

Treré, E. & Mattoni, A. (2016) Media ecologies and protest movements: Main perspectives and key lessons, *Information, Communication & Society*, *19*(3), 290–306, DOI: 10.1080/1369118X.2015.1109699

2   The business of popular culture

Introduction

Disney has emerged as an astonishingly successful media corporation of recent years, particularly its feature film productions. The Disney formula is simple and utterly transparent: Mine the properties of the company by remaking or slightly rebooting beloved movies of the past (see Figure 2.1).

The list of Disney remakes and reboots over the last several years seems comically long: It includes *Beauty and the Beast, Aladdin, The Lion King, 101 Dalmatians, The Jungle Book, Lady and the Tramp, Mulan, Winnie the Pooh, Cinderella, Finding Nemo, Alice in Wonderland, Mary Poppins, Pinocchio, Snow White and the Seven Dwarfs,* and *The Little Mermaid.*

Figure 2.1 Scene from *The Lion King* (2019).

DOI: 10.4324/9781003372943-2

While some of these films are huge blockbusters and some are pretty forgettable, for the most part they all make money. Simultaneously, the Disney company has acquired the intellectual property rights to other beloved franchises, such as *Star Wars*, and churned out movies, TV shows, theme park rides, and merchandising on brand.

Though it may seem like we're singling out Disney, we want to be clear—Disney is simply following the formula that the entire media industry took over the last decade or two. Other companies like Warner (*Harry Potter* and *Batman* franchises) and Universal (*Fast and Furious* and *Jurassic World* franchises) shamelessly stick with sequels, prequels, remakes, and reboots as the lowest-risk, highest-profit movies and TV shows. This was not always the case. In fact, as recently as the 1980s, sequels and reboots were associated with cheesy low-quality "B" movies (think of sequels to *Jaws*, *Robocop*, and *Friday the 13th*). As a result of the fixation of existing properties, studios have all but eliminated the mid- to lower-budget dramas and comedies that were once staples of movie theaters. In fact, looking at the top five highest grossing films of each year from 2004 to 2022, the number of original films is barely into double digits (at 12)—and most of these films now anchor branded franchises, including *The Incredibles* (2004), *Cars* (2006), *Avatar* (2009–2010), and *Frozen* (2013).[1] The ten highest grossing films from 2004 to 2022 are all sequels, prequels, spin-offs, or reboots, from existing property (see Table 2.1). Feature films are very difficult to get made within the current studio system unless a filmmaker is interested in superheroes, princesses, or aliens.

All of popular culture is embedded in the business of a few giant corporations and these companies play an important role in deciding what pop culture gets made, who makes it, and where and how we see and hear it. From this viewpoint, popular culture is a business designed for money-making, and, some would argue, exploiting the system to make the

Table 2.1 Top ten highest grossing films, 2004–2022

Film title	Gross box-office totals (US dollars)	Year of release
Avengers: Endgame	$858,373,000	2019
Star Wars Episode VII: The Force Awakens	$742,208,942	2015
Black Panther	$700,059,566	2018
Avengers: Infinity War	$678,815,482	2018
Jurassic World	$652,270,625	2018
The Avengers	$623,357,910	2012
Spider-Man: No Way Home	$613,600,664	2021
Incredibles 2	$608,581,744	2018
The Lion King (live action)	$543,638,043	2019
The Dark Knight	$531,001,578	2008

maximum profits possible. Our focus in Chapter 2 is less on the critique of power difference here (because we take that up in other chapters), and more on helping readers navigate what has become a very complicated set of business practices. We want to "open the curtain" for readers on how corporate convergence, intellectual property, branding, and algorithms affect how we are able to access popular culture, experience and produce it.

Chapter 3 will get into more of the individual level of consumption, but before that we must take the perspective of someone flying in an airplane—or, more appropriately perhaps, hitching a ride on a satellite orbiting the Earth—to understand the business of popular culture. From this perspective, giant media companies and tech behemoths like Amazon and Apple are controlling much of the production and flow of popular culture. These companies decide where, how, and what popular culture content is available to consumers. In this chapter, we'll focus on the business aspects of production in the United States; in Chapter 9, we expand the scope of this system to the global level, with implications not just for economics, but also politics, culture, and the environment.

From our satellite perspective, an individual media consumer is a tiny, imperceptible datapoint in a massive sea of information determining the value of billions of dollars of popular culture content across distribution channels worldwide. Though you are just a tiny datapoint in this global system, corporate interests impact your experience as a producer and consumer of popular culture in countless ways: the increasing cost of a Netflix subscription and high speed Internet access, the musical styles filling pop radio stations and playlists, the types of stories and characters featured in movies, why some people get rich from intellectual property (while others, including those who post to social media, make little or none) are all outcomes of this system. So, let's get to know the system a little better, first, with an overview of popular culture production (to contrast the dream of "pure art" we often envision when we imagine "breaking big" as an artist or creator in the system). We then complicate popular culture production through a political economy perspective, which focuses attention on today's prevailing business practices in popular culture. The practices, which we devote some time to for the remaining chapter, include corporate convergence, branding, intellectual property, and algorithms.

Popular culture production versus the myth of "pure art"

Some of us like to think of the emergence of our favorite songs, movies, novels, video games, and TV shows as independent of business interests—a kind of "pure" art. We've seen stories like this reinforced over and over again in films like *Eight Mile*, *Bohemian Rhapsody*, and *Walk the Line*, with talented artists, to be sure, rising to fame and wealth through their vision and persistence. But for the majority of people—even very talented ones—breaking (and staying) big in music, acting, dancing, or writing, is just a myth. One of the great contributions of hip hop, we think, is valuing the fair compensation for an artist's labor. Whereas anti-corporate 1990s grunge artists claimed they would never "sell out," today's rappers brag about deals they strike with large corporations to ensure that they are not exploited. Perhaps we, as social media users, should take a cue from today's hip-hop artists, since we receive no compensation for our posts, while social media companies like TikTok earned $4 billion in advertising revenue in 2021 (with an expected $12 billion in 2022) (Solon, Shaw, & Turner, 2022).

Pop music, like all popular culture, is riddled with examples of artists earning millions for others while seeing relatively little money for their work, including beloved artists like Chuck Berry, Elvis Presley, the Rolling Stones, N.W.A, Tyga, and TLC. More recently, in echoes of predatory recording contracts, artists only make $0.0033 to $0.0054 per stream on Spotify (Dellatto, 2022). Today, pretty much anybody, even people with virtually no musical talent or training, can write, record, and distribute music—in fact, a young friend of our son produces his own songs with simple computer software and posts them on Spotify (we'll withhold any comment on the quality of his music). On the other hand, *almost no one* can make a living writing, recording, and distributing music. Even major artists make the bulk of their income by touring.

In fact, partly due to the reliance on touring for revenue, ticket prices for concerts have quadrupled in the last 20 years which means fans now have to pay large sums of money to see their favorite band, singer, or rapper perform (Shaw, 2019). When trying to purchase Bruce Springsteen tickets in the spring of 2022, we were shocked to discover that most tickets were priced around $2,000–$5,000 (for tickets that would typically cost $100–$200 for a major tour) due to new "dynamic ticket pricing" developed by algorithms to gauge the demand of buyers at any given moment. A few months later, the US Congress called hearings on Ticketmaster, after the company not only inflated prices for Taylor Swift's 2023 football stadium tour, but withheld tickets from consumers. Such outcomes are not an accident, nor are they the work of some monocled man twirling his mustache and laughing at the suffering of Swifties and fans of The Boss. Rather, this is the logical consequence of contemporary business practices.

In the past, concerts were viewed primarily as promotion for album sales, so ticket prices were, by today's standards, astonishingly affordable. To see the Beatles in 1965 cost $5.65, to see Led Zeppelin in 1980 cost $12. The increases in ticket prices perfectly represent an ecological approach to pop culture, as a number of disparate factors led to the current concert ticketing situation. Digital online ticketing enabled promoters to track demand in real time. Promotion shifted from regional small businesses to massive multinational conglomerates such as Ticketmaster. Spectacular multi-media concert performances and massive festivals such as Coachella drew greater interest from fans. Resale apps such as Stubhub offered new business opportunities for ticket scalpers that did not require standing outside a venue in the rain or dodging cops to re-sell tickets they'd purchased. Further, artists needed new revenue streams in an era of little profit from file sharing and music streaming. The confluence of all these forces have created conditions for ticket prices to skyrocket.

As noted in Chapter 1, by definition, all popular culture is, and always has been, inextricably associated with business. In many ways, these inherent business dimensions of popular culture are reminiscent of the old cliché about Congress—many of us don't want to see how the sausage gets made. Behind your favorite artist and their song, movie, novel, or video game are corporate lawyers, market analyses, contracts, economic projections on spreadsheets and graphs, tedious meetings in lifeless conference rooms, etc. For the people in media corporations, a movie or video game is really no different from any other consumer product. The basic principles are the same: efficiently manufacture uniform products to meet consumer demand. Imagine an assembly line, probably featuring automated robots, producing uniform tubes of toothpaste. The toothpaste's qualities were decided by careful market analysis to predict consumer demand (size/shape of the package, new flavors, featured ingredients such as fluoride and whitening agents, etc.) and efficiently shipped to stores and warehouses. Similarly, Disney analyzes market interest of movie goers and sees nostalgia and spectacle are popular among audiences. The 2017 remake of *Beauty and the Beast*, a remake of one of Disney's most beloved animated films, made $1.2 billion at the box office. Disney efficiently produces a line-up of spectacular, nostalgic live action remakes to fill consumer demand.

The idea that popular culture production functions as a kind of assembly line producing uniform products relates to **a political economy approach**, which critiques the "culture industries" promoting capitalism and mindless consumerism. Championed by scholars like Theodor Adorno and Max Horkheimer, the political economy approach is grounded in a broader critique of capitalism strongly influenced by Karl Marx (see Chapter 5). Miller (2000) summarizes this line of reasoning: as formulaic mass production, the film industry uses production systems designed for relatively identical products (e.g., genre movies, sequels, etc.).

Some of these formulas seem to work remarkably well across generations. Take, for example, boy bands. A long time ago, record producers realized that if you find a few attractive young men, dress them in fashionable (often uniform) outfits, choreograph some dance moves, and have them sing love songs, fans (particularly teenage girls) will buy a lot records. This formula reached its zenith in the late 1990s and early 2000s with the phenomenal success of the Backstreet Boys and NSYNC. While the boy bands of the 1990s may have mastered the formula, they definitely did not invent it. In fact, the formula dates back to the 1950s and 1960s with the Four Seasons, Crew Cuts, Dion and the Belmonts, and the Monkees, continued into the 1970s with the Jackson Five, Bay City Rollers, and Osmonds, and extended into the MTV era of the 1980s with New Edition, Wham, and New Kids on the Block. Of course, more recently, boy bands such as One Direction and BTS show that the US is not the only home for the formula's success.

Our formulaic factory production metaphor does not hold for all of popular culture. While all industries are mercurial with changing tastes of consumers, popular culture can radically change, almost overnight. For instance, after only a few years, most of the boy bands described above were discarded as uncool, mercilessly mocked and parodied (then to return to the nostalgia tour circuit years later). As a style of music explodes in popularity and is copied by countless other artists, it quickly falls out of favor with music consumers. Needless to say, refrigerator or laundry de-tergent styles do not change so quickly. At the peak of dance synth-based pop at the start of the 1990s (think Michael Jackson), Nirvana exploded in popularity and marginalized the MTV styles of the 1980s. Then, grunge was mass produced with countless copycat groups quickly resembling a kind of self-parody. In the wake of this oversaturation of alt rock styles, charismatic rap superstars like the Notorious B.I.G and Tupac burst on the radio and left grunge behind, permanently ushering in the hip-hop era with its ever-changing subgenres and styles. Today, with interesting new music posted on TikTok every day, musical styles come and go in the blink of an eye, which leads us into the era of convergence.

Convergence: Introducing the business logic of pop culture

Here's a sort of weird observation: media companies seem to routinely change their names. Viacom is now Paramount, Time Warner is now Warner Media, 20th Century Fox is now Disney, NBC is now Comcast. These name changes are probably pretty meaningless to most regular folks outside the media industry, just a bunch of corporate maneuvers by old fo-geys in suits. Actually, in some ways, these name changes represent the key to understanding the current business of popular culture. Media compa-nies need to change their names as they are constantly merging with other large companies, as well as acquiring new, smaller companies, including TV networks and movie studios, telecommunications and Internet service providers, social media giants, etc. Even looking just a few years prior to a name change can reveal a good deal about business practices hiding behind today's big hits.

Not long ago, different types of popular culture production were largely differentiated by medium. Movie studios were separate from TV networks, Internet providers were separate from book publishers and newspapers, etc. For the reasons described above, this "medium-specific" model was volatile and unpredictable. For instance, when TV became popular in the 1950s, movie attendance declined dramatically reducing movie studios profits. Further, when Internet use grew in popularity in the 2000s, newspaper subscriptions plummeted. The response of corporations to the relatively unpredictable nature of popular culture consumption is to merge into giant conglomerates to control as much of the process of distribution and production as possible. The logic is that when one giant corporation controls movie production, TV networks, radio and pop music, news, social media, Internet access, etc., then the companies (now one entity) are protected from the variability across different types of popular culture consumption. Consumers are affected by these mergers in a lot of ways, such as when a favorite show or movie franchise suddenly jumps from one streaming service to another. Just as we can chart mergers through name changes, so, too, can we see corporate convergence by following the flow of favorite franchises such as *Spiderman, Harry Potter, Lord of the Rings, James Bond,* and *Star Wars* across platforms.

The term for these mergers is "convergence" or "the flow of content across multiple media platforms" (Jenkins, 2006, p. 2). These two terms—content and platform—are key to understanding **convergence** in recent years. First, the idea of **content** appears straightforward enough: units of pop culture to be consumed, be they movies, TV shows, songs, social media videos, etc. But, today, for media companies, "content" really means intellectual property that can be monetized or turned into revenue. When Disney bought *Star Wars*, they weren't primarily interested in just owning old *Star Wars* movies. They wanted to buy the intellectual property, the exclusive legal ownership of the characters, storylines, logos, etc., of *Star Wars*, allowing them to make new content and merchandise to spread across their platforms. At its most basic, a **platform** is where a consumer finds their popular culture content such as a streaming app (e.g., Netflix or Spotify), social media site (e.g., YouTube or Instagram), a cable or broadcast television network, radio station, or a retailer (like Amazon, a record store, etc.).

For many decades, companies have been trying to merge content and platform with movie studios sometimes buying theater chains or television networks producing their own TV shows. This ended up as a kind of disparate and ever-changing patchwork that was far from seamless or consistent. Today, corporations can control content and platforms in much more sophisticated and dependable ways. Netflix was a trailblazer emphasizing original content on its own platform rather than paying massive costs for content such as the enduringly popular sitcoms *Friends* or *The Office*. In fact, this former DVD-rental service turned down a $50 million offer to merge with Blockbuster in 2001, and rode the waves of the digital economy through the 2000s, which included innovating its DVDs-by-mail service with streaming and algorithms (discussed more below). Netflix is also now famous for creating hits like *Orange Is the New Black*, and expanding to 222 million subscribers worldwide with $24.9 billion in revenue for 2021 (Iqbal, 2023). Critics and audiences question the quality of Netflix original series like *Fate: The Winx Saga* or *Emily in Paris*—but with 57 and 58 million views as of August, 2021 (Fish, 2021), the profitability and power of Netflix's convergence is without question. Challenging Netflix, of course, is Disney, which has probably the most fully integrated platform and content. Disney+ exclusively offers Disney movies and TV shows to streamers, and rakes in profits with on-demand events such as *Hamilton* (which Disney paid $75 million to acquire) (Rogers, 2020).

The emphasis on controlling platform and content through convergence has real consequences on what types of popular culture get produced. Companies are so focused on pulling consumers into their "universe" of content and their specific platform, all efforts are directed at developing series designed for binge watching (watch multiple episodes in rapid succession), preferably within the intellectual property of a franchise, rather than any other type of content such as original feature films or new situation comedies. As a result, with a massive reduction in the production of non-sequel, non-reboot, mid-level budget films, movie stars are shifting to streaming, bingeable content. The biggest movie stars of the 2000s such as Will Farrell, Reese Witherspoon, Julia Roberts, and Jim Carrey have all shifted their careers to binge content on streaming services such as Netflix, Apple TV+, and Hulu. Perhaps more telling, the biggest *current* movie stars such as Chris Pratt, Zendaya, Chris Evans, and Benedict Cumberbatch have all starred in bingeable content for streaming services.

But, in practice, the "platform" of contemporary popular culture in not just the subscription-based streaming service but the Internet as a whole. For many consumers, between Wi-Fi in their home and cell service for their phone, Internet access is the single most expensive part of their popular culture consumption. Further, while one might cancel Netflix or Disney+ for a few months to save money, most consumers would never consider interrupting Internet access for even a few days. Unsurprisingly, media companies have sought to control consumers' Internet access. For instance, Warner Media owns AT&T (for Internet and cell phone service), Universal and DC Pictures (among many, many other media properties), and HBO Max (as a streaming service) which means they control content and platform from top to bottom. The concern is simple. By serving as a kind of monopoly of its platform and content, Warner Media can set any price to watch the latest *Batman* movie, *Game of Thrones* spin-off, or acclaimed HBO shows such as *Barry* or *Hacks*. Consumers have felt this pinch. "Cord cutting" was once heralded as a cheaper option than cable, but by the time consumers pay subscription fees for Netflix, HBO Max, Hulu, and others, access to their favorite shows easily exceeds many cable packages (especially when coupled with the growing price of high speed Internet). Some consumers respond to the growing cost of streaming services by pirating copies of their favorite shows and movies illegally via Torrent sites and sketchy streaming services, requiring media companies to carefully price their services to avoid consumers cancelling or switching en masse. The point we are stressing here is that behind the great "art" in popular culture are convergence logics that give rise to content and your ability to access it on platforms.

The other side of giant media conglomerates like Disney and Warner Media are technology companies who produce and distribute TV, movies, and music primarily to promote their central business model, which is definitely not making movies and TV shows. Apple and Amazon treat their streaming services such as Apple+, Amazon Prime Video, Apple, and Amazon Music as ways to pull consumers into their larger branding experience to sell, in the case of Apple, phones, tablets, and computers; and in the case of Amazon, loyalty to the online retail subscription service. This represents convergence on an even larger scale when impossibly large companies, companies literally wealthier than the vast majority of *countries* in the world, can fund a $100 million-plus movie or TV show (like Amazon's *Lord of the Rings*) as a tiny part of their overall business. This leads us to supplement the logics of convergence with a discussion of advertising and branding as part of today's business of popular culture.

Advertising and branding

It is hard to exaggerate the ubiquity of contemporary advertising. Some experts estimate that most Americans are exposed to 4,000–10,00 advertisements *per day* on our smartphones, computers, televisions, and in public spaces via billboards and digital screens (Simpson, 2017). Advertising is everywhere we turn in a culture filled with people staring at screens. Advertising is wed to popular culture in a wide variety of ways, beginning with marketing and advertising pop culture artifacts themselves. Advertising is also infused into many popular cultural experiences such as the commercials during television broadcasts and YouTube videos and product placements in movies. Further, advertising itself (as we elaborate through examples like *Old Spice* in Chapter 7) is a form of popular culture, created to encourage spreading over social media and as an expression of identity. Advertising is a clever and engaging product in its own right. Finally, by infusing meaning into automobiles, soft drinks, and almost anything else, advertising transforms everyday objects into popular culture, a process referred to by Jhally (1987) as **fetishizing**.

Advertising spending by corporations continues to grow annually now reaching $763 billion per year (Graham, 2021). Why do companies spend so much money on advertising? If you spend a few moments watching advertising on your phones and televisions, it rarely focuses on the actual function of a product (e.g., what a beer tastes like or the nutritional value of a hamburger), but rather depicts the pleasurable lifestyle associated with a brand. Jhally (1987) described how advertising erases the actual function or use of a product, such as running shoes, and fills the object with elaborate new meanings. The purpose is simple. If we only purchase products for their function, we would only have one comfortable pair of shoes for getting from point A to point B. There would be no consumers left to buy any totally unnecessary new shoes. Of course, most people own a closet filled with shoes and the market seems infinitely renewable because we really don't think about the function of shoes anymore. We think about the meaning constructed by brands like Nike or Skechers or Keen. We buy shoes to express facets of ourselves at work, when we hang out with friends, while we are exercising, and when we dress up for a formal event. Certainly, stiletto high heels seem light years from the function of walking comfortably or efficiently. Taking this to its logical endpoint, "sneakerheads" now purchase expensive Nike basketball shoes and leave them in their packaging to be displayed in their homes. The shoe has been completely removed of its function. Fetishizing fills products with powerful, even magical and mystical, meanings. Nike fills its shoes with almost superhuman power tied to the athletic excellence of highly compensated athletes such as Michael Jordan, Lebron James, and Serena Williams (see Figure 2.2). Consumers fill in this carefully cultivated meaning every time they see a Nike swoosh on a pair of shoes or t-shirt (we elaborate on logos and meaning in Chapter 7).

Perhaps the clearest example of an object that has been filled with a fetishized meaning via branding is the diamond. Diamonds are not particularly scarce and have no obvious function—they don't quench your thirst or mow your lawn. People purchase diamonds only because of the fetishized meaning behind the object, a meaning carefully constructed by the diamond industry over decades (see Figure 2.3).

For a moment, consider: what does a diamond mean? A few things probably come to mind: committed monogamous love, wealth, or status. You may recall the rituals associated with the diamond such as a marriage proposal, anniversary gift, etc. This entire meaning system was crafted and cultivated by the diamond industry (Friedman, 2015). The slogan "a diamond is forever" was coined in 1947 by an intrepid copywriter at

Figure 2.2 Nike commercial featuring Serena Williams.

Figure 2.3 Kay diamond engagement ring ad.

an advertising agency to bolster lagging sales of the relatively common jewel. This worked quite famously. "A diamond is forever" was eventually named the "slogan of the century" by *Advertising Age* magazine.

Elaborate meaning systems which include advertising transform various products (diamonds or sneakers, movies, or songs) into popular culture which brings the owner pleasure. Popular culture artifacts are invested with meaningful stories, communities of identification, and escapist fantasies for fun, pleasure, and play (all of which are considered further in this book).

When Tom and Donna on the television show *Parks and Recreation* declare a "Treat Yo Self" day, they are expressing the pleasurable experience of shopping for consumer products as a popular cultural event comparable to a Super Bowl party or music concert.

Perhaps no aspect of the business side of popular culture has more deeply seeped into our everyday consciousness than the idea of branding. People now talk about individuals as brands such as a celebrity (the Ariana Grande brand) or the average person selling "their brand" on social media to prospective employers or clients. The negligible line between advertising and branding and other forms of popular culture is most visibly observed in paid product placements in movies, TV shows, and video games. Today, virtually all movies produced by major studios, especially the big budget blockbusters with superheroes, dinosaurs, aliens, and the like, prominently feature product placements especially for automobile, fast food, clothing, alcohol, soft drink, and technology brands. Further, in an era of streaming with limited or no commercials, advertisers have more aggressively integrated product placement into shows on Netflix, Amazon, and Hulu. When a company pays for a brand to be placed in a movie or TV show, for the time the product is on the screen the audience is watching a mini-commercial as the star of the movie enjoys a cold Bud Light or drives a gleaming brand new Ford truck. Product-placed cars are never dirty or break down. Product-placed sodas and pizza are always delicious.

In a now notorious example, Apple has aggressively placed its products in films and television for years as film characters are often using phones and computers. Apple has stipulated that the villain of a movie can never use an iPhone, so, when a movie is a murder mystery such as the film *Knives Out*, the audience can simply look for the only character using an Android phone to find the murderer. Examples such as these are important because they reveal how the branding process always supersedes any artistic decisions by directors, writers, actors, or producers. The movie or TV show is a brand experience first and an entertaining story second. Corporations use branding as a way of control the meaning of products (i.e., content) in consumers' everyday lives. Branding offers easily recognizable signs to keep consumers "stuck" to content and platforms. In particular, from the perspective of the corporation, the movie or song is simply another vehicle or commodity from which to make revenue. This leads to a more focused discussion on intellectual property, which is at the heart of convergence and branding.

Intellectual property

Intellectual property allows us to commodify popular culture, as the creation of mental, artistic efforts. Intellectual property can be monetized in a wide variety of ways, such as the endless movies, TV shows, theme park rides, stage productions, and merchandise of a given franchise. In addition to using company's own properties, licensing intellectual properties to others has proven to be enormously profitable. Back in the 1970s, George Lucas creatively licensed *Star Wars* to toy makers for a fortune. Since then, corporations have scoured their properties for new and unexpected revenue streams.

Back catalogue music has unexpectedly emerged as a particularly profitable form of intellectual property. In the 1980s, in an era when new music was the overwhelming focus, record companies realized that repackaging dusty old songs on greatest hits albums could be quite profitable, especially when The Eagles' *Greatest Hits* became the top-selling album of all time. When John Fogerty released an album of all new songs in 1988, Fantasy Records, the owner of his Creedence Clearwater Revival hits, sued for copyright infringement believing the new songs were too similar to old Creedence songs. In a strange twist, due to a terrible record contract that gave full copyright ownership to his record company, Fogerty was sued for plagiarizing *himself*. Also in the 1980s, rap artists began scoring huge hits that prominently sampled old songs. When hit songs such as "You Can't Touch This" from MC Hammer and "Ice Ice Baby" from Vanilla Ice heavily sampled old hits from Rick James and Queen, the music industry took notice. Today, to prominently sample an old song usually requires giving over much of the song's royalties to a media conglomerate (the rights to old music is rarely owned by the original artist). Artists who fail to secure these rights will surely be sued and face massive legal fees as well as eventually hand over royalties (i.e., any revenue from the use or re-recording of their music), as happened with Robin Thicke with his appropriation of Marvin Gaye's music in his song "Blurred Lines." When an artist obviously appropriates an old song, such as Ariana Grande's clear reworking of the Broadway classic "My Favorite Things" in her song "Seven Rings," 90% of the royalties can go to the copyright owner (Blaise-Billy, 2019). Similarly, realizing the value of immediate nostalgic recognition, songs from the Beatles, Rolling Stones, or Bob Dylan can cost a movie producer or advertiser millions, even tens of millions, in licensing fees. In the business of popular culture, who *owns* the song is far more important than who wrote or performed a song, especially when copyright owners have legions of lawyers.

Unsurprisingly, artists have resisted their creative work being reduced to intellectual property and taken out of their control. Recently, Taylor Swift had a very public dispute with her former record label who owned the copyright of her master recordings. Feeling she was unfairly compensated and lacked control over how her music was being used, she began a process of re-recording all of her older songs with full ownership and control. She has directed her fans to only stream the new versions of her music. This represents a key dimension of the business side of popular culture that recurs in this book: corporations seek greater and greater control, but as they acquire control, artists and fans resist and defy these corporations for greater freedom in their popular cultural experiences.

The history of music streaming represents a compelling example to demonstrate consumers' resistance to corporations' attempts to control intellectual property for greater profit. To understand the current streaming business model, we need to chart a series of business decisions by the music industry. In the late 1990s and early 2000s, when albums transitioned from cassette to compact disc, the music divisions of media companies were setting record profits. Compact discs were priced two or three dollars higher than cassettes as consumers were both buying new albums on CD and replacing their favorite older albums with new CD versions. In an act of astonishing hubris, breaking an expectation established in the 1950s, record companies also stopped releasing cassette or CD singles of popular songs (usually priced at $2–$3), so consumers had to buy an entire $15 CD for a song they liked. In a climate when music consumers were particularly disillusioned by this price gouging, file sharing on the Internet exploded. Record companies were quite slow to offer any online music content as this, in their minds, would diminish, rather than enhance control of content and platform. Simultaneously, Apple's iPod offered an easy and fun device on which to listen to music. The iPod seemed like a bargain compared to those overpriced CDs. Consumers could easily rationalize downloading pirated music when they had been overpaying for years. In the wake of file sharing on websites like Napster, the record industry faced an unprecedented financial crisis with revenues plummeting. When Apple created iTunes in 2003, they had all the leverage to set the prices and conditions (Steve Jobs famously wanted 99 cent songs for marketing purposes). As streaming to smartphones emerged in the 2010s, again, Spotify and other streaming services set the conditions, leaving the record companies helpless to accept the business model established by Apple and now the expectation of consumers. The music industry still has not regained control of the platform of pop music. This represents affordances and business practices in a nutshell. A wide range of cultural conditions determine when one technology (CDs) is abandoned for a new technology (downloaded and streamed music). No matter how hard they try, corporations cannot control this process. Algorithms simply represent the latest attempt.

Algorithms

The concept of algorithms is quite difficult to define as its meaning changes from the realm of computer scientists to the more common, colloquial uses of the term. For this discussion, as a popular culture experience, we are primarily interested in *what* algorithms do (and why they do it), not *how* they do what they do (which is the focus of computer scientists). Simply, **algorithms** are "logical series of steps for organizing and acting on a body of data to quickly achieve a desired outcome" (Gillespie, 2016, p. 19).

Algorithms are ever-present when using mobile apps, playing video games, or searching the Internet. To illustrate one important, common algorithm to the business of popular culture, let's explore recommendation systems.

For the user, algorithms are the invisible mathematical processes that automatically generate Google search results, suggested videos on You-Tube and Netflix, and personalized playlists on Spotify. When searching on Google, or receiving recommended videos on YouTube or Netflix, ultimately, algorithms answer the question of what's relevant (Gillespie, 2016). In other words, recommendation algorithms curate content (Born, Morris, Diaz, & Anderson, 2021), performing a role once offered by critics or local institutions (think of how movie or music critics make recommendations, DJs chose songs for radio broadcasts, or record and video rental stores displayed recommended movies and albums). Algorithms are both intellectual property and a means of regulating and controlling users' relationship to both platform and content. Recommendation systems are not so much trying to suggest "good" or "quality" videos or songs, but, content that will keep the user on Netflix, Spotify, or YouTube—commonly referred to as being "sticky," as algorithm recommendations attract and lock users in the platform. The primary goal of the algorithm is to keep the user within the platform's boundaries and keep them consuming the company's content for long stretches of time.

For instance, YouTube's algorithm works to direct users toward specific types of sticky content, such as conspiracy theories or partisan political videos, because this content so effectively keeps the user watching content within the platform for longer periods of time. Thus, the user is exposed to the advertising which pays out revenue to the platform owner (Popken, 2018). Similarly, the recommendation algorithms for music streaming services such as Spotify are largely based on the user's previous song choices, classifying the user into groups of similar music fans (Born, Morris, Diaz, & Anderson, 2021). In other words, the algorithm gives users familiar music, quite similar to songs they (or people like them) have listened to in the past. The result is to keep the music playing endlessly on the platform by never suggesting anything unexpected and challenging outside of musical genres and styles familiar to the user. Second, by curating content, algorithms can direct users to the corporation's intellectual property. Within this logic, Disney creates a "universe" of *Star Wars* content such as the television series *The Mandalorian* and *Obi Wan Kenobi*, which are recommended whenever a user shows interest in *Star Wars*, or adjacent, content. Disney's algorithms keep the user within both the company's platform and intellectual property content. The user thus remains exposed to a brand and/or exposed to advertising, which earn revenue for the platform owner in the short term and long term.

As we wrap up the business practices of pop culture, we revisit where the chapter began. Recall that our goal was not just to identify the easy conclusion that corporations like Disney are "in it for the money." By exploring algorithms, intellectual property, advertising and branding, as well as convergence, we have gotten to know better how content creators make money to know how to navigate this system. This leads us to the style of question that media ecologists may inspire us, as tiny datapoints within this global system, to ask: when are the business practices of media corporations serving me well? When are these businesses exploiting my time and energy, or limiting my popular culture options? When and why should I accept, resist, or opt out of this system? To punctuate these questions, we present a final case study that demonstrates the logical extreme of convergence logics in pop culture.

Conclusion: Cultivating brand loyalty in children's popular culture

As Disney represents, children are a much-desired market for popular culture. In the 1980s, savvy toy companies realized that cheaply produced cartoons for action figures, such as *Transformers* and *He-Man*, served as effective advertising to children. In the 1990s and early 2000s, the Disney Channel and Nickelodeon dominated the popular culture landscape for children, representing early versions of convergence processes. Today, YouTube Kids has colonized the free time of millions of children with personalized content determined by algorithms.

Children are especially desirable to corporations as they have not yet formed their brand loyalty. A clever marketer can make a kid brand loyal to Cheerios, Adidas, Doritos, or Coke for life. Further, children's brains are unable to detect advertising tricks and are highly susceptible to colorful images, fun jingles, and recognizable characters like Sponge Bob or Minions. Because children are so vulnerable to manipulative advertising, many countries such as the United Kingdom, Greece, Norway, and Belgium have significantly restricted marketing directed at children under 12.

Entertainment media starts to feel inescapable for parents of even very young children. For instance, over 20 years ago, the movie *Shrek*, released by Disney competitor Dreamworks (which is a subsidiary of Universal), was marketed as a kind of anti-Disney alternative for family entertainment. With knowing parodies of both Disney fairy tale movies and theme parks, *Shrek* vacillated between silly broad comedy for children (plenty of bodily noises and Smashmouth songs) and clever references to the corporate machinery of Disney's empire. The film, for instance, mocked the long lines at Disneyland, the irritating "It's a Small World" ride, and the antiquated gender roles of Disney princesses.

Now, decades later, somewhat ironically, the *Shrek* franchise has successfully followed the Disney blueprint of corporate convergence. With three sequels (to date), two spin-offs (including our favorite, *Puss in Boots*), theme-park rides, a Christmas and Halloween special, a Broadway show, television series, multiple video games, and innumerable toys and other products, *Shrek* has never needed to be rebooted—it never left the public consciousness with plenty of new content in the works. *Shrek* even functions as nostalgia for Millennials sharing with their kids both the newest and classic *Shrek* content. As parents, we know that Shrek is inescapable. He appears on bandages, t-shirts, pajamas, board books, Cheez-its, Eggo waffles, countless YouTube videos, etc. Kids know who Shrek is before they can walk.

In many ways, corporations are so determined to reach children that, as a parent, resistance seems futile. And, just as the beginning of *Shrek* as the "anti-Disney" suggests, the aggressive marketing to kids through convergence is nothing new: *Spongebob, Minions, Kungfu Panda, Toy Story* join *The Muppets* and *Star Wars* as the latest brands seeking to get family audiences to "stick" to their content, with the potential to cultivate a lifetime of treasured family memories (and all the dollars that go with them). Do you believe that it is ethical for a company like Disney to market so heavily to children? Why/not? We invite you to reflect more on the business of pop culture more as we conclude Chapter 2.

Reflecting on the business of pop culture in your everyday life

- Are you "brand loyal" to any popular culture content (e.g., a sports franchise, Marvel movies, Disney princesses, etc.) or platform (Netflix, TikTok, Spotify, etc.)? Why?
- View a sequel, prequel, and/or spin-off of one of your favorite films. Do you believe it has as high a quality as the first film you saw? Why/not? How do you see convergence logic at work in this film?
- Keep a list of the advertisements you see in a single 24-hour period. How subtle or explicit do these messages appear to you as "ads"? What influence does all of this exposure to advertising have on our culture?
- Do you believe that artists should be able to sample selections from others' songs without having to pay royalties toward copyright? Why/not?
- What algorithms do you interact with every day (YouTube, Spotify, Netflix, Instagram, etc.)? How do these algorithms influence your popular culture consumption habits? Have you ever attempted to break the algorithm, or obtain recommended content in new ways? How did that go, and what did you learn?

When emphasizing the goals and tactics of the business side of popular culture, it can make consumers seem like mindless drones being directed by corporate puppet masters via advertising, algorithms, etc. Hopefully, you are already questioning this simplistic view. For every Marvel, Disney, and YouTube that seem to effortlessly produce revenue within a formulaic system, there are giant movie flops, struggling music companies, and bankrupt social media start-ups. Further, suddenly, when a popular culture experience no longer offers affordances to consumers, a revenue-generating formula can begin to fail, such as the music industry in the 2000s, with a new formula emerging in its wake (in fact, there are signs that both Facebook and Netflix's strategies or formulae may be starting to fail). In this chapter, we explored the business of popular culture production, the significant role of convergence in contemporary media companies, and the value of intellectual property and algorithms for media corporations. In the following chapter, we flip the perspective by focusing on the consumer's active role in the popular culture experience.

Note

1   Data compiled using annual searches with "Box Office Mojo" from Internet Movie Database (IMDb, https://www.boxofficemojo.com/year/2004/).

Suggested readings

Discenna, T. A. (2016). The culture industries. In G. Burns (Ed.), *A companion to popular culture* (pp. 441–460). John Wiley & Sons. https://doi.org/10.1002/9781118883341.ch24

Hallinan, B., & Striphas, T. (2016). Recommended for you: The Netflix Prize and the production of algorithmic culture. *New Media & Society*, *18*(1), 117–137. https://doi.org/10.1177/1461444814538646

Klinger, U., & Svensson, J. (2018). The end of media logics? On algorithms and agency. *New Media & Society*, *20*(12), 4653–4670. https://doi.org/10.1177/1461444818779750

Lanham, R. (2006). *The economics of attention*. University of Chicago Press.

Tryon, C. (2009). Reinventing cinema: Movies in the age of media convergence. Rutgers University Press.

References

Blaise-Billy, B. (2019, March 19). 90% of Ariana Grande's "Seven Rings" royalties go to Rodgers and Hammerstein. *Pitchfork*. https://pitchfork.com/news/90-of-ariana-grandes-7-rings-royalties-go-to-rodgers-and-hammerstein/

Born, G., Morris, J., Diaz, F., & Anderson, A. (2021, June 1). *Artificial intelligence, music recommendation and the curation of culture*. University of Toronto. https://841.io/doc/BornMorrisDiazAnderson%20%20Artificial%20

Intelligence, %20Music%20Recommendation, %20and%20the%20Curation%20of%20Culture%20(2021)%20-%209.pdf

Dellatto, M. (2022, April 14). Spotify say it paid 7 billion in royalties in 2021. *Forbes*. https://www.forbes.com/sites/marisadellatto/2022/03/24/spotify-says-it-paid-7-billion-in-royalties-in-2021-amid-claims-of-low-pay-from-artists/?sh=1bf9d238a0db

Fish, T. (2021, August 22). The 13 most watched Netflix series. *Newsweek*. https://www.newsweek.com/most-watched-netflix-original-TV-series-1621212

Friedman, U. (2015, February 13). How an ad campaign invented the diamond engagement ring. *The Atlantic*. https://www.theatlantic.com/international/archive/2015/02/how-an-ad-campaign-invented-the-diamond-engagement-ring/385376/

Gillespie, T. (2016). Algorithm. In B. Peters (Ed.), *Digital keywords: A vocabulary of information society and culture* (pp. 18–30). Princeton University Press.

Graham, M. (2021, December 6). Advertising market keeps growing much faster than expected. *Wall Street Journal*. https://www.wsj.com/articles/advertising-market-keeps-growing-much-faster-than-expected-forecasters-say-11638784800

Iqbal, M. (2023, January 9). Netflix revenue and usage statistics. *Business of Apps*. https://www.businessofapps.com/data/netflix-statistics/

Jenkins, H. (2006). *Convergence culture: Where old and new media collide*. New York University Press.

Jhally S. (1987). *The codes of advertising: Fetishism and the political economy of meaning in the consumer society*. F. Pinter.

Miller, T. (2000). Introduction: Class and the culture industries. In R. Stam & T. Miller (Eds.), *Film and theory: An anthology* (pp. 539–551). Blackwell.

Popken, B. (2018, April 19). As algorithms take over, YouTube's recommendation highlight a human problem. *NBC News*. https://www.nbcnews.com/tech/social-media/algorithms-take-over-YouTube-s-recommendations-highlight-human-problem-n867596

Rogers, T. N. (2020, July 3). Lin-Manuel Miranda has made millions off "Hamilton" in its 5-year run. *Business Insider*. https://www.businessinsider.com/lin-manuel-miranda-hamilton-money-earnings-disney-career-2020-2

Shaw, L. (2019. September 10). Concerts are more expensive than ever. *Bloomberg*. https://www.bloomberg.com/news/articles/2019-09-10/concerts-are-more-expensive-than-ever-and-fans-keep-paying-up

Simpson, J. (2017, August 25). Finding brand success in the digital world. *Forbes*. https://www.forbes.com/sites/forbesagencycouncil/2017/08/25/finding-brand-success-in-the-digital-world/?sh=7ee71fca626e

Solon, O., Shaw, L., and Turner, G. (2022, November 8). TikTok is on track to earn $12 billion this year. *Fortune*. https://fortune.com/2022/11/08/tiktok-profits-record-industry-wants-increase-royalties-revenue/.

3   Consuming popular culture

Introduction

A generation ago, most popular culture experiences were selected and scheduled by large institutions outside of an individual's control. TV viewers watched one of the shows on three networks only at a time scheduled by the networks. Music lovers only heard the songs played by radio programmers and disc jockeys, on a limited number of stations (dictated not by satellite, but by towers and signals). Movie fans waited for a movie to be screened at their local theatre. While these limitations were experienced within the lifetimes of most Americans, it feels like a distant memory in this era of overwhelming choice. Of course, now, particularly in the last ten years, virtually every song, movie, TV show, book, and video game ever created is available *immediately* at the touch of a screen (for a nominal fee). If we were to ask you, in this era of unprecedented consumer choice, why do you watch a certain TV show, listen to a certain song, read a certain book, etc., you would probably simply say, "I like it." As we introduced in Chapter 1, most of us don't spend a lot of time investigating *why* we choose one TV show or movie over another. It just makes sense to us. We might even find ourselves in curious conversations with friends saying things like, "How could you like that terrible song?" To which our friend would likely reply, "Because it's soooo good!"

In this chapter, we turn to two traditional resources for understanding why people, viewed as consumers, choose popular culture, even in our era of excessive choice: uses and gratifications theory and cultural capital. Consumers turn to popular culture that gratifies needs, including needs for intimacy (as we discuss through the idea of parasocial relationships). A second traditional resource, cultural capital, tells us that consumer choice is not just a matter of individual psychology, but has to do with the ways popular culture products are marked as "quality" or "tasteful" choices to their social groups. A Carl's Jr. bacon double cheeseburger and fries may meet the same need of sustenance as a kale and quinoa bowl from Whole

DOI: 10.4324/9781003372943-3

Foods. But we immediately know the different senses of taste and quality attached to the foods, which relate to class identities as both income and cultural capital or knowledge about "quality" food choice within one's class.

Chapter 3's focus on consumer preference, built from two theories that look at how individuals have agency (or the ability to act) to determine popular culture experiences, may seem like a contradiction to Chapter 2, which offered more of a structural determinist view. Recall that in Chapter 2, we demonstrated how powerful corporations seek to control consumers' choices of both content and platform, getting consumers to "stick" to *their* popular culture through branding, intellectual property, and recommendation algorithms. These apparent contradictions are related to an important principle of our approach in this book—exploring popular culture experiences from multiple perspectives. Taken together with Chapter 9 on globalization, Chapters 2 and 3 suggest that businesses and consumers *both* determine popular culture experiences in a kind of ebb and flow within this global system. Our chapter's closing case study gets us thinking, though, about the consequences of popular culture as this global system stretches desires and wants into "needs," and encourages us to meet them through consumption. Reality networks like Home & Garden Television (HGTV) may satisfy needs for closeness, but they also repeat messages that confuse needs and uses with desires, leading to potential harm for people and the planet.

Understanding consumer choice through uses and gratifications

For decades, researchers have tried to better understand (and even predict) how consumers interact with media. Early research into radio and television tended to treat audiences as a kind of unified whole that consumed media just as producers designed it. Over time, researchers realized people listen to the radio or watch TV for a wide range of reasons. This followed advertisers' interest in understanding who was tuning in at specific times of day so they could better target their commercials (e.g., to daytime game show versus late night talk show audiences). Instead of a passive "mass" audience, viewers and listeners were categorized into niches with unique qualities. Today, market research has become even more "niche," using psychographic techniques (and algorithms) to see how consumers in very specific identity groups (e.g., middle- to upper-class Latinas who are environmentally conscious, enjoy crossword puzzles, and vote Democratic) respond, positively or negatively, to certain genres of music or television shows.[1] Such data helps get very specific individuals to look at, click, or otherwise engage platforms, allowing businesses to predict content preferences for delivery to advertisers.

As researchers grew more interested in seeing consumers as individuals with choice and agency, they began to explore the psychology behind consumer interactions with media. **Uses and gratifications** theory assumes that individuals and groups of consumers seek out media that is useful to them, or fulfills some purpose (Whiting & Williams, 2013). Uses and gratification theory shifts away from systemic and deterministic economic structures (as in Chapter 2), and toward internal psychological processes of audiences, as they help explain why someone would like *Grey's Anatomy* season 19, or watch old Vine clips from 2013. Rather than mindlessly consuming whatever powerful forces (like media corporations) dish out, uses and gratifications theory argues that individuals consciously seek out popular culture to fulfill specific needs. Moreover, if media and popular culture regularly gratify someone's needs, they tend to continue choosing it from amongst the myriad options available. If how-to videos on YouTube help someone solve problems with broken toilets or smoke detectors, someone will likely continue to look them up when they need to solve household problems. This is referred to as the **information seeking** function of media, and is an important type of use/gratification within popular culture.

If you have had an especially stressful day, what popular culture do you choose to relax? A playlist of mellow songs, a favorite episode of *The Office*, a reality show, something else? Popular culture gratifies the need for relaxation (Menon, 2022), but also serves to connect people. Consumers turn to popular culture, like the *Harry Potter* and *Hunger Games* franchises, to support identity formation, cultural identification, and coping (Garmon, Glover, & Vozzola, 2018). Popular culture can also fulfill status needs within convergence logics: fans of stigmatized pop culture, like video games (see Chapter 11), may feel validated when they see *Assassin's Creed* and *Warcraft* turn into films (Banks & Wasserman, 2019).

People also use popular culture to organize, give, and receive social support in the face of such traumas as racist policing and sexual violence (which affects Black women at disproportionately high rates): Francis and Finn (2022), for instance, found that viewers of the TV drama *Queen Sugar* used the hashtag #QueenSugarTalks to create a space for conversations about mental health and supporting others through trauma. The authors suggest that popular culture could be a tool in which to clear space to talk about "taboo topics," and even steer people toward healthy coping, in culturally responsive ways.

One of the more powerful needs that popular culture fulfills is the need for intimacy, a close connection to other people, which can bring feelings of personal validation through sharing emotions (Şot, 2022). Interestingly, different social media platforms use affordances to foster a sense of intimacy, with users in Turkey, for instance, selecting TikTok as it helped them promote "trustful bonds," and "a safe and cozy space" with others (Şot, 2022).

Indeed, the participants in Şot's study gravitated away from airbrushed, photoshopped photography of Instagram, and toward TikTok, showing how affordances relate to uses and gratifications. Users seemed to translate the "true to life" appearance of TikTok with a greater acceptance of diverse body types, for instance, and greater support for people of different social identities.

The ability of pop culture to foster intimacy through media has a history that predates social media. With increased time spent viewing television through the 1970s and 1980s, as well as greater significance of celebrity culture, researchers studied parasocial relationships to account for how people who are mediated in popular culture could meet the need for intimacy.

Think back on a tragic and untimely celebrity death. When a celebrity such as Prince, Paul Walker, Whitney Houston, or Kobe Bryant dies unexpectedly, legions fans mourn the death like a loved one has passed away. TV reports show gatherings of hundreds of fans in cities across the world openly weeping or creating impromptu memorials. Of course, these fans have never met the celebrity. By all reasonable measures they were strangers. Yet, the fan *feels* like a friend has died. Why? In the tradition of uses and gratifications research, the term **parasocial relationship** was coined to describe the imaginary relationship between media consumers and popular culture personalities. At first glance, the idea of a parasocial relationship with a celebrity might sound a bit weird. You might think of the Eminem song "Stan" (see Chapter 5) or the many movie depictions of fans obsessively stalking an actress or sports star. In fact, research has indicated that parasocial relationships are a *normal response* to watching the same media personality regularly. In other words, if someone watches a talk show host, YouTube influencer, or TV character day after day, they will almost certainly develop some type of parasocial relationship.

Millions of people—averaging 3.25 million in 2021, to be precise—start their days watching *Good Morning America* (Katz, 2022). Why don't people grow bored watching the same people doing the same things daily? From a uses and gratifications perspective, the incredibly routine conventions of morning shows cultivate feelings of intimacy in viewers, fulfilling the interpersonal needs of companionship. The incredibly routine conventions even enhance this effect, making it seem as though Robin Roberts, George Stephanopolous, and Michael Strahan are right at the kitchen table with us—the *Good Morning America* stars of 2023 are often seen seated with a cup of coffee, sharing stories from their weekends, gossiping about current events, and looking forward to changes in the weather, just like we are.

Similarly, talk show hosts like Oprah Winfrey seem to cultivate parasocial relationships with legions of fans. Oprah would stare directly into the camera, making eye contact with the viewer, and regularly disclose details from her life such as her relationship with her husband, struggles with weight loss, or experiences with racism. Reality television shows like *The Real World* and *The Bachelor* further expanded affordances of intimacy, especially with the convention of the "confessional," in which the performers talk about deeply personal experiences directly into the camera (often in a "private" interview away from other contestants). When private information is disclosed, it develops feelings of closeness with others (Greene, Derlega, & Mathews, 2006). Today's celebrities seem well aware that sharing the intimate experiences of their lives (often on the pages of *People* magazine and *Us Weekly*) will foster greater loyalty and affection from their fans: details of wedding plans, a child's birth, or battling a life-threatening disease enhance parasocial relationships.

Today's social media influencers take the lessons from parasocial relationships past, often placing the camera within inches of their faces and blending private details of their lives with suggestions for beauty products and home décor (see Figure 3.1). Interestingly, though, social media make parasocial relationships a bit more of a two-way street. Viewers can directly respond to celebrities via @ handles and comments. In the aggregate (with hashtags, likes and sharing), fans can also inspire interactions with celebrities, who often record videos in response to fans.

As this discussion of uses and gratifications, particularly in terms of how pop culture can fulfill the need for intimacy, suggests, consumers make use of popular culture through the affordances of media or communication technology. As introduced in Chapter 1, at their simplest, affordances are the technological features that shape and enable how consumers use the technology. Affordances help explain how a technology does, or doesn't, do

Figure 3.1 Video from YouTube influencer Emma Chamberlain.

the thing users want it to do at any given time (Schrock, 2015). As Norman (2013) writes, an **affordance** is "the relationship between properties of the artefacts and capabilities of the users that establishes the way that the artefact would be used" (p. 11). For instance, when Apple first introduced the iPhone in 2007, its design was radically different from other cell phones by featuring a touchscreen rather than a keypad (think of a flip phone). Other phone makers followed suit, and soon smartphones moved from mobile telephones to the interface for interacting with any number of applications (or "apps"). Today, the Apple and Google app stores have *2–3.5 million* applications available to meet any number of needs, from navigating the streets while driving (thanks, Google Maps!), to checking weather conditions, to keeping us in touch with friends and family (Messages, Facebook, etc.).

Affordances matter to our discussion of uses and gratifications, because consumers often make decisions based on them, as much as the content they deliver. Consider the process of choosing a music streaming app. Users weigh a wide range of factors such as the cost, the interface, the accuracy of the music recommendations, the catalogue of music and podcasts in the app's database, etc. As these conditions change, the user re-evaluates their apps and perhaps decides to choose something new. To return us to the ebb and flow of consumer choice and structural determinism, the user's decisions about streaming music are limited by price, legality, etc., which is constrained by business practices described in Chapter 2. Though we may want to watch *White Lotus* for free, we may fear the legal consequences of finding pirated content, lack the technical ability to use Torrent sites, or prefer to pay the subscription fee for the easier interface of HBOMax.

This leads us to reflect critically on uses and gratifications theory. Popular culture can gratify a wide range of needs, from the mundane to the significant, through the affordances of media technology. Some uses, like seeking out credible information during the COVID-19 pandemic or hitting play on an up-tempo hip-hop song to get energized for a workout, are rather straightforward. Others, though, require a bit more self-reflection, or a knowing awareness of our activities at a given moment, and self-reflexivity, adapting our behaviors in the moment to align with our values (Nagata, 2005). Uses and gratifications theory argues we first choose a media form or technology with a conscious decision, but over time this initial decision can become an unconscious habit.

If you're one of the estimated 85% of Americans who owns a smartphone (according to the Pew Research Center, 2021), you might reflect on how useful it is to you, and why. What mobile apps do you use multiple times every day? How do you use these apps? What affordances help you use these apps to meet your needs?

Though social media users may initially turn to Instagram, for instance, to meet the needs for social interaction, self-expression, or being perceived as cool or creative (Kircaburun, Alhabash, & Tosuntaş, 2020), Instagram users may eventually develop a monotonous habit of flipping through images whenever there is a "pause" in movements throughout the day. In other words, gratifying needs can give way to grabbing one's phone whenever and wherever one doesn't know what else to do, such as when standing in line, waiting for an appointment, eating in the break room at work, etc. If this sounds familiar, you're not alone. And, as we hope to inspire by Chapter 13, self-reflexivity helps consumers recognize and even change: why am I choosing this YouTube video, TikTok, or game, right now, in this specific place? Should I stare at my screen right now? Is this serving a need in my everyday life? Is this app distracting me from another focus that would be more beneficial? Is staring at my phone actually making me feel *more* dissatisfied or bored?

Along with self-reflexivity in when, where, and how we consume popular culture, we leave this section on uses and gratifications by raising the issue of *what* we choose to consume. For instance, we often hear people say they choose a TV show or movie because it is "entertaining," which is actually a pretty ambiguous statement. *How* is the movie or TV show entertaining? A Vin Diesel movie featuring muscle cars jumping over giant canyons definitely offers an escape from the real world. A Sandra Bullock romantic comedy involving a couple finding love after facing overwhelming obstacles can nicely meet the emotional needs associated with relationships. A Matt Damon political thriller featuring a whistleblower exposing a conspiracy of powerful figures in Congress and the White House perfectly reinforces ideas about the dangers of corruption in democratic institutions. All of these movies are "entertaining," just in ways that depend on the uses and gratifications one seeks to satisfy. And, as we see with our second major theoretical answer to the question, "Why do people chose to consume specific popular culture?," what appears to be "entertaining" to consumers changes based on their levels of income, knowledge, and taste, or cultural capital.

Cultural capital and consumption: Taste, quality, and class

Consumers' popular culture choices are tied to a wide variety of factors beyond individual psychology (the needs that they satisfy with popular culture). Taste and quality affect a consumer's decision to choose a "guilty pleasure" (like reality TV or a cheesy old pop song). Taste and quality are not just individual sensations and determinations. They are discourses, that is to say longstanding conversations that may contain words, images, stylistic conventions, and other symbols or signs, which communicate a worldview (Fiske, 1987). In contrast to uses and gratifications, then, the theory of cultural capital, taste, and quality look to how a whole cultural meaning system surrounds popular culture artifacts, allowing us to make judgments. The system of ranking and classifying pop culture artifacts includes formal reviews and recommendation algorithms (Chapter 2), but is far more complex than that. Judgments of taste and quality are shared by members with similar income levels and social capital—the resources, from formal and informal education, to make sense of the reality marked within a social class. In Chapter 4, we consider in more depth the ways that social identities like class (as well as race, gender, and ability) shape experience with popular culture.

An influential figure in media studies, Pierre Bourdieu (1984), described popular culture as a form of cultural capital. **Cultural capital** refers to "a person's cultural values, habits, and tastes acquired both explicitly and tacitly; it includes things such as education and style of speech and dress" (Reagle, 2015, p. 2866). Whenever we choose a product, we are classifying ourselves and others are classifying us. For instance, the simple act of choosing a beer at a restaurant or bar immediately suggests a certain classification: the working-class Miller Lite, the upscale Stella Artois, the hipster, politically liberal local microbrew. We all choose popular culture within this system of meaning, whether we aspire to its prestige or not.

Food demonstrates this notion quite clearly. Elites seek to perform prestige by eating at elegant "Michelin star" restaurants. Other folks might perform their taste by shopping at Whole Foods and choosing the latest trendy ingredients, perhaps quinoa, organic kale, or heirloom tomatoes. On the other hand, some people might deliberately reject this elitism and gleefully enjoy a Carl's Jr. bacon double cheeseburger and fries. Whether rejecting or embracing the desire for prestige, we are all ranked and classified by others. In all likelihood, you would have little trouble naming "high class" brands of automobiles, clothing, or perfume, even if you have no interest in purchasing these items. When someone is impressed by a musician's training at Juilliard, an actor's background performing with the Royal Shakespeare Company, or a writer's Pulitzer Prize, they are fully immersed in the discourse of quality. Popular culture works in a similar manner. We may or may not particularly like "quality" TV shows, movies, or music, but we can easily identify them.

Scholars have used the term **quality** to describe the performance of respectable popular culture, especially film and television. Historically, particularly before the 1960s, TV and film were largely perceived as populist mediums and unconcerned with being viewed as "art." Over the last several decades, film and TV producers have sought to designate particular genres (historical epic, biopic, film noir, etc.) and stylistic conventions (lighting, music, costumes, acting, camera movement, etc.) as among its highest quality. The creators of these TV shows and movies self-consciously perform these stylistic conventions of quality with "an air of selectivity, refinement, uniqueness, and privilege" (Caldwell, 1995, p. 106).

Specifically, Hollywood has effectively marketed films as quality for decades, developing a bit of a stylistic formula. Think of movies that are routinely referenced as high quality, such as *The Godfather*, *Shawshank Redemption*, or *Schindler's List*. These movies share a lot in common: they are set in the past and have "historical" significance, emphasize a heroic character overcoming great obstacles, explore literary themes of war, morality, and existence, feature award-winning male actors, involve a dramatic orchestral music score, advance moderate liberal values, etc. Similarly, HBO has cultivated a reputation as the premier network for quality television. Consider the types of shows that are often celebrated on HBO: *Game of Thrones*, *Chernobyl*, *Boardwalk Empire*, and *The Sopranos*. Uncoincidentally, these shows share many of the same characteristics of quality films. And, as we consider more in Chapter 8, the quality markers include not only content matter, but also color palette, camera focus and pacing, musical score, costume and set design features—visual and aural cues that can be read within a discourse, just as words can.

The conventions of "great acting" have been repeated so frequently to filmgoers and TV viewers in promotional material and at awards ceremonies, it almost feels preordained that quality aesthetics will be rewarded. For instance, actors such as Daniel Day Lewis or Joaquin Phoenix are celebrated for dramatic physical transformations like weight loss/gain or speaking in a new dialect. Actors whose characters face tremendous grief, suffering, and/or mental illness (as we elaborate in Chapter 4) are also frequently singled out for their performances, such as Jeremy Strong in *Succession* (see Figure 3.2).

Figure 3.2 Ad for HBO's *Succession* highlighting awards.

Finally, great acting is in "serious" movies featuring moments of intense emotional expression, especially weeping uncontrollably or violently shouting in anger. Many of such performances appear in films directed by widely celebrated "auteur" directors (i.e., filmmakers with a distinctive singular vision) like Martin Scorsese, Quentin Tarantino, or Steven Spielberg.

These conventions reveal some interesting biases in what we most value about movie and TV acting. For instance, comic performances are rarely awarded by Hollywood, even though many actors will confirm that comedy acting is harder than dramatic acting (the actor must create a believable character *and* have impeccable comic timing). Further, the incredible physicality demanded of action movies, especially martial arts films (think of Jackie Chan), requires years of training and expert timing, but is not usually treated as great acting.

In the sense-making processes of popular culture, "quality" is defined in many respects by what it is not—the lowbrow entertainment for unrefined tastes (which have been historically viewed as working class) such as broad comedies or slasher horror movies. Just as a kale quinoa bowl connotes a different quality than a McDonald's Big Mac, consumers make choices in popular culture based on different quality and taste of films, television, and musical artists. Even the mention of professional wrestling, *Real Housewives*, or Vanilla Ice brings a giggle or eye roll, perhaps the recognition of a shared "guilty pleasure." We count ourselves among the millions of people who enjoy some of these "low quality" forms of popular culture each day.

Dance pop, with traditions in disco and 1980s club music, is a genre that has often been denigrated as low quality, especially by disc jockeys and music critics. In 1979, a radio DJ even organized a "disco demolition" rally at a Chicago White Sox game, featuring the explosive destruction of disco records, which devolved into an angry riot. In contrast, quality pop music is associated with the singer-songwriter styles exemplified by Bob Dylan, Bruce Springsteen, and the Beatles. To further demonstrate this bias, pop stars have pivoted toward "quality" singer-songwriter styles when seeking greater public credibility. For instance, Taylor Swift and Lady Gaga have both emphasized their singer-songwriter credibility in recent years (playing alone with a guitar or piano) while artists such as Dua Lipa, Selena Gomez, and Kendrick Lamar have partnered with singer-songwriters from the past such as Elton John, Coldplay, and U2. We find it curious that to demonstrate an artist is "talented," people will often highlight their performances alone at a piano singing, as though singing and dancing in complicated choreographed routines with dozens of dancers in elaborate costumes does not demonstrate their enormous talent (the latter seems much harder than the former).

Recently, a number of critics have highlighted the ways discourses of quality reaffirm the prestige of certain styles of popular culture, usually associated with privileged White men. For instance, the growing poptimism movement (briefly described in Chapter 1) is a response to these biases, celebrating music genres often created and performed by people of color and members of the LGBTQ+ community. "Lowbrow" film genres (horror, broad comedy, and action) have historically had more diverse filmmakers and stars, and dance pop and disco grew from LGBTQ+ artists. In just the last several years, a lively conversation has emerged over what is truly quality popular culture, whether it conforms to "quality" discourse or not.

Poptimism helps address how social identities affect our perceptions of what is valuable (artful, moving, and thus worthy of awards and celebration) in pop culture. Social media, too, allows consumers to celebrate work that would have been marginalized decades ago. The success of recent films (like the horror comedy *Get Out* and the horror drama *Parasite*) represents change, where films outside the White mainstream are not only popular with consumers, but also with critics. Further, the unfortunate and very long tradition of critically acclaimed and award-winning "White savior" movies such as *The Help*, *Dances with Wolves*, *The Blind Side*, *The Last Samurai*, etc. has been harshly criticized across the Internet, especially after *Green Book* won the Academy Award for Best Picture in 2019.

As this discussion of quality aesthetics in food, film, and music underscores, "good" popular culture is not simply a matter of an artist's vision matching with objective standards for "quality" art. The social capital perspective calls our attention to the ways that income provides access to pop culture experiences, but also relates to knowledge and sensibilities. The poptimism movement expands the critique of quality to include other social identities (notably, race, gender, and sexuality), suggesting that what we often celebrate as valuable popular culture relates to White, masculine, or male, straight privilege as much, or more, than aesthetically and morally valuable forms of expression. We elaborate on these ideas in Chapter 4. For now, we conclude the discussion of cultural capital by elaborating on consumers' power in the digital economy.

The tradition of fulfilling audience desire for entertainment through popular appeal, rather than gatekeepers' ideas of aesthetically and morally valuable art, continues in the digital economy. Interestingly, digital affordances seem to be a kind of "match-maker" for lowbrow stars, genres, and audiences. For instance, Adam Sandler's movies (e.g., *The Waterboy* and *The Wedding Singer*) are unlikely to be taken seriously by critics and audiences seeking "quality" film experiences. Indeed, his filmmaking had hit a lull, with weak box-office returns in the early 2010s. But Netflix signed a four-movie deal for $275 million with Sandler in 2015 because of his popularity with subscribers. By 2019, Sandler's comedy *Murder Mystery* (co-starring *Friends* star Jennifer Aniston) was the most watched film on Netflix (Ruimy, 2020). Just as audiences may have voted with their dollars in yesterday's penny cinema, today's audiences can access content that comports to their tastes in the digital economy.

Along with streaming subscriptions, rating systems feel like a natural part of our popular culture consumption routine. Amazon includes user reviews of movies, TV shows, and music on their platform. Similarly, IMDb includes aggregated ratings from thousands of users of the website. Even Rotten Tomatoes includes an "audience score" alongside its aggregated rating from mainstream critics. "Crowdsourcing," the act of soliciting data and/or labor from large groups of people through digital affordances (like a website or a mobile app), on platforms like Amazon and Rotten Tomatoes, began in the late 1990s. Rating systems offer an important metric through which to view consumer tastes; but like other affordances, rating systems exceed the original intended design of popular culture producers.

The five-star quantitative review, as well as longer qualitative user comments, aggregate (or pull together) and archive (maintain in the long term) data, which is then accessed by other consumers. Ratings systems provide the "stuff" of cultural capital. Consumers can use ratings systems to gather information, share stories and insights, react to critics, etc. Interestingly, and perhaps in response to the growing power of consumers, Netflix discontinued user reviews in 2017, and shifted entirely to corporate-owned algorithms to determine content recommendations. In other cases, companies are seeking to expand consumer power, allowing consumers to put their money where their values are. Filmmakers have used Kickstarter as a way to raise money from fans for feature films such as *Veronica Mars* and *The Babadook*. Crowdfunding is an important form of crowdsourcing, where consumers work outside conventional corporate structures, in a sense becoming producers. Indeed, as digital affordances show, the once clear boundaries between consumer and producer in popular culture is now quite blurred: when someone watches YouTube, posts comments, and responds with their own video, are they a consumer or a producer?

In conclusion, we've seen the ways that cultural capital—particularly the stylistic conventions that distinguish "lowbrow" from "high quality" popular culture—can affect consumer decisions to select artifacts. Within digital media logic, as well as uses and gratifications theory, it may be more accurate to refer to people as *users* or *experiencers* of popular culture, rather than as *consumers* who passively take in what producers create. Yet, as our final case study invites us to consider, popular culture producers will continue to confuse needs and desires as they strive for brand loyalty.

Conclusion: Distinguishing needs and desires in lifestyle branding and reality television

HGTV is a popular basic cable network that averaged 826,000 total viewers daily, making it the 11th most popular channel on television in early

2023 (USTVDB, 2023). The network began in 1994, and its most popular shows include *Home Town*, *Fixer to Fabulous*, and *House Hunters*, all of which pull audiences of 892,000–1.5 million. The content of the different series varies, but the top performers on HGTV have learned the lessons of the convergence economy. *Home Town*, particularly, is a branded franchise that has spin-off shows: 2022's *Home Town Kickstart*, for instance, sees hosts Erin and Ben Napier traveling from their home in Laurel, Mississippi (which they share with young daughters, Helen and Mae), to small towns like Buffalo, Wyoming, and LaGrange, Kentucky. Partnering with *People* magazine, *Home Town Kickstart* is hoping to foster a "small-town renaissance" (HGTV, 2022). The Napiers own Laurel Mercantile, which is not only a store in their Mississippi town, but also a website where people from all over the world can purchase kitchenware, home décor, clothing, and other "lifestyle" items (including candles from Erin Napier's "Scent Library"); and where people can link to *Home Town* episodes. Each episode in season four features the Napiers working on home remodels and telling stories of the home owners. Viewers can conveniently locate materials used in the various remodels on the website, laurelmercantile.com, including Sherwin Williams paint, floor lamps from Target, drapery and hardware from Pier 1 and Lowe's, and art from Southern Antiques.

In some ways, such details matter less than the parasocial interactions networks like HGTV cultivate. HGTV reminds us of scholarship that connected TV to warmth and domestic life due to its audio-visual affordances and its constant presence in the intimate spaces of our homes (namely, the living room) (Spigel, 1992). Along with fostering intimacy between HGTV personalities like the Napiers and their viewers, the shows normalize design practices, making it seem as though we should be constantly working to achieve a quality, tasteful space. In fact, more and more homeowners are renovating their homes using the materials (inexpensive flooring, paint, etc.) and appliances featured in HGTV shows (Mull, 2022). Renovating and redesigning have become so normalized over time that real estate and design professionals coined the term "HGTV effect" to account for their clients' expectations that remodeling and/or selling a home is a quick, convenient, and flawless process (Chappell, 2020).

Along with the HGTV effect, for people who watch the shows regularly, the *desire* for a home that looks generically "new" (like a house ready to be shown for prospective buyers or an Airbnb ready to be photographed for prospective clients) seems to become a *need* for redecorating and/or remodeling the home. As real estate blogger, Jon Gorey (May 3, 2019) cites, people in the US were projected to spend $337 billion on remodeling in 2019, with 58% of homeowners planning a home improvement project (per a 2018 LightStream Survey). In terms of this chapter, Gorey worries that repeated viewing of HGTV has led people to not just gratify needs, but to "feel like your life is incomplete without stone counters and an open living space."

The trendy products featured on HGTV are replaced each new season. Most media consumers spend time and energy choosing products, especially popular culture products, that are largely disposable. Like other consumer products, we are encouraged to experience some fleeting pleasure from popular culture, then throw it away. Gorey cites an EPA study that finds remodeling a typical kitchen and dining room would generate more than two tons of construction debris, and likely result in kitchen appliances (the "standard" of a range, dishwasher, refrigerator, microwave) ending up in the landfill—since most (42% of them, per the Environmental Protection Agency or EPA) do end up in the landfill. This doesn't even account for the cost of many of the products featured on shows like *Home Town*. So while the Napiers likely have the best of intentions, like many other lifestyle entrepreneurs, they are quite successful at navigating today's pop culture economy to support their own livelihood (to the benefit of anyone investing in, or employed at the top of, HGTV and networked companies). Though it seems like their recommendations for freshening one's flooring, window treatments, and paint job, are coming from a friend, we encourage anyone to look at whether this parasocial relationship has a reciprocal interaction before spending a lot of money on home improvement projects likely to lead to a good deal of waste.

Reflecting on consuming pop culture in your everyday life

- What needs are met by your favorite mobile apps, TV shows, movies, and video games? Compare these pop culture artifacts to those which you identify as equipment for living in communities of which you are a part. How is equipment for living similar to, and different from, uses and gratifications?
- What characteristics do you associate with quality TV, movies, and music? Do you tend to choose quality popular culture? Why or why not?
- Do you have a "guilty pleasure" in pop culture? If so, how does this chapter's discussion of cultural capital, what makes certain pop culture "low brow," change your understanding of the guilty pleasure?
- Do you spend time consuming popular culture that is quickly forgotten? Why? What factors make popular culture re-watchable and treasured over many years?
- What are the potential effects (sometimes hidden) of our popular culture consumption habits? Who benefits from these habitual patterns of consumption? Who suffers?
- Have your desires ever felt like "must have" or "must do" needs, similar to our case study with HGTV?

Just like the latest clothing trends or model of a phone, we are conditioned to gobble up whatever new, forgettable content is popping up on our streaming apps based on a corporation's recommendations. Of course, most of us have favorite movies that we love re-watching over and over. We have songs we can sing by heart, always make us cry, and/or that we play at our wedding or anniversary. Popular culture can be deeply appreciated and interpreted, providing much deeper meaning. As we explore throughout this book, popular culture can build communities, offer emotional support, even define our cultural history. This inherent contradiction, like so many associated with popular culture, helps us understand how popular culture can feel so totally trivial and disposable, as well as deeply momentous and enduringly meaningful *at the same time*.

In conclusion, Chapter 3 offered two traditional answers for the question of why consumers choose the pop culture they consume: uses and gratifications and cultural capital help us understand both the uses (and psychological needs) met by pop culture, as well as taste making. Along with recognizing consumer agency (or power to choose to meet their needs), in Chapter 4, we consider how pop culture isn't simply a profit-making endeavor—it is closely tied to who we are as individuals and collectives.

Note

1 Pop culture producers have a long history of using test screening, audience preference surveys, and other marketing techniques to gauge consumer preference. Test screenings often influence the editing of films, in some cases even changing a movie's ending or removing characters from the film entirely. In television, research has shifted away from sweeping generalizations about what "women" think of a program, to more particular qualities of psychology in groups: "behaviors, attitudes, interests, values, opinions, feelings, etc." (Abzug, 2011, p. 7). In order to get inside the heads of consumers, audience researchers may start with specific questions about a brand: How would you feel about a TV show in the *Star Wars* universe featuring Yoda? Market research may show a commercial, TV show, or other artifact, and get real time reactions from consumers who move dials from one to a hundred (Ivala, 2007). Psychographic research of today reflects trends discussed in Chapter 8, as marketers want to know the sensations experienced around brands to keep people "stuck" to content.

Suggested readings

Baumann, S. (2007). *Hollywood highbrow: From entertainment to art*. Princeton University Press.

Jankovich, M. (2008). *Quality popular television*. British Film Institute.

Ruggiero, T. (2000). Uses and gratifications theory in the 21st century. *Mass Communication & Society*, 3(1), 3–37. 10.1207/S15327825MCS0301_02.

References

Abzug, R. (2011, December). The future of television audience research: Changes and challenges. USC Annenberg, The Norman Lear Center. http://learcenter.org/pdf/futureoftvaudience.pdf

Banks, J., & Wasserman, J. A. (2019). The big screen treatment: Gratifications sought in game to film transmedia. *Poetics*, *73*, 72–83. https://doi.org/10.1016/j.poetic.2019.01.004

Bourdieu, P. (1984). *Distinction: A social critique of the judgement of taste* (R. Nice, Trans.). Harvard University Press.

Caldwell, J. T. (1995). *Televisuality: Style, crisis, and authority in American television*. Rutgers University Press.

Chappell, C. (2020, February 2). They slap lipstick on a pig: What Chicago real estate experts think of the HGTV effect. *Chicago Tribune*. https://www.chicagotribune.com/real-estate/ct-re-0216-windy-city-rehab-hgTV-myths-20200210-nnrsvxaqancspkm7hl337o3na4-story.html

Fiske, J. (1987). *Television culture*. Methuen.

Francis, D. B., & Finn, L. (2022). A theoretically based analysis of Twitter conversations about trauma and mental health: Examining responses to storylines on the television show *Queen Sugar*. *Health Communication*, *37*(9), 1104–1112. https://doi.org.aurarialibrary.idm.oclc.org/10.1080/10410236.2021.1888454

Garmon, L. C., Glover, R. J., & Vozzola, E. C. (2018). Self-perceived use of popular culture media franchises: Does gratification impact multiple exposures? *Psychology of Popular Media Culture*, *7*(4), 572–588. DOI:10.1037/ppm0000153

Gorey, J. (2019, May 3). America, you've lost your freaking mind about remodeling. *Apartment Therapy*. https://www.apartmenttherapy.com/home-remodeling-negative-effects-260749

Greene, K., Derlega, V., & Mathews, A. (2006). Self-disclosure in personal relationships. In A. L. Vangelisti & D. Perlman (Eds.), *The Cambridge Handbook of Personal Relationships* (pp. 412–413). Cambridge University Press.

HGTV. (2022, April 19). HGTV to expand *Home Town* to multi-series franchise. HGTV. https://www.hgtv.com/shows/home-town/hgtv-to-expand-home-town-into-multi-series-franchise-#:~:text=In%20HGTV's%20new%20Home%20Town, to%20six%20small%20towns%20nationwide

Ivala, E. (2007). Television audience research revisited: Early television audience research and the more recent developments in television audience research. *Communicatio*, *33*(1), 26–41. DOI: 10.1080/02500160701398961

Katz, A. (2022, September 20). Here are morning show ratings. *Ad Week*. https://www.adweek.com/TVnewser/here-are-morning-show-ratings-for-2021-22-TV-season-and-q3-2022/514894/

Kircaburun, K., Alhabash, S., & Tosuntaş, Ş. B. (2020). Uses and gratifications of problematic social media use among university students: A simultaneous examination of the big five of personality traits, social media platforms, and social media use motives. *International Journal of Mental Health Addiction*, *18*, 525–547. https://doi.org/10.1007/s11469-018-9940-6

López, C., Hartmann, P., & Apaolaza, V. (2019). Gratifications on social networking sites: The role of secondary school students' individual differences in loneliness. *Journal of Educational Computing Research*, *57*(1), 58–82. https://doi.org/10.1177/0735633117743917

Menon, D. (2022). Purchase and continuation intentions of over-the-top (OTT) video streaming platform subscriptions: A uses and gratification theory perspective. *Telematics and Informatics Reports*, *5*, https://doi.org/10.1016/j.teler.2022.100006.

Mull, A. (2022, August 19). The HGTV-ification of America. *The Atlantic*. https://www.theatlantic.com/technology/archive/2022/08/hgTV-flipping-houses-cheap-redesign/671187/

Nagata, A. L. (2005). Promoting self-reflexivity in intercultural education. *Journal of Intercultural Communication*, *8*, 139–167.

Norman, D. (2013). *The design of everyday things*. Basic Books.

Pew Research Center, (2021, April 7). Mobile fact sheet. *Pew Research*. https://www.pewresearch.org/internet/fact-sheet/mobile/

Reagle, J. (2015). Geek policing: Fake geek girls and contested attention. *International Journal of Communication*, *9*, 2862–2880.

Ruimy, J, (2020, January 31). Netflix signs Adam Sandler to $275 million movie deal. *World of Reel*. https://www.worldofreel.com/blog/2020/1/netflix-signs-adam-sandler-to-275-million4-movie-deal-claims-its-viewers-spent-2-billion-hours-watching-his-movies

Schrock, A. (2015). Communicative affordances of mobile media: Portability, availability, locatability, and multimediality. *International Journal of Communication*, *9*, 18. https://ijoc.org/index.php/ijoc/article/view/3288

Sot, İ. (2022). Fostering intimacy on TikTok: A platform that "listens" and "creates a safe space." *Media, Culture, & Society*, *44*(8), 1490–1507. https://doi.org.aurarialibrary.idm.oclc.org/10.1177/01634437221104709

Spigel, L. (1992). *Make room for TV: Television and the family ideal in postwar America*. University of Chicago Press.

USTVDB. (2023). US Television Database. *HGTV*. https://usTVdb.com/networks/hgTV/

Whiting, A. & Williams, D. (2013). Why people use social media: A uses and gratifications approach. *Qualitative Market Research*, *16*(4), 362–369. https://doi.org/10.1108/QMR-06-2013-0041

4 Identity and popular culture

Introduction

In 2020, the National Football League (NFL) team based in Washington, DC, after almost 90 years, eliminated the mascot from its franchise. The decision followed a decade of high schools, colleges, and other professional sports teams across the US deciding to change their mascots from those that featured the names of tribal nations or images/names relating to Indigenous People. And this was after years of debate and criticism, including public protests from Native groups, who argued that the team names appropriated sacred cultural symbols and included centuries-old stereotypes that were demeaning to Indigenous People. Some fans saw the protests as liberal political correctness gone wrong, advocating that the mascots were "celebrating" Native American culture.

Contrasting the Washington NFL team, Florida State University continues to use the Seminole mascot with the support of, and interaction with, the Seminole tribal nation. The Seminole nation is involved in the choices concerning the depiction of the mascot during games, on team uniforms, and in promotional materials. The University and Seminoles have also collaborated on educational outreach programs concerning Seminole cultural history, making the relationship more reciprocal than simply a monetary transaction (Baker, 2020).

The mascot controversy demonstrates how central identity is to popular culture. Identity in this example includes sports fans and corporate brand identity, as well as political identifications. But even more important for our purposes in Chapter 4, it includes social identities (like race and ethnicity) and questions of power: Who has the power to represent another group of people? And who can financially gain from these representations? We prepare you to join complex conversations on identity by walking through different dimensions of identity as individual, social, and intersectional. At each step, we discuss how identity is a social construction and performance. Centering a Black feminist perspective, we consider how representations of identities have (and can continue to) exclude or even

DOI: 10.4324/9781003372943-4

harm groups based on their identities; but also how popular culture has the potential to reimagine identities outside of domination. We conclude the chapter with an extended discussion of "cancel culture," to promote reflection and reflexivity concerning identity and power.

Identity as a social construction and performance

As we've established, popular culture is worthy of our attention not only because we spend so much time and money consuming it, nor just because it brings joy. Rather, pop culture is a reflection of lived experience, which also creates lived experience. Popular culture is both a mirror and a stage to the larger communities and societies of which it is a part. As such, popular culture is a generator and purveyor of meanings, the basis for much of human reality.

Identity refers to the sense of one's self, a collection of who one "is," how one experiences oneself, and how one performs that sense of self to the world. As sociologists in the Chicago school (like George Herbert Mead) put forth, there is no essential core to who we are as individuals. Mead (1934) argued, against the prevailing theories of the time, that humans act on more than just instinct. Though the sensations of hunger and thirst, or the desire for warmth and comfort, motivate individual action, they do not explain the complexity of human relationships. Mead and others assumed that an individual is born as *tabula rasa*, a blank slate, whose sense of self emerges through communication with others. More particularly, significant others like parents, friends, romantic partners, and teachers, reinforce over time who a person performs as, their sense of self. Symbolic interaction, or an exchange between people using words and images, gives meaning to who "I am" and who "you are."

Popular culture, too, influences how we view and perform our sense of self. Have you ever shifted your "go to" genre of music? We have. We remember different music "phases" that we went through over time, including Christina, who was really into country music as a teen and young adult. She wore "roper" jeans and black leather cowboy boots, a patterned Western button-up shirt, and went line dancing at the bars of Manhattan, Kansas, in college. Maybe you stored all your old gear in your parents' basement, too, and became a fan of Cake, Weezer, and Counting Crows. Maybe you have gravitated more toward hip hop, emo and goth music, or have "discovered" punk styles (which haven't changed much since they attracted our friends in the 1980s and 1990s). A change in music and fashion can often bring out a change in personal identity—maybe you drop your plan to marry your high school sweetheart and live in a small town. Maybe you spend less time with friends who enjoy line dancing, and more time with friends who enjoy talking politics or philosophy. The point is that popular culture can help motivate, and reflect, a change in the story of who you are, or could be.

This relates to another important facet of identity through a popular culture perspective, and a reason why popular culture is so worthy of study: Identity is a performance (Conquergood, 1983). Building on the social constructionist premise that there is no "essence" to who/what the self is; and that the self is built through interactions with language and other symbols; we consider identity as expression, built with others (and built with others in mind). The range of available performances of identity are set, in part, by social identities (discussed more below). The meanings that have accreted over time for physical markers (such as skin tone), as well as resources accessible through money and education, mean that identity is not a "limitless" play that all people participate in equally.

With other communication scholars (see Madison & Hamera, 2005), we consider the word "performance" not to mean a fictional or formal event (like a concert or movie screening). Rather, **performance** is a heightened aesthetic occasion which occurs in everyday life. It is "heightened" due to greater attention and intentionality, often on the part of the one initiating performance (but also including others viewing and joining in on the performance), and aesthetic because performance tends to celebrate the artistic flow, the emotional and non-instrumental qualities of the moment. Identity performances are also context specific—so the version of self we present at work will likely differ from the self we present with friends, which will differ still from the version of self we present with family, and so on.

Identity performances are not limited to immediate, face-to-face contexts. Perhaps you have joined a virtual reality (VR) dance club where avatars from around the world meet to dance, as VR DJs share electronic dance music (EDM), in an entirely virtual space (see Chapter 8). Whether virtual or face-to-face, contemporary popular culture offers ample opportunity to play with identity performances. When we choose an avatar in a video game, when we change our @ handle and profile pic in Instagram, we are presenting a version of who we are for others to engage.

But the performative nature of identity is not only a matter of storytelling and play. Identity performance can lead to "social validation," as well as determine "who one should" and should not "socialize with" (Walker & Caprar, 2020, p. 1081). When we consider the layer of profit on top of play, too, the stakes of popular culture raise. Looking back on the sports mascot controversy described at this chapter's opening, we may ask: What does it mean for a football team owned by a wealthy White man to be literally profiting off the likeness of Indigenous People? This leads us to another important dimension of who we are, which is created and expressed within popular culture: social identity.

Social identities: Representations and standpoints

Social identity refers to long-standing social constructions of groups, often with connections to physical, mental, and/or cultural differences between people. As we considered with individual identity, popular culture is a site inundated with social identity performances. Importantly, as we consider in this section, social identities are vehicles through which groups of people (in dominant or majority identities) maintain their privilege—sometimes by subjecting other groups of people (in non-dominant identities) to marginalization or even oppression (Allen, 2023). The identities of people who create and perform popular culture, as well as the ways that popular culture *represents* social identities, can perpetuate dominance, or/and imagine and perform ways of being outside of dominance. Finally, in this section, we consider social identities as a *resource* for members of different groups to interpret and express their worldviews in popular culture.

An easy shorthand for social identities is demographic information, like data you may have shared in applications or on a census form. Age, socioeconomic status (such as average annual income), race and ethnicity, gender and gender identity, sexuality, ability, nationality or immigration status, and religion or faith community, tell prospective employers or schools about your background. Did you grow up in a house with more income and thus a greater likelihood of access to quality education and health care? Does a physical or mental disability affect the way that you learn and work, requiring accommodation to access learning or work? Social locations like socioeconomic status and ability give us information about power, privilege, and marginalization that affects an individual's experience.

Social identities demonstrate the *systemic* ways that group differences align with differences in power. Critics of Hollywood circulated a hashtag in 2016, for instance, to challenge the Academy of Motion Picture Arts and Sciences (AMPAS) to recognize the creative achievements of people of color. #OscarsSoWhite publicized the privilege that White actors, directors, writers, etc., have in their industry, including their disproportionately frequent appearance on the award stage. The AMPAS is the institutional face of a complex network of interconnected pieces, a popular culture system that includes content development (writing, storyboarding, animation), storytelling (acting, directing, filming, editing), distribution (advertising, public relations appearances and campaigns), and commentary or reflection on the system (reviews, journalism, awards). If Hollywood continues to hire White and cisgender male content creators to tell the stories of White and cisgender male characters, with production and distribution being dominated by White cisgender men, that all seems beyond individual control. To some degree, it is. But, as with all systems, this one is not beyond change. Individuals, and especially collections of individuals, have the ability to change systems: indeed, a study released by UCLA (2022) shows that women characters are about proportionate to men characters in broadcast, cable, and digital television, with women writers about equal to men across platforms. People of color are also gaining parity, though still underrepresented two to one in television. Not only do people have the ability to change systems. We believe that it is up to *all* of us to support a system that works for everyone—not just some at the continued exclusion of others. This is why conversations about social identities are so important.

Peggy McIntosh (2003) famously compared White privilege to a knapsack (or backpack), "an invisible package of unearned assets which," she reflected, "I can count on cashing in each day, but about which I was 'meant' to remain oblivious" (p. 191). McIntosh lists 26 unique privileges that she, as a White person, can count on daily, which range from life and death matters (like encounters with police), to financial and job well-being, to ordinary moments of popular culture. For instance, when she visits grocery or music stores, she can expect a variety of foods that relate to her culture, and an ample selection of content produced by people who look like her.

Here, McIntosh demonstrates why **representation** matters. To represent someone, as in a legal matter, means the act of speaking for or on behalf of that person. In the context of popular culture, representation refers to the ways that content projects a reality. While popular culture projects many facets of reality (like places, rituals, habits, and stories), our focus in this chapter is on identity. And as we have said, given that individual and social identity as a construction and a performance, popular culture has a very important role in representing social identities like ability, race and ethnicity, and gender. Popular culture has the power to **other**, that is to separate and devalue those who appear different on the basis of social identities. In McIntosh's invisible knapsack, she includes the ability to find plastic bandages in her skin tone. Bandage manufacturers like Band-Aid (a Johnson & Johnson brand) modeled their product after White skin tone, othering (separating and devaluing) darker skin tones.

One form of othering is rendering a group of people invisible in public discourse. A sheer lack of **visibility**, as a refusal to speak of, recognize, or represent a social identity in popular culture, can lead to feelings of inferiority for members of identity groups. The Gay and Lesbian Alliance Against Defamation (GLAAD), one of the US's largest advocacy organizations for the LGBTQ+ community, describes its choices to initiate a social media campaign with Netflix, #FirstTimeISawMe, in response to a lack of visibility for trans folks. Trans-identified people share (in tweets collected on GLAAD's site) how seeing trans or genderqueer characters helped foster connection and positive views of themselves. Further, as GLAAD (n.d.) notes, "multiple polls show that approximately 20% of Americans say they personally know someone who is transgender. Given this reality, most

Americans learn about transgender people through the media." Visibility in popular culture is particularly important given the uptick in laws (especially at the state and local level) designed to deny trans people the right to play sports, seek health care, or even use the bathroom, consistent with their gender identities (see ACLU, 2023, January 24).

Another harmful form of representation in popular culture is the **stereotype**. A stereotype is a simplified perception of an individual, based on their membership in an identity group. Stereotypes are widely held beliefs about members of a group, for instance people of a socioeconomic class or sexuality. "Gay men are stylish and neat," "rich people are snobs" are two examples of over-generalizations. When we apply these over-generalizations to individuals (without considering an individual's unique characteristics), we stereotype them. Stereotypes also mar public perception of entire groups of people, as in discourse around so-called "bathroom bills," which make it illegal to enter a public restroom that is not consistent with sex assigned at birth. Discourse around bathroom bills has invoked stereotypes of trans folks (particularly transwomen) as deviant, even dangerous predators.

We can see how attitudes toward people in marginalized identities have changed by revisiting old films, such as Disney's *Dumbo*, *The Jungle Book*, and *Lady and the Tramp*, which have scenes that, as Internet commentators put it kindly, "don't age well." Racist stereotypes of African American Vernacular English as being inarticulate or a sign of lower intelligence, of Asian characters as conniving or untrustworthy, are difficult to watch because the negative over-generalizations are so obvious, and so hateful.

Other stereotypes are more subtle, perhaps because they have been around for so long that they seem natural, normal, and beyond question. For instance, watching *Sleeping Beauty* and *Snow White* end with a "true love's kiss," in which a Prince Charming character "awakens" a girl from her "slumber" seemed harmless to our eyes as kids growing up in the 1970s and 1980s. However, stereotypes that men are chivalrous saviors who may kiss girls without consent, pursue instant heterosexual attraction that leads to marriage, etc., have "not aged well." These stereotypes are not identities for men or women that we want our children to enact. As Ono (2017) notes, "the meaning of a stereotype is not fixed" (p. 106), because it is an outcome of different cultural forces, and these forces change. The idea of Asians and Asian Americans as a "yellow peril" or massive force poised to overthrow the US government was later joined by the "model minority" stereotype, in which Asian American characters were depicted as studious, quiet, and happy to assimilate to US culture. Ono and Pham (2009) show how racist discourses combined the two stereotypes in characterizing Asian American students at California high schools and universities.

Through persistent critique, advocates have pushed content creators to stop producing blatant and subtle stereotypes. In the hopes of augmenting the quantity of representation, though, some films are guilty of using token characters. A **token** is a singular representative of someone in marginalized identity/ies, who is not a fully realized character or a meaningful part of the story. *Saturday Night Live* lampoons tokens in its parody of *Frozen 2*, where Kenan Thompson portrays Arendelle's lone soldier of color: "In rural Norway? In 1840?" Questioning whether or not his presence creates "a real rainbow of colors now," Thompson's sketch comedy calls out why tokenism is harmful. Including the "one Black character" others Black people. Token characters suggest that roles and actors are *only* or *primarily* included because of their race, and not by virtue of who they fully are as individuals.

Reliance on stereotypes and tokens to populate stories owes to formulaic (and, frankly, lazy) business practices as well as longstanding patterns of discrimination. Remember the toothpaste factory analogy we introduced in Chapter 2? Producers are more likely to retain the same stories and characters that brought successful profits, a formula which will be able to appear in lots of different content across different media and products. Here, if a conventionally attractive, thin, White girl with blonde hair and blue eyes earned money last year, she will be the template to try to make money this year. Given the assembly line of popular culture, it is no surprise that stereotypes and tokens persist in often unconscious ways.

Along with pointing out harmful representations (like othering, stereotypes, and tokens), critics of representation often look at both the quantity and quality of how social identities are represented to evaluate popular culture. For instance, disability rights advocates followed the #OscarsSoWhite hashtag with their own analysis of Hollywood's poor representation. In 2016, the Ruderman Family Foundation released a study that concluded "people with disabilities are the most unrepresented minority in Hollywood" (Wagmeister, 2016). Disability rights advocates make this claim on the basis of the low number of people with disabilities employed in the creation and production of film and television, as well as the poor number of, and quality representations of, disabled characters. The study showed that 95% of disabled characters in prominent television shows are played by able-bodied actors. To put that differently, even though 20% of the US population lives with disabilities, only 5% of disabled characters on television are performed by actors with disabilities.

The Annenberg Inclusion Initiative elaborates on poor quantity and quality of representation with their analysis of the top 100 grossing films of 2019. First, only 1.5% of characters in these films experience a mental health condition, in contrast to 21% of the general population (Oganesyan, 2022). We might say, then, that Hollywood fails to represent (or reflect) the number of people with mental disabilities. Further, the study found that "over half of characters with mental health conditions were perpetrators of violence" in their storylines. So in the few cases in which characters live with mental illness, they are shown in stereotypical ways. Here, we might say that representation fails to align with the reality that many experience, and further stigmatizes disability.

Spotlight on questioning representation in a pop culture artifact

Interested in evaluating a pop culture artifact's representation of social identities? Remember that both quantity and quality are important. As one of our mentors would say of changing the culture of toxic masculinity in a workplace, "you can't just add women and stir." For any piece of popular culture, "you can't just add minorities and stir" to achieve a high-quality representation of social identities—the quality and quantity both matter.

Quantity of representation:

- Does a pop culture artifact reflect the compositional diversity of its audience, and/or of the community in which it is set? Put differently— can audience members see themselves in the social identities of the actors cast? If one were to look at demographic percentages of the community where the show or film is set, would one see LGBTQ characters, folks of different abilities, races, ethnicities, gender and gender identities, etc. reflected as a percentage of the cast?
- Can you see the composition of social identities, such as people of color (which includes not only generic "non-White people," but recognizable racial minorities, like Asian American, Black, Indigenous, Latine folks), women, LGBTQ folks, and folks of different income levels, in the artifact?

Quality of representation:

- Does the artifact avoid stereotypes, controlling images, and token characters?
- Is identity marked as "otherness," or a facet of a character's identity as an individual? Put differently: Are characters from marginalized identities fully realized, authentic characters whose social identities are just another part of who they are?
- Are characters from marginalized backgrounds in positions of authority in the story? Or are they further marginalized through their roles?
- How does the story treat social identities like gender, race, and sexuality? Does the story treat social identity as not only a kind of box to check off, but perhaps as a source of power and perspective?
- Does the story center privileged identities, and if so, how?

To suggest that social identities reveal systemic patterns of power, privilege, and marginalization or oppression shows just how widespread and long-lasting these patterns are. You might recall in film history how disability enhanced stories of "overcoming adversity," with performances from typically abled actors performing characters with mental and physical disabilities. Indeed, as mentioned in Chapter 3's discussion of "quality" acting, the AMPAS seemed to take an abled actor's ability to "transform" themselves into a disabled character as a sign of quality acting—as did Daniel Day-Lewis, 1990 Best Actor Oscar winner who played a painter living with cerebral palsy, or Russell Crowe, who portrayed a mathematician living with schizophrenia in the 2002 Best Picture *A Beautiful Mind*. As one headline concluded, "History suggests that an Oscar-nominated actor in a physically or emotionally afflicted role has nearly a 50 percent shot of a win" (Thompson, 2017).

McIntosh's knapsack metaphor suggests that social identities deliver privilege to individuals in ways that are largely outside of individual control; but that individuals of privileged identities often make use of privilege without reflection. The invisibility of the knapsack, and the unconscious use of its contents by people of privileged social identities, are important ways that people in privileged identities maintain their group's status, often to the detriment of other groups. Disrupting ableism—the dominant way of thinking, acting, and seeing the world which suggests that a person of "sound mind and body" is the norm—will take more than ignoring harmful representations. It will take more than stating that "everyone is normal," or "I don't see the wheelchair, all I see is the person." Social identities like race, gender, and ability may be social constructions, but that does not mean that they can be so easily waved away. In the words of Eric King Watts, "there are plenty of 'fictions' that structure our subjectivities and social relations that are quite stubborn" (Squires et al., 2010, p. 215). We can't simply wave away power, privilege, and oppression by ignoring the social identities that organize them. It is up to all of us to ask how representations of a social identity (like ability) affect our perceptions of the people who happen to have such identities; and to center the voices of people on the margins to more accurately represent their experience.

As disability rights advocates argue, hiring more disabled writers, actors, directors, producers, etc. can help bring more, and higher-quality, representations of people with disabilities. Put differently, compositional diversity (or the make-up of a group of people, by social identities) matters in the popular culture workplace. August Pritchett, who blogs on disability issues, argues that accuracy is the best standard when evaluating whether an abled person can perform a disabled character. Certain roles dictate accuracy, and the experience of someone with disability can enhance their ability to accurately perform a role: "A sighted actor doesn't have the years of navigation by touch skills that blind people have ... Paralyzed bodies move differently than non-paralyzed bodies" (Pritchett, n.d.). Though some disabilities make it challenging to cast actors in a one-to-one match between a person and a characters' social identities, accurate representation is a standard to which Hollywood should aspire.

This leads us to a final important premise when studying the identities in popular culture. Social identities are more than discourses through which privilege and marginalization are leveraged. Social identities are **standpoints**, providing and organizing important resources for interpreting the world and expressing ourselves within it.

In late August 2020, professional athletes in the National Basketball Association (NBA) decided to walk out of their first-round play-off game between the Milwaukee Bucks and Orlando Magic, following Kenosha, Wisconsin police shooting and seriously injuring Jacob Blake, an unarmed Black man who was arrested following a "domestic incident" call (see Figure 4.1). Bucks guard Sterling Brown stated, "There has been no action, so our focus today cannot be on basketball." Soon, more teams joined the boycott, with the NBA Coaches Association releasing a statement: "The baseless shootings of Jacob Blake and other [B]lack men and women by law enforcement underscores the need for action ... Not after the playoffs, not in the future, but now" (Mahoney & Reynolds, 2020). The actions followed the league's racial justice messages in the wake of Black Lives Matter protests in response to the murder of George Floyd in Minneapolis in late May of the same year. Individual players opted to replace their last

Figure 4.1 Members of the Milwaukee Bucks host a press conference.

names with slogans like "Say Her Name" and "I Can't Breathe," a move supported by the NBA organization. Los Angeles Laker, LeBron James, tweeted messages of support to his 46 million followers, as former NBA player Jalen Rose told ESPN: "I wish America loved [B]lack people as much as it loves [B]lack culture … We're not here designed only to entertain. We're actually living and breathing human beings" (Woike, 2020).

NBA athletes like Brown, Rose, and James use their social identities as Black men, along with their roles as professional athletes, to be responsive to racism and injustice. James, in particular, has donated millions to Akron, Ohio (his hometown), including paying tuition and opening a school for grades 3–8. He also organized protests in 2014, as the Cleveland Cavaliers wore t-shirts that said "I Can't Breathe" (following Eric Garner's death at the hands of New York City police) (Bunn, 2020).

Not everyone appreciates James's integration of his social identities and professional roles to support personal commitments. In 2018, Fox News host Laura Ingraham told James (and Kevin Durant, another NBA player who had also been critical of President Donald Trump) to "shut up and dribble." James pointed out that Ingraham was not critical when NFL quarterback Drews Brees criticized Collin Kaepernick (who took a knee during the national anthem to protest racism). In other words, James pointed out the Fox News personality's double standard when it came to a White conservative athlete using his platform in politics. James retweeted Ingraham's segment ("Jocks on Politics") with a new tweet: "CHANGE!!! #ShutUpAndDribbleThisPowerfulBlackManComingFullSteam" with five steam emoji. Here, we see that social identities help organize a power with and a power to, not just a power over. James embraces his race and gender standpoints as a source of knowledge and power which continues to connect him to a community beyond himself and his role in the NBA. Put differently, James combats Ingraham's use of his social identities to shut him down, by asserting his social identities as a source of strength and connection (Bieler, 2020).

As noted earlier, social identities are a performance with a range of possibilities for those who happen to be born within them (Stowell, 2022). LeBron James's identity performance is a marked departure from the "Michael Jordan" era of athletes, who never talked about politics. James appears to perform Black masculinity closer to Muhammad Ali. Ali won a gold medal for boxing in the 1960 Olympics at the age of 18. In 1964, the heavyweight champion of the world converted to Islam, spoke out against racism and the Vietnam War, and later refused to join the Army: "My conscience won't let me go shoot my brother, or some darker people, or some poor hungry people . . . for big powerful America. And shoot them for what? They never called me [the n-word], they never lynched me," Ali stated (Scott, 2016). Ali was stripped of his title and boxing license in every state until 1971, when the Supreme Court overturned his conviction, arguing that the federal government had not specified why they denied his conscientious objector application.

Kareem Abdul-Jabbar, like Muhammad Ali, is outspoken in his support for racial justice. He boycotted the 1968 Olympics on principle, even though he believed it would "probably [have] very little impact" (Medina, 2016). Abdul-Jabbar contrasts his ethos to Michael Jordan who is arguably the greatest basketball player in NBA history, but made the Forbes' billionaires list. Jordan remained silent on several racial injustices and political controversies, including one of the most famous from his home state of North Carolina—when he refused to endorse a Black candidate for Senate against a racist incumbent, Jesse Helms (Howard, 2015). Muhammad Ali and Kareem Abdul-Jabbar illustrate the long roots of Black men in professional sports using their platforms to speak out against injustice, while also representing their communities through the resources available to them through social identities.

Individual identity is socially constructed, and social identities are also such enduring constructions that they have and continue to constrain experiences in powerful ways. We've seen how, like a knapsack of privileges, social identities can provide groups (and the individuals who share those demographics) unearned access and resources (like money, education, time, and health). We've also seen how social identities can marginalize and even oppress groups (and the individuals who share those demographics), denying them access and resources. Lastly, we've considered how social identities are not only the symbolic means through which power, privilege, and oppression are organized—they can provide resources, like knowledge, experience, and community. In order to understand identity in relationship to popular culture, we have a final key idea: intersectionality.

Intersectionality

In her popular TED Talk, "The Urgency of Intersectionality," Professor Kimberlé Crenshaw shares the story behind her choice to use an analogy of intersecting roads to describe discrimination Black women face. Emma DeGraffenreid sought a job at an automobile manufacturing plant, but was turned down, as DeGraffenreid argued, due to her identities as a Black woman. The automobile manufacturing facility defended itself, showing that it hired Black men to work in the factory, and White women to do administrative and secretarial work. Unfortunately, because the court did not consider the intersection of race and gender in DeGraffenreid's case (it only saw discrimination in a single-axis, like race alone), it did not allow DeGraffenreid to proceed with her discrimination claim. With over 5.3 million views, Crenshaw's TED Talk demonstrates the power of popular culture to disseminate new ways of thinking. As she concludes in the talk, without a name, one cannot see a problem, nor can one begin taking steps to solving it: and given the disproportionate violence affecting Black women, and women of color, naming **intersectionality** and using it to be responsive to racism, sexism, and other forms of marginalization and oppression as they overlap and intersect, is an urgent matter indeed (Crenshaw, 2016).

Another important figure in Black feminist thought, sociologist Patricia Hill Collins (2000), describes a "matrix of domination" that constrains Black women's experiences. Like Crenshaw, Collins's framework demonstrates the need to see not only race or gender or sexuality or ability or any other social identity in isolation, but rather, in combination for how it constrains and enables identity performances. Collins and Crenshaw provide a very important framework for exploring social identities, one which contrasts mainstream White feminism.[1]

Earlier in this chapter, we discussed how #OscarsSoWhite inspired disability rights advocates to analyze representations of people with disability in film and television. An intersectional approach would advance questions such as: How do race, gender, and other identities complicate the representation of people with disability? How might a Black person who is on the autism spectrum, for instance, be read differently than a White person on the spectrum?

Recognizing the intersections of identities like race, gender, and ability are a way to promote higher-quality representations, which can create more just and humane realities. In order to better appreciate this potential in popular culture, we consider Black feminist thought in conversation with popular Black women artists of the 2020s. Award-winning, popular and successful Black women artists like Megan Thee Stallion and Lizzo demonstrate a Black feminist consciousness speaking against a history of racism and sexism particularly affecting women of color in hip hop and pop music.

Foremost, Black feminism recognizes that individuals stand at complex intersections in their own lives, as multiple different social identities converge to structure their understandings of themselves, their experiences, and the world around them. There is no monolithic "Black woman" as an identity category, and oppression will not affect all oppressed people in the same way (Collins, 2000). Nonetheless, Black women can still share a consciousness—a "group knowledge" inspired by "collective memory," "shared history," and "common daily experiences" (Alinia, 2015, p. 2337). When Beyoncé joins Megan Thee Stallion in the remix of the latter's breakout single "Savage," the two singers reflect on the diversity of appearance, body type, voice, and experience that Black women in general have; but also the potential that everyday experiences of marginalization (like fashion) can inspire a shared consciousness. After suggesting that fans will have a chance to "see some real" dancing (("left cheek, right cheek, drop it low, then swang (Swang); Texas up in this thang (Thang)"), Beyoncé sings, "If you don't jump to put jeans on, baby, you don't feel my pain."

The shared consciousness that Black women develop is a means of social support, to be sure; but it can go beyond "feeling others' pain," to antagonizing dominant discourses, like the music industry which limits how Black women can perform who they are. Hunter and Soto (2009) performed a content analysis of popular rap song and music videos (from the 2002 and 2003 Top Rap Singles of the Year), particularly following the transition "from 'message rap' like Public Enemy to 'gangsta rap' like Snoop Dogg"—a mainstreaming of rap that seemed to trade "political content" for "racial and gender stereotypes" (Brown, 2018). Hunter and Soto (2009) note that roughly a third of songs positioned women (almost all women of color) "as strippers, prostitutes, and positioned men as pimps" (Brown, 2018). Here, we are reminded of another key term in Black feminist thought, the **controlling image**. Controlling images are stereotypes that dehumanize and exploit Black women, and they come from binary thinking that cuts Black women out of traditional values and performances of White femininity, such as piety, purity, and virtuous domestic care-giving. The controlling image of the jezebel, for instance, depicts Black women as hypersexual, often exotic or deviant.

Controlling images set the tone for the Black women playing that role, as well as anyone present in the frame (Collins, 2000). Even for the few women allowed as "respectable girlfriends" or loyal "partners in crime" with men in rap videos and songs, lyrics and imagery treat them as ready to perform as sex workers for their men (as in Nelly's *Hot in Herre*, whose plotline can be summed up by the chorus—"It's getting' hot in here (so hot) So take off all your clothes"). Moreover, women voiced the hooks or choruses of songs over 40% of the time, suggesting a kind of consent. Outside the content of rap videos, women like Dani Stevenson do not seem to rise to the same level of fame and wealth as the people they performed with (like Nelly); and, as Hunter and Soto (2009) argue, their appearances seem to legitimate or soften the sexist representations from male artists.

Contrast this representation of Black women from about 2018 through today, where some of the biggest stars in the world perform social and individual identities very differently. Dr. Jennifer Turner and Dr. Melissa Brown, two scholars influenced by Collins's work, shared their interpretation of the controversial Billboard Number One from August, 2020 "WAP" (Turner & Brown, 2021). The collaboration marked a third Number One for Cardi B and a second for Megan Thee Stallion. "WAP," of course, drew controversy for its explicit lyrics and provocative sexual content in the music video (see Figure 4.2).

Figure 4.2 Cardi B and Megan Thee Stallion perform in the "WAP" music video.

As Cardi B and Megan Thee Stallion have joked on late-night appearances, there isn't an easy way to produce a "clean" version of "WAP." Growing up around guys who listened to Easy-E and 2 Live Crew, we didn't find "WAP" terribly shocking. "Gimme that Nut" and "Me So Horny," released by the aforementioned male artists in the 1980s, covered similar explicit territory—earning 2 Live Crew a #1 on Billboard's rap chart and #26 on the Hot 100. So when popular artist CeeLo Green criticized the "shameless" explicit content of the late 2010s, compared to "a time when we were savvy enough to code certain things," we wonder who he was listening to in the 1980s. Green later affirmed "WAP" creators as "powerful, beautiful and influential women ... and professionals" (VanHoose, 2020), demonstrating the range of meanings possible in a song like "WAP."

On the one hand, we agree with Green. The in-your-face descriptions of sex acts, the explicit naming of body parts, can come off as a bit too descriptive. On the other hand, the song and video confront us with two Black women who are unabashedly accounting for what brings them pleasure, declaring their power over men with pretty clever word play. Megan Thee Stallion makes no bones about her prowess as a businessperson, rapper, and woman when she describes a man who will "pay [her] tuition just to kiss [her] on this" WAP. As Professors Turner and Brown elaborate, "WAP is a song that has this message about race, gender, sexuality, and money that doesn't map onto historically what the Americas claim to value from Black women." The vulgarity of "WAP" can't be read outside the historic intersections, Turner and Brown argue, not only of rap music, but also chattel slavery, in which Black women's bodies were denigrated and displayed, and in general treated as non-human.

Another noteworthy artist, Lizzo, is further pushing pop culture (and surrounding realms) to make more space for intersecting identity performances, particularly, as she states (in Pantony & Feroze, 2021), for "[B]lack women, big [B]lack women, [and] [B]lack trans women." Lizzo further demonstrates the ways that social identities provide resources for aesthetic self-expression, personal empowerment, and collective support. As she states, "as a [B]lack woman, I make music for people, from an experience that is from a [B]lack woman … I'm making music that hopefully makes other people feel good and helps me discover self-love" (Pantony & Feroze, 2021). Lizzo released "Truth Hurts" in 2019, followed by several additional hits, including 2022's "2 Be Loved" and "About Damn Time." Lizzo is known to post provocative photos of herself on Instagram, including an unedited nude selfie alongside her appearance in advertising for Dove. Her performances demonstrate her commitment to embracing a diversity of body types as not only normal, but also beautiful (see Figure 4.3).

In 2019, Lizzo collaborated with Cardi B to release "Rumors." When we first heard the song, it felt like it was more of a calculated business decision—it just didn't speak to us musically the way "Good as Hell" and "Truth Hurts" had (though we found the music video, with its gorgeous aesthetic and dance numbers featuring women of color with diverse body types, skin tones, and hair, to be pretty engaging). But after the song's release, a strange moment in which life imitated art took over. The song

Figure 4.3 Lizzo's music video for "2 Be Loved."

"Rumors" names and takes control over gossip on such topics as who Lizzo has sex with, how she gives women a bad name, and so forth. Following the release of the song and video, Azealia Banks (a rapper based in New York who is famous for having been banned from Twitter multiple times over trolling comments) accused Lizzo of being a "mammy." Others on social media followed, claiming that Lizzo performed for the White fan gaze (Muhammed, 2021).

Lizzo responded with a brilliant Instagram live video. Appearing in a gray hoodie, full make-up, and wig cap, Lizzo shares, tearfully, how down she feels due to social media trolls. Defying many controlling images (especially the Angry Black Woman or Sapphire), Lizzo speaks to the camera with a vulnerability that is often reserved for White women. Later, she becomes steely, performing a persona more like Megan Thee Stallion. She tells haters that they can "suck" her, and concludes by cementing the identity politics inherent in much trolling, stating that she won't stand for "y'all doing this to Black women over and over and over again, especially us big Black girls. When we don't fit into the box you want to put us in, you just unleash hatred onto us. It's not cool" (Lizzo, 2021).

A Black feminist view sees that "for most of the people who experience [oppression, it] is 'not an intellectual issue' but 'a lived reality' that 'is felt in the body in myriad ways'" (Alinia, 2015, p. 2337; citing Collins, 2000, pp. 292–293). Other theoretical lenses, like Marxism and liberal feminism, can offer a strong critique of marginalization; but they tend to ignore the complex matrix of domination that includes systems of power intersecting in social identities. A Marxist lens may hone in on the fact that Lizzo (as a multi-millionaire) is earning positive attention through this moment, particularly developing and performing her "brand" as what *Glamour* called "the most relatable woman on the planet" (Pantony & Feroze, 2021). A liberal feminist perspective may see the incident involving Banks as an unfortunate outcome of patriarchy, which pits women against each other in a competition for public attention. In contrast, Black feminism views social identities in their complex intersections.

Along with holding racist, sexist, and other voices of hate accountable, as Patricia Hill Collins (2000) notes, supporting safer spaces with, by, and for Black women chips away at generational systems of oppression. As we have tried to illustrate in this section, what might appear to dominant standpoints as vulgar ("WAP") or self-branding (Lizzo's Instagram response to trolls) looks quite different from a Black feminist lens. Here, artists like Megan Thee Stallion (2021) use their music, videos, social media presence, fashion, business sense, political platforms, and so much more to provide spaces outside of dominant ideas about who Black women are and should be. We hope that their creativity and critique can inspire others to reimagine ways of being in the world outside systems of domination and oppression, as we consider throughout this book. But not everyone has a platform like these amazing artists; so for those of us who are more everyday users of pop culture, what is our role in interrupting intergenerational domination? We address this question through recent controversies around "cancel culture" and "wokeness" in pop culture.

Conclusion: Evaluating identity politics in pop culture

In this chapter, we have walked through many levels of identity to arrive at some of the most divisive controversies in the US today. "Cancel culture" refers to decisions (often by large groups of individuals) to boycott, disavow, and call out (sometimes through shaming) a public figure or public creative endeavor—typically, because that person or performance marginalized one or more social identities. For instance, Azealia Banks has been "cancelled" on more occasion than one, meaning that fans have stopped listening to her content. Some of them have publicly decried her racist statements. As we noted, Banks has also been banned from Twitter and Instagram, which is a different type of cancellation based on violation of a platform's rules.

McGrady (2021) shares the history of cancel culture from its origins in Black music and culture, as well as its uses in Black Twitter, complicating the characterization of "cancel culture" in contemporary politics. McGrady traces the first appearance of "cancel" to a 1981 Chic song, "Your Love Is Cancelled." The Chic song was inspired by the lead singer watching television after a bad date. Later allusions to the Chic song connote a similar action: cancelling someone means "You stepped out of line, and now I'm done with you" versus what White folks appropriated it into today, which seems more like a public shaming or organized boycott. In McGrady's words, "Saying someone was 'canceled' was more like changing the channel—and telling your friends and followers about it—than demanding that the TV execs take the program off the air." As McGrady continues, following the #MeToo movement and Black Lives Matter (BLM) protests, "online 'call-outs,' aimed more at public accountability than low-key channel-changing, really took hold." With "greater consequences" to these call-outs, "some people became nervous about how social media had changed power dynamics in the court of public opinion." Thus, "cancel culture" became politicized, connoting a kind of "mob" mentality with egregious public shaming. McGrady interviews BLM activist Johnetta Elzie, who notes, "'Cancel' is now just another word that White people have taken and run into the ground."

In different ways, celebrities like Demi Lovato and politicians like President Donald Trump have used "cancel culture" to advocate for the type of culture they would like to see in the US. The term is everywhere, and it's difficult to sort out what it does and should mean for popular culture. The Pew Research Center (2021) released interesting data that shows demographics and party affiliations affect how people perceive cancel culture. Perhaps unsurprisingly, people over the age of 50 do not have as much knowledge about cancel culture as folks 20 years old and younger. People who identify as liberal Democrats with an undergraduate degree or higher interpret cancel culture as a form of accountability, particularly to point out marginalizing statements and representations. People who identify as conservative Republicans with an undergraduate degree or higher perceive cancel culture as an encroachment on free speech, with chilling effects for our ability to debate publicly. Republican lawmakers have declared individual and community acts of conscience—such as taking down memorials to White supremacist historic figures, and ceasing performances of the national anthem before sporting events in protest of US imperialism—as "cancel culture" (Vasilogambros, 2021). "Cancel culture" is such a powerful motivator that GOP lawmakers in five states have introduced bills to ban the 1619 Project curricula, which are based on a series of essays to consider how racism and slavery are central to the US experience (1619 America Slavery).

We find the original meaning of cancelling popular culture to be the most powerful, as an act of conscience one makes (and shares with others) to "change the channel" on creators or content. Not all gaffes or representations are worthy of the levels of public shaming they have received, nor are they worthy of calls to banish someone to "cancellation island." For instance, we argue that there is a difference between comedian Bill Cosby's serial predatory behavior and Taylor Swift's apparent mocking of ex-boyfriend John Mayer on TikTok (Barilla, 2021). Evidence against Cosby had circulated informally for years, eventually resulting in a trial and conviction (which was later overturned on a technicality). Cosby's behavior enacts the power of men over women, especially women of color, while systems maintained his ability to do so. The Swift–Mayer feud seems to be more controversy stirred by social media affordances that seek to get users to "stick" to platforms (see Chapter 2). We hope that "Swifties" and members of John Mayer's Fan Club can take a breath before performing more public shaming. But at the end of the day, should a member of the Fan Club decide to skip Swift, that's their prerogative. We only hope it's for good reason, and not to join the cancellation bandwagon.

In conclusion, we have explored the ways that pop culture creates and reflects identities, viewing identities as both a social construction and performance at the level of individual, social, and intersecting identity. Social identities like race, gender, and sexuality, among others, provide standpoints that organize power, privilege, oppression, and marginalization; but also resources through which to know the world and express oneself.

A Black feminist lens promotes complexity, as we saw in how artists like Lizzo expand the range of how Black women can perform their social identities, along with their art.

Along the way, we've considered why representation matters: harmful representations, like othering, stereotypes, and tokens denigrate groups of people and perpetuate harm for those in marginalized identities, and for everyone. People in marginalized identities have led the charge in demanding better representations, which, as we have seen, includes both a quantitative component (to ask if pop culture reflects the social identities of its audience, or the reality it relates to) and qualitative component (to ask what are the characters within pop culture doing, how are they representing social identities through their stories?). Our chapter ended by raising critical questions about cancel culture, echoing views that "changing the channel" on content that perpetuates harm is one way to hold producers accountable. In the next chapters, we consider how popular culture might imagine new ways of being and relating to each other, through such tools as story and community.

Reflecting on pop culture and identity in your everyday life

- Chapter 4 sets forth the idea that identity is a social construction and a performance. What do you take that to mean? How do you perform your own sense of identity (be it your individual identity or some aspect of your intersecting social identities)? How might pop culture (the clothes you wear, the music you listen to, etc.) help you perform who you are?
- Chapter 4 begins with a discussion of the use of Indigenous Peoples' identities in sports mascots. Why do you think it took so long for the Washington NFL franchise to change its mascots to the Commanders? What does this tell us about power and popular culture, especially the power to represent identities?
- Chapter 4 asserts that social identities are not only the vehicles through which marginalization and oppression occur. Social identities provide resources to the people who inhabit them. Sometimes, these resources are unearned and invisible (as in McIntosh's knapsack); sometimes, these resources are aesthetic styles and social capital that people put into action for the betterment of their community (as in LeBron James). Reflect on the intersecting social identities you inhabit (e.g., the social class, race and ethnicity, gender and gender identity, sexuality, ability, age, religion, immigration status, etc. that you have claim to). What resources do these

social identities make available to you? How does popular culture relate to these resources, perhaps providing equipment for living to those in various social identities?

- What might lead someone to "break it off" or stop choosing pop culture in their everyday life? How might others perceive one's decision, or/and declaration, that they are cancelling a creator or content? Do you believe that "cancel culture" is fairly represented in political discourse and on social media, given Chapter 4's discussion of identity in pop culture? Why or why not?

Note

1 Social identities like gender have inspired entire bodies of knowledge and practice in universities, politics, and culture. Feminism is the everyday practice and belief that women are equal to men, and should have equal opportunity to live regardless of their sex or gender identity performance. We often hear of the "waves" of feminism in the US, which begin with suffrage activism to secure women a right to vote (ratified with the 19th Amendment in 1920). Though feminist history contains diverse activists, theories, and practices (including lesbian feminism, radical feminism, and Black feminism), mainstream public memories of feminism's first and second waves are often limited to White liberal matters or frameworks. For instance, women's concerns that their domestic lives were unfulfilling and they should be granted access to work and public life, cut out concerns of Black women, lower-income women, and LGBTQ+ women, who were already working, or did not participate in White feminine virtue. A White liberal feminist framework may prioritize equality for women in ways that do not consider the unique intersections of race, sexuality, and social class. We concur with hooks (2015), who writes, sisterhood begins when we grapple with our past socialization, acknowledging that, "American women, without exception, are socialized to be racist, classist and sexist, in varying degrees ... and labeling ourselves feminists does not change the fact that we must consciously work to rid ourselves of the legacy of negative socialization" (p. 157).

Suggested readings

Bennett, P., & Griffin, R. A. (2016). Dehumanized and empowered? Black women, reality television, and *Love and Hip Hop Atlanta*. In D. Allison (Ed.), *Black women's portrayals on reality television: The new sapphire* (pp. 169–190). Lexington.

Cisneros, J. D., & Nakayama, T. K. (2015). New media, old racisms: Twitter, Miss America, and cultural logics of race. *Journal of International and Intercultural Communication, 8*(2), 108–127. DOI: 10.1080/17513057.1025328

Lovelock, M. (2019). *Reality tv and queer identities: Sexuality, authenticity, celebrity*. Palgrave Macmillan.

Morris, C. E., III, & Sloop, J. M. (2006). "What lips these lips have kissed": Re-figuring the politics of queer public kissing. *Communication & Critical/Cultural Studies, 3*(1), 1–26. DOI: 10.1080/14791420500505585

Morris, C. E., III, & Sloop, J. M. (2017). Other lips, whither kisses? *Communication & Critical/Cultural Studies, 14*(2), 182–186. 10.1080/14791420.2017.1293953

References

1619 America Slavery (2019). *The New York Times.* https://www.nytimes.com/interactive/2019/08/14/magazine/1619-america-slavery.html

ACLU. (2023, January 24). Mapping attacks on LGBTQ rights in US state legislature. American Civil Liberties Union. https://www.aclu.org/legislative-attacks-on-lgbtq-rights

Alinia, M. (2015). On *Black Feminist Thought*: Thinking oppression and resistance through intersectional paradigm, *Ethnic and Racial Studies, 38*(13), 2334–2340. DOI: 10.1080/01419870.2015.1058492

Allen, B. J. (2023). *Difference matters: Communicating social identity* (3rd ed.). Waveland.

Baker, M. (2020, July 10). Why Florida State, Seminole Tribe stand behind Seminole nickname. *Tampa Bay Times.* https://www.tampabay.com/sports/seminoles/2020/07/10/why-florida-state-seminole-tribe-stand-behind-the-seminoles-nickname/

Barilla, C. (2021, March 22). Some Twitter users are trying to cancel Taylor Swift. *Distractify.* https://www.distractify.com/p/taylor-swift-canceled

Bieler, D. (2020, June 4). LeBron James, told by Laura Ingraham to "shut up and dribble," calls her out over Drew Brees. *Washington Post.* https://www.washingtonpost.com/sports/2020/06/04/lebron-james-calls-out-laura-ingraham-over-drew-brees/

Brown, M. (2018). Women of color in hip hop: The pornographic gaze. *Black Feminisms.* https://blackfeminisms.com/women-color-hip-hop/.

Bunn, C. (2020, June 23). How LeBron James has become a leading voice for social justice in a racially divided nation. *NBC News.* https://www.nbcnews.com/news/nbcblk/how-lebron-james-has-become-leading-voice-social-justice-racially-n1231391

Collins, P. H. (2000). *Black feminist thought: Knowledge, consciousness, and the politics of empowerment.* Routledge.

Conquergood, D. (1983). Communication as performance: Dramaturgical dimensions of everyday life. In J. J. Sisco (Ed.), *Jensen lectures in contemporary studies* (pp. 24–43). University of South Florida Press.

Crenshaw, K. (2016). The urgency of intersectionality. Ted Talks. https://www.ted.com/talks/kimberle_crenshaw_the_urgency_of_intersectionality?language=en

GLAAD (n.d.). GLAAD transgender media program. *GLAAD.* https://www.glaad.org/transgender

hooks, b. (2015). *Ain't I a woman: Black women and feminism.* Routledge.

Howard, A. (2015, November 5). Kareem Abdul-Jabbar: Michael Jordan chose "commerce over conscience." MSNBC. https://www.msnbc.com/msnbc/kareem-abdul-jabbar-michael-jordan-chose-commerce-over-conscience-msna717846

Hunter, M., & Soto, K. (2009). Women of color in hip hop: The pornographic gaze. *Race. Gender, & Class, 16*(1–2), 170–191.

Lizzo. (2021, August 15). Lizzo Instagram live. YouTube. https://www.youtube. com/watch?v=RuZTrfWTRA8.

Madison, D. S., & Hamera, J. (Eds.). (2005). *The SAGE Handbook of Performance Studies*. SAGE Publishing.

Mahoney, B., & Reynolds, T. (2020, August 26). NBA playoff games called off amid player protests. NBA. https://www.nba.com/news/bucks-protest-nba-postpones-games

McGrady, C. (2021, April 2). The strange journey of "cancel," from a Black-culture punchline to a White-grievance watchword. *Washington Post*. https://www. washingtonpost.com/lifestyle/cancel-culture-background-black-culture-white-grievance/2021/04/01/2e42e4fe-8b24-11eb-aff6-4f720ca2d479_story.html

McIntosh, P. (2003). White privilege: Unpacking the invisible knapsack. In S. Plous (Ed.), *Understanding prejudice and discrimination* (pp. 191–196). McGraw-Hill.

Mead, G. H. (1934). *Mind, self, and society*. University of Chicago Press.

Medina, M. (2016, November 9). Kareem Abdul-Jabbar remains passionate about political and social activism. *Los Angeles Daily News*. https://www. dailynews.com/2016/11/09/kareem-abdul-jabbar-remains-passionate-about-political-and-social-activism/

Muhammed, M. (2021, August 17). Lizzo is not a mammy, you're just fatphobic and colorist. *The Garnett Report*. https://thegarnettereport.com/art/music/lizzo-not-mammy-youre-just-fatphobic-colorist/

Oganesyan, N. (2022, May 3). Hollywood still stigmatizes mental health issues, USC study says. *The Wrap*. https://www.thewrap.com/usc-annenberg-inclusion-initiative-mental-health-stigma/

Ono, K. A. (2017). The shifting landscape of Asian Americans in the media. *Japanese Journal of Communication Studies, 45*(2), 105–113.

Ono, K. A., & Pham, V. N. (2009). *Asian Americans and the media: Media and minorities*. Polity Press.

Pantony, A., & Feroze, M. (2021, April 21). Lizzo: An icon of our time. *Glamour*. https://www.glamourmagazine.co.uk/article/lizzo-body-dysmorphia

Pew Research Center. (2021, May 19). Americans and "cancel culture": Where some see calls for accountability, others see censorship, punishment. *Politics online*. https://www.pewresearch.org/internet/2021/05/19/americans-and-cancel-culture-where-some-see-calls-for-accountability-others-see-censorship-punishment/

Pritchett, A. (n.d.). Should non-disabled actors play disabled characters? URevolution. https://www.urevolution.com/blogs/magazine/should-non-disabled-actors-play-disabled-characters

Scott, E. (2016, June 4). The political fights of Muhammad Ali. CNN. https://www.cnn.com/2016/06/04/politics/muhammad-ali-political-moments

Squires, C., King Watts, E., Douglas Vavrus, M., Ono, K. A., Feyh, K., Calafell, B. M., & Brouwer, D. C. (2010). What is this "post-" in postracial, postfeminist… (fill in the blank)? *Journal of Communication Inquiry, 34*(3), 210–253. https://doi.org/10.1177/0196859910371375

Stallion, M. (2021, October 13). Why I speak up for Black women. *The New York Times*. https://www.nytimes.com/2020/10/13/opinion/megan-thee-stallion-black-women.html

Stowell, O. (2022). "It's *Top Chef*, not a personality contest": Grammars of stereotype, neoliberal logics of personhood, and the performance of the racialized self in *Top Chef: New York*. *New Review of Film and Television Studies*, 20(4), 569–587. DOI: 10.1080/17400309.2022.2133920

Thompson, A. (2017, September 25). Here are 59 actors who landed Oscar nominations for portraying characters with disabilities. *Indiewire*. https://www.indiewire.com/2017/09/actors-oscar-nominations-disabilities-afflictions-1201879957/

Turner, J., & Brown, M. (2021). What the Wap: Black feminist scholars on Black women's popular culture. *Black Feminisms*. https://blackfeminisms.com/wap-part-one/

UCLA (2022). Hollywood diversity report 2022: A new, post-pandemic normal? *UCLA Social Sciences*. https://socialsciences.ucla.edu/wp-content/uploads/2022/10/UCLA-Hollywood-Diversity-Report-2022-Television-10-27-2022.pdf

VanHoose, B. (2020, August 25). Cardi B defends "WAP" against those who claim song is too vulgar: "It's for adults." *People*. https://people.com/music/cardi-b-defends-wap-against-haters/

Vasilogambros, M. (2021, February 26). GOP targets "cancel culture" in school lessons, political speech. Pew Research. https://www.pewtrusts.org/en/research-and-analysis/blogs/stateline/2021/02/26/gop-targets-cancel-culture-in-school-lessons-political-speech

Wagmeister, E. (2016, June 13). Able-bodied actors play 95% of disabled characters in top 10 TV shows, says new study. *Variety*. https://variety.com/2016/tv/news/disabled-actors-television-study-1201813686/

Walker, B. W., & Caprar, D. V. (2020). When performance gets personal: Towards a theory of performance-based identity. *Human Relations*, 73(8), 1077–1105. https://doi.org/10.1177/0018726719851835

Woike, D. (2020, May 31). NBA players and coaches plead as loud as ever against racial injustice. *Los Angeles Times*. https://www.latimes.com/sports/story/2020-05-31/nba-players-lebron-james-michael-jordan-statement-racial-injustice-george-floyd-death

5 The communities of popular culture

Introduction

In 2000, rapper Eminem released "Stan," a song that told a dark story from the perspective of an obsessive fan. The verses are a series fan letters from Stan, who has an unhealthy fixation on Eminem's personal life. Stan becomes angry when Eminem does not reply to his letters. Stan describes the murder of his girlfriend, and an attempted suicide, loosely recreating the lyrics of one of Eminem's songs. At the end of the song, in a shocking twist, Eminem realizes Stan actually committed the murder/suicide. Weirdly, the word "Stan" has shifted meanings from an unhealthy fan, to largely being just a synonym for fan. The term Stan is most frequently used on social media to express a commonality with other passionate fans of the latest pop culture trend, as in "stanning" Harry Styles. Fandom, once stigmatized as the dangerous and weird activities of isolated and alienated individuals, is now normalized, especially among *communities* of fans.

In this chapter, we explore how people build community through popular culture, particularly via fandom. After defining community and its connections to popular culture, we recognize the influence of cultural studies in understanding popular culture. The cultural studies tradition spotlights meaning-making, interpretation, and critique as a foundation for community-building with and through popular culture. We stress the importance of community members (and not just experts!) critiquing domination and imagining new ways of being in the world. Then, we discuss how fandom helps build community in an era of fragmentation, before turning to social capital and production in fan communities to demonstrate how digital affordances shape fandom today. This framework gets put to use as we close the chapter exploring fan communities, LGBTQ+ meaning-making, and Queen Elsa in *Frozen II*.

Cultural studies and "reading" popular culture in communities

To begin, what is a **community**? This might seem painfully obvious—groups of people who share interests or goals, etc. A few clarifications

DOI: 10.4324/9781003372943-5

about the meaning of community might be in order, though. First, for a very long time, the term community simply meant a place where people lived. With the developments of communication technology and transportation, people began to feel connectedness with others outside of their immediate neighborhood or town, thus expanding the notion of community. Further, the word "community" has expanded in usage largely because it is generally seen as overwhelmingly positive. For instance, politicians and corporations state that they wholeheartedly support "building stronger communities." We tend to think of communities coming to together to help families after a natural disaster or some other crisis. But, are communities always positive? Without question, White supremacist groups, cults, and terrorist organizations are usually very tight-knit communities. Collective meaning-making and action can be a force of tremendous good and tremendous harm.

For our purposes in this chapter, we are interested in how popular culture brings people into community with others. Popular culture is tied to community in a number of ways. It creates occasion for people to gather together, as we see with sporting events (Chapter 12) and gaming (Chapter 11). Popular culture prompts refection and conversation on shared challenges or histories (Chapter 1, Chapter 6). Popular culture represents who people are, and how they might be together in the world (Chapter 4). In Chapter 5, we focus primarily on fandom and community (with connections to social identities, stories, and points of focus in other chapters).

As we introduced in Chapter 1, popular culture has not always been viewed as a legitimate course of study. You may experience raised eyebrows from family members who hear about your popular culture class when they ask what courses you're taking for college credit. The biases against popular culture not only come from traditions that contrast it with high art, but also the associations between popular culture and fan communities (including those who hold non-dominant identities). Marxist scholars in the United Kingdom turned to the study of popular culture in the late 1950s and early 1960s, in part, to push back on the ways dominant social classes maintained their power over lower income folks. Cultural studies as a field was born as professors saw popular culture as a means of organizing and expressing identities, meanings, power, and aesthetics, from the bottom-up. Popular culture provides ways for ordinary people to build and enact *their* culture, rather than simply enacting a given social order as it was designed and maintained by powerful forces, to the benefit of the powerful.

An important cultural studies scholar, Stuart Hall (1980), introduced key terms to the understanding of popular culture to account for how communities did not passively consume the meanings fed to them: **encoding** and **decoding**. Anyone who has studied communication may recognize the terms encoding and decoding as the activities of expressing a message (encoding) and interpreting a message (decoding). For Hall, encoding/decoding are *collective* activities, which rely on shared knowledge frameworks, a system of infrastructure or channels of communication, and economic systems of production. In terms of popular culture, producers encode the "proper" or, in Hall's terms, **dominant readings** of an artifact. For instance, when watching a movie, the audience is encoded to "ooh and aah" at the impressive special effects or laugh at the punchline of a lead character's joke. In more subtle ways, the audience is also supposed to cheer on the underdog boxer in the big fight as a personification of the American Dream (e.g., in the eight, and counting, *Rocky* franchise movies). On the other hand, sometimes audiences perform **resistant readings**, decoding popular culture in excessive ways, as when a viewer laughs at cheesy special effects or groans at a punchline that falls flat. More complexly, viewers ridicule the White savior mythology of *Green Book*, interpreting the civil rights era movie as (ironically) racist, which is definitely not the intended meaning of the producers. Communities decode popular culture artifacts within the boundaries of meaning encoded by producers; but in ways that serve them as they navigate life together (recalling equipment for living from Chapter 1).

British scholars wrote about how youth subcultures formed identities through popular culture, including the clothes they wore, the music they listened to, and the places they hung out (Hebdige, 1979). Youth subcultures like the mods and the punks built their identities in sharp contrast to "respectable" British identities (we could imagine hip-hop culture as a comparable example in the US). It was too easy to denigrate popular culture, along with the young people from working-class backgrounds, as vulgar and even dangerous. British cultural studies scholars turned to Marxist theories to help explain why popular culture was not only a legitimate form of expression, but also rich with potential to change society. Notably, cultural studies honed the analysis of ideology and hegemony in popular culture. Let's walk through these key terms and their importance to how communities interact with popular culture, using a more contemporary example—the $4 billion dollar per year brand Disney princesses (Setoodeh, 2007).

Ideology refers to a dominant system of ideas that appears natural and normal (Eagleton, 1991). It is like the "given" way of the world, and becomes so taken for granted, that we do not question where it came from. Ideology is an important tool to explain why workers continually get exploited by the upper class, who own the means of production or benefit from the system more than those whose labor makes the system run (consider Jeff Bezos making billions off the labor of low-wage Amazon warehouse and delivery employees). Ideology isn't just any system of ideas that we take for granted. It is comprised of **dominant** ideas, which is to say it comes from and supports a group of people who benefit from "an un-equal distribution of power within society" (Terray & Serrano, 2019, p. 412), while other people systematically do not share in the benefits. Domi-nant groups tend to have easy access to resources that leverage power, like money or flexible time; they occupy roles in which they can move an organization to enact their power; and they tend to have more education to be able to put symbols and media to work for their interests.[1] Dominant groups sit atop a **hierarchy**, which is a vertical ordering from best to worst that ranks groups of people. Hierarchy can become domination, and even-tually **oppression**, where one group holds other groups down in order to retain control over the social system (and benefit from that control).

The Disney princesses are so normalized, it is hard to imagine a world where they weren't everywhere, from their movies, to toys like the En-chanted Cupcake Party Game, to costumes and coloring books, even breakfast cereal and plastic bandages. But the "Disney princesses" didn't begin as a group. In fact, Walt Disney told creatives that they could never take a character out of its original story and put that character into another story. Cinderella was to remain in her world, toiling away for an unloving family and escaping this life through the lightning bolt of romantic love (with a little help from the fairy godmother). She was to never cross paths with, say, Snow White. But in 1999, Disney hired a former Nike executive (Andy Mooney) who noticed that little girls attending *Disney on Ice* shows dressed in different princess costumes. He pitched the idea to market the princesses as a group, violating Mr. Disney's rule, but earning the company astronomical profits—from $300 million in 2001 to $3 billion in 2012 for Mooney's division (Ng, 2021). It's no surprise, as a Brigham Young study of 200 kids aged 3–4 revealed, that 96% of girls and 87% of boys knew about Disney princesses (Paquette, 2016).

So what do the Disney princesses have to do with dominant ideas? The same study mentioned above found that girls who engaged with Disney princesses placed "a higher importance on appearance." Sociologist Charu Uppal did a study with girls aged 8–15 from China, Fiji, India, Sweden, and the US. She asked the girls to draw a "princess," and 61 out of 63 drew a light-skinned Disney-esque princess. In reporting the study, Neilson (2019) noted that "some girls from … India, Fiji, and China said in their interviews with Uppal that they could not be a princess because their skin was too dark and they were not beautiful enough." Minimally, then, the Disney princesses relate to a dominant system of ideas about what women or girls are beautiful, and what beauty means.

When we consider the typical Disney princess story, a conventionally at-tractive girl or young woman, who is demure and kind (feminine virtues), gets swept up in romantic love. The story often unfolds as convention-ally attractive young man, who is physically strong and brave, "saves" her from some outside force (like an unloving, even abusive, family in the case of Cinderella; or the spell of a jealous old crone, in the case of Snow White or Aurora from *Sleeping Beauty*). The details here don't matter as much as the lessons learned, which, again, reinforce the idea that light skin and Whiter features (untextured, straight, long hair and noses with small nostrils, for instance) are beautiful; that girls and women should embody White femininity (being good caregivers); that romantic love should take place between people born as male and female (who are still assumed to be cisgendered); and that the nuclear family they will start takes priority over other social configurations (such as extended family networks, friendships with neighbors, or close-knit cultures). In a nutshell, Disney princess stories tend to embody an ideology known as **White heteropatriarchy**, a dominant system of ideas that makes White, male-headed straight households the default for society.

Ideology is sometimes described a "veil of false consciousness," which means it is like a cloth that dominant classes placed over the working class to distract them from their reality (Marx & Engels, 1947). In the example above, ideology obscures the view of girls and women as a marginalized group, suggesting that jumping into marriage with a man is the normal thing to do. The stakes of this story seem highest in *The Little Mermaid*, where 16-year-old Ariel is subject to a rather violent fight with her father, King Triton, and seeks comfort with Prince Eric (see Figure 5.1). This is quite literally White heteropatriarchy at work, where a girl leaves the household headed by her traditionally masculine White father, to assume her place as part of another household headed by a traditionally masculine White man.

Figure 5.1 Scene from *The Little Mermaid*.

If Karl Marx were alive to watch *The Little Mermaid*, he may note that the catchy songs, a funny crab, and an evil sea witch are all complicit in the ways that social and cultural phenomena distract people. Ideologies keep marginalized people in their place, even when they see that the system does not serve their best interests and keeps others like them down. One study, for instance, estimates that a girl living in the US who drops out of high school is 11% more likely to be in a family below the poverty line, and girls who marry young as teens are 31% more likely to live in poverty (Dahl, 2010). The promise that a prince will rescue a girl from her current situation and they will live "happily ever after," especially as it is repeated over and over again, hides other possibilities for how girls and women, as well as people of all gender expressions, might navigate the world.

Marx's writings often positioned experts (scientists) as the best defense against ideology, since ordinary people could be fooled so easily. But as cultural studies scholars like Stuart Hall argued powerfully, people are not dupes—they can make sense of popular culture in a variety of ways, and not just as dominant groups want them to. Hall and other British cultural studies scholars found the work of Antonio Gramsci inspiring. Gramsci was an Italian Marxist who was imprisoned by the Fascist dictator Benito Mussolini in order to silence the threat that Mussolini believed Gramsci posed to his control over the country. Gramsci died in prison 11 years later, but his notebooks (Gramsci, 1976) would inspire new ways of carrying out class struggle, including the importance of "organic intellectuals." Organic intellectuals were members of marginalized communities who critiqued ideology from within their communities, in order to overthrow domination. Even though British cultural studies scholars did not follow Marx in his dismissal of culture, they saw ideology as an important tool to understanding how hierarchies built on class, race, gender, and other social identities can last for so long.

With Gramsci, cultural studies scholars developed another tool to explain how systems of domination maintain themselves for so long: **hegemony**. Hegemony, as Gitlin (1979) argued, is like a vaccine for the larger social body. Dominant groups allow for a small amount of change or difference in order to give the appearance that the whole system is changing, when in actuality the system remains intact. A character will deviate from a standard formula slightly, as in Belle from *Beauty and the Beast*. She appears to be undeterred by other girls' pursuits of romantic love, uninterested in being pretty. Indeed, Belle begins the story as bookish and aloof. She is, in other words, not your "typical" Disney princess. But, by story's end, Belle "civilizes" Beast with her feminine virtue. Even nerdy girls can't resist romantic love with a man who they help transform.

When Disney, using convergence, reboots its princess movies from the past, they face an ideological dilemma. On one hand, the logic of formulaic reboots is to stay achingly close to the original movie for the nostalgic fan community (see Chapter 2). On the other hand, contemporary sensibilities make these narratives, such as *Beauty and the Beast* or *Cinderella*, seem wildly out of step with today's gender roles. The result is often awkward, with vaguely "tough and independent" princesses still resolving their problems with the love of a man.

But, as cultural studies scholars show, hegemony can show others "cracks" in ideologies. In the metaphor of the vaccination, a social system's antibodies don't eradicate the "virus" of social change fully. Over the course of years, Belle becomes Queen Elsa or Moana, characters who further deviate from the ideological norm of girls consumed by beauty who fall in love with men. We agree with rhetoric scholars like McKerrow (1989) who suggest that, as members of communities, it is up to us to point out the ways that domination maintains itself through ideology and hegemony; but also it is up to us to point out the possibilities for freedom and justice. What possibilities exist in popular culture, for relating and acting in the world, without replicating hierarchies and domination? This is the work of communities of popular culture, which is quite apparent in fandom.

Fandom as community

Fans or, more fully expressed, *fanatics* are, by definition, excessive. Their interest in a form of popular culture or specific media personality extends outside prescribed, relatively passive, consumption practices. Fans watch movies and TV shows over and over, memorize obscure facts, dress as their favorite characters, paint their faces and bodies the colors of their favorite sports team. The history of fandom is complicated, largely because of these excesses. In a now famous *Saturday Night Live* (*SNL*) sketch from 1986, William Shatner, the actor who played Captain Kirk on *Star Trek*, is speaking at a science fiction convention filled with stereotypical nerds. After a series of increasingly obscure questions about the TV series, in frustration Shatner (playing himself) exclaims, "Get a life" to the *Star Trek* fans. The *SNL* audience howls with both laughter and approval, as though someone finally named the problem of these abnormal, lonely, isolated fans. For decades, fans were the source of ridicule, pity, and even fear, as "obsessive" and violent fans (or Stans) were a common trope in movies and TV. Of course, today, the phrase, "I am a huge fan of . . ." is sprinkled into everyday conversation without a second thought. Why is fandom, once stigmatized by the larger culture, now considered normal and prevalent? A number of factors have fostered this changing perception of fandom, but a media ecology lens brings two into focus: emergent digital technology and the eroding of community.

Prior to around the 1990s, fandom could be a pretty isolating experience. If someone was the only fan of *Lord of the Rings*, Joan Jett, or the New York Knicks in their town or school, they really didn't have anyone to talk to about their interests. Very large cities might have an annual convention of comic book or science fiction fans, but this would only be a few days. Fans were especially stigmatized because they seemed to be alienated individuals cut off from others in their community obsessing over something very few people cared about. Then came the Internet.

Almost as soon as people could search for content online, people gathered on the Internet to discuss popular culture they loved. These groups, referred to as **virtual communities**, often only interacted online primarily via asynchronous, text-based discussion forums that nonetheless allowed people to transcend time and space (Rheingold, 1993). In other words, no matter where they lived or what time of the day it was, fans could continue the threaded conversation. As computer-savvy people were often also comic book, fantasy, and science fiction fans, fan communities in these genres started growing especially quickly. In the 1990s and early 2000s, Hollywood became increasingly aware of the intensity of these groups and catered to their interests, with shows such as *The X Files* and *Lost* (with storylines that offered plenty of ambiguous twists and turns, perhaps a precursor to the "drillable" texts we discuss in Chapter 7). No longer did folks feel isolated or alone. As the Internet expanded into social media, these fan communities became increasingly specialized, well outside the stereotypical "fanboy" (superheroes, science fiction, etc.) interests, moving across the spectrum of interests from Evangelical Christian literature to 1970s grindhouse horror movies, from University of Minnesota hockey to yacht rock.

As the Internet was growing in popularity, academics began to track the weakening of community ties in the US. Chief among the sources of this decline were fewer opportunities for socializing outside of work and one's home, or what Putnam (2000) famously called *Bowling Alone* in his book of the same title. Putnam argues that social capital—or the "connections among individuals' social networks and the norms of reciprocity and trustworthiness that arise from them" (p. 19)—is declining, evidenced first by the decline in afternoon and evening bowling leagues. The erosion of social capital, Putnam demonstrates, can be seen in other areas of bondedness, including political and civic participation, workplaces, religious groups, and more informal connections based on mutual trust.

Putnam's argument reflects the "dark side" of the contemporary culture, where suburban development patterns, configurations of work, and media have led to isolation. People have little to no free time for socializing, or cannot afford to not work multiple jobs (Saccaro, 2015). Rather than spend time visiting with neighbors at a café below the apartment building, we end a 40–60-minute commute to the suburbs in a McDonald's drive-through before collapsing on the couch. Our routines appear to be set by sitting alone at home, channel surfing or scrolling social media. Here, the fragmented self seeks out resources to fill the void of identity once woven together through family and community ties, in the form of churches, civic clubs (like the Rotary Club), sports leagues, and just getting together with friends.

All humans have a basic need to feel connected to some form of community. To fill the void left from community participation described by Putnam, fan communities have flourished, especially with digital communication. Popular culture is a common reference point for people longing for community. In other words, strangers can feel an immediate connection when sharing a common object of fandom. A stranger can notice a Pittsburgh Steelers' jersey and quickly start up a conversation about their starting quarterback. Seeing a Taylor Swift sticker on a classmate's laptop creates an easy opening to social interaction about her new album. People want to feel a sense of community and popular culture is increasingly the conduit for their social connections.

In an era of community decline, large public events such as music festivals and Broadway shows are growing in popularity (see Chapter 12). Popular culture quite literally brings people together, and one of the more interesting venues for authentic fan culture are conventions. Comic-Cons (conventions for fans of comic books and related genres) first emerged in the 1970s in a few small hotel conference rooms gathering a few hundred people. These conventions grew steadily over the decades, but through the 1980s and 1990s, remained the purview of intense fans. Of course, Comic-Cons today are massive events attracting thousands of fans and A-List celebrities. Major media companies carefully monitor the response of fans at Comic-Cons to their latest big budget superhero or fantasy films as these fans serve as taste makers online, capable of building positive buzz leading to a huge opening weekend (*Black Panther*) or negative buzz leading to a giant flop (*Batman vs. Superman*). The ability to alter the decisions of executives producing movies for Marvel or DC leads us to consider more closely the power of fans today.

Social capital and production in fan communities today

In Chapter 3, we discussed social capital as it pertained to understanding why consumers of popular culture choose some artifacts over others. You may recall that social capital refers to the resources, such as education and styles of talk and dress, that relate to social class or income levels. "Quality" aesthetics and taste provide a means of moving up the "cultural ladder" and gaining prestige or status. Cultural capital functions in unique ways in the realm of fandom, as fans are typically interested in gaining the prestige of other fans. Jancovich (2002) draws a useful distinction important to the ranking and status of fan communities—**authentic** and **inauthentic fans**. Fan communities use cultural capital to differentiate someone with casual interest in an artifact, star, or team (i.e., someone who "likes" the Denver Nuggets) from the true or authentic fan. Authentic fans are not merely a "consumer" but also an active producer of cultural capital within a fan community (Fiske, 1992).

Cultural capital is really any performance that demonstrates the labor (time and money) of fandom. It can include displaying a rare edition of a comic book, reciting the detailed statistics of a sports team, or quoting lines of dialogue from movies. Authentic fans can identify inauthentic fans with a few quick questions (What's your favorite album? Who is your favorite character?), or even by how another fan dresses or talks. For instance, inauthentic fans would rarely dress in a highly detailed, homemade costume of a movie character or wear a limited edition jersey of a basketball player. At a music concert, only authentic fans loudly sing lines in unison from favorite deep-cut songs, publicly demonstrating their acquired cultural capital.

Sports fans perfectly represent cultural capital, particularly fantasy sports. Fantasy leagues, and gambling apps featuring fantasy-like games, typically involve drafting individual players from the NFL, MLB, or NBA and accumulating points based on their statistical performances. Fantasy sports have exploded in popularity and can require an astonishing amount of specialized knowledge such as daily game match-ups, injury probabilities, and statistical trends over seasons (interestingly, as fantasy sports became more popular in the 2000s, corporate behemoths overtook the fan-created fantasy leagues, which shifted the experience of fantasy sports from local communities of fans to individual gamblers playing games independently). Given the necessary labor involved, winning in a fantasy league is a visible marker of one's authentic fandom.

Similarly, collecting is a physical manifestation of cultural capital. Fans of the rock band the Grateful Dead are well known for collecting hundreds of bootlegs of concert recordings. For "Dead Heads," the ability to effortlessly reference tracks from bootlegs is clear marker of authentic fandom. Of course, fans are especially interested in objects once used by the creator of their favorite popular culture texts. In this respect, cultural capital within fandom sometimes is literally economic: a jersey Michael Jordan wore in a game sold for $10 million and Marilyn Monroe's dress sold for $5.6 million (Stebbins, 2022; Duke, 2011).

Fan communities not only perform and collect to display their authentic commitments. Building on the cultural studies discussion above, fans also engage in complex interpretive practices, leading pop culture producers to have an ambivalent relationship with fans. On one hand, a fan base that will regularly buy tickets, stream TV shows, and spend as much time "stuck" on a brand as they can (Chapter 2) definitely helps pay the bills. On the other hand, especially in an era of social media, fans often challenge producers' business decisions and content. For instance, fans have swayed the endings of films, and even gotten NBA and NFL coaches fired.

As introduced above, the systems of production try to determine the "appropriate" ways of reading or "using" media texts, e.g., viewers passively sitting in a movie theater or in one's home, flinching at the killers' reveal at the intended time, or listening to the algorithm's recommended songs "just for you." As the premise of decoding would suggest, though, some media consumers still find unique, perhaps defiant, ways of using media texts even within the strict parameters of business. These "excessive readers" (Fiske, 1992), often "interact" with media texts in alternative or creative ways—and, in digital media logic, they readily share such excessive interpretations with other fans, who can appreciate and play with new **excessive readings** themselves, for further engagement with other fans. The pleasures of interpreting popular artifacts together (see Chapters 7 and 13) builds community, as fans decode together, sometimes in excessive ways, and share those excessive readings with each other.

Excessively interpreting "bad" popular culture has become an increasingly pleasurable activity. In the 1970s and 1980s, midnight movies (literally shown at midnight at local movie theatres) featuring low-budget, strange and beloved movies such as *Rocky Horror Picture Show* or *Pink Flamingos* attracted a cult following of fans who sometimes talked to the screen or dressed in costumes. Today, this midnight movie fandom has gone mainstream. For instance, the popular podcast "How Did This Get Made" discusses movies that are poor quality (remember Chapter 3's discussion) and find pleasures in the strange and excessive aspects of these failed movies. The podcast celebrates the eccentricities of an oddball Nicolas Cage performance or rule breaking of over-the-top, low-budget action movies and musicals. Further, fans have incorporated weird and excessive songs from the 1980s such as "Total Eclipse of the Heart" by Bonnie Tyler and "Never Gonna Give You Up" by Rick Astley into memes and TikToks that somehow both love and mock the songs simultaneously. Parodic fandom can take on a life of its own, with devoted followings to *On Cinema* (a webseries and podcast featuring Tim Heidecker and Gregg Turkington, kinds of caricatures of themselves, who provide fairly meaningless reviews and lots of "meta" comedy), that include faux community conflicts between "Timheads" and "Greggheads" throughout digital media.

As these examples attest, digital media radically changed fandom and the relationship between fans and media producers. Once viewed as a marginal oddity, fan communities are now often a central feature of producers' marketing campaigns. At the beginning of many projects, producers first consider how to best please their most loyal fanbase, beginning by monitoring online activity. Fan service is a term that began in anime and manga communities to describe animators showing romantic encounters between characters or glimpses of nudity based on pent-up demand among fans (RT Staff, 2021). Now, fan service involves, more or less, giving fans exactly what they are desiring, especially based on their online discussions. This can involve a romantic encounter between TV characters who fans have been "shipping" online or releasing Zach Snyder's four-hour director's cut of *The Justice League* to appease fans clamoring on social media. Increasingly, films are filled with "Easter eggs" for authentic fans, with obscure references to previous movies (we explore Easter eggs more in Chapter 7). As a brief example, Pixar regularly inserts brief images of characters or objects from older Pixar films, a little "treat" for authentic fans to notice. Some critics feel this emphasis on the most vocal and intense fans is largely based on fear in an era of convergence, as when a giant media corporation is betting its streaming platform on a reboot of a franchise such as *Star Wars* or *Spiderman*. Ironically, the thing that originally pulled the fan into a franchise, a sense of wonder and surprise, is removed if all they receive is fan service.

Along with changes to the business of popular culture, digital media affordances can change the scope of fandom. Fandom can bring about shared identities and commitments beyond popular culture, with positive implications for social justice, as fans of celebrity activists like Lady Gaga or BTS support LGBTQ+ rights or Black Lives Matter. However, social media can also create an echo chamber in which the same ideas get repeated over and over again, encouraging angry or hateful talking points and tones repeated by fans. Sometimes, this is criticism of a movie or TV show, such as the intense reaction to *The Last Jedi* in which very vocal fans felt the movie deviated too far from previous *Star Wars* mythology (Abad-Santos & Wilkinson, 2019). The intensity of these criticisms spread into personal attacks on actress Kelly Marie Tran (who portrayed Rose Tico in *The Last Jedi*) that were so severe she had to delete her Instagram account. Similar hostility toward female performers occurred toward the cast of the *Ghostbusters* reboot when the trailer was first posted on YouTube. In a trend that seems motivated by sexism, vocal fans have been especially critical of female actors cast in franchise films, such as Brie Larson as *Captain Marvel* (Sims, 2016). Relatedly, in a series of controversies widely referred to as Gamergate, a group of gamers threatened women in the video game industry because these toxic fans felt video games had become too politically progressive (Romano, 2021). Toxic fandom, which reflects a sense of ownership or entitlement over popular culture content and/or social identity privileges, is a dark side to the communities of popular culture.

Toxic fandom understandably concerns celebrities. The intensity of some fans' online behavior recalls Eminem's song Stan and in the present era celebrities feel especially vulnerable to fans' emotional devotion, often fueled by the parasocial relationships described in Chapter 3. In sort of the opposite of a parasocial relationship, celebrities who are facing personal turmoil such as Lindsey Lohan, Amanda Bynes, and Ezra Miller become a source of amusement through ridicule on social media. We consider the ethics of treating a person in dehumanizing ways in social media further in Chapter 7.

Fans not only build community through decoding activities (which can be playful or unethical, as these examples show). Fan communities also extend their reach and power through encoding or production. For decades, fans of *Star Trek* and *Star Wars* challenged intellectual property ownership of the franchises by appropriating the stories and characters into homemade costumes and videos. Cultural studies scholars turned to the work of Michel de Certeau (1984), who was interested in how people made new meanings, often in creative and unexpected ways. Drawing upon the work of de Certeau, Jenkins (2000) described how fans could make new meanings with images and sounds, in creative and unexpected ways. Fans will play with pop culture, "poaching" or "tak[ing] away only those things that seem useful or pleasurable to the reader" (p. 449).

For instance, in the past, teenagers cobbled together magazine photographs of their favorite musicians, athletes, and actors on their bedroom walls. Today, through digital media, fans can create all kinds of new content from existing popular culture to be posted on social media. Digitization allows for variability or an object that "can exist in different, potentially infinite versions" (Manovich, 2001, p. 36). For this reason, "electronic information seems to resist ownership" (Lanham, 1993, p. 19). Increasingly, in a digital era, fans seem unconcerned with an author or creator's intent and encoding in their favorite popular culture texts. Fans have re-edited movies, such as *Star Wars: The Phantom Menace*, removing entire storylines or characters they disliked. Music fans remix songs, reimaging a ballad as a pulsing dance tune. TV fans have cobbled together clips to provide evidence of a theory about the meaning of a TV show in a YouTube video. And, of course, there's TikTok, which seems like a ready-made platform in which to playfully poach snippets of songs, dances, visual images, and ideas.

Fan communities bring their social identities (amongst other shared resources) into the interpretation of popular culture; and sometimes, the excessive readings they share can inspire new stories. The LGBTQ+ and allied community demonstrates well the cyclical nature of encoding and decoding. Queer readings take many forms and are often quite lively online, but, for the sake of clarity, we'll focus on one type: fan fiction. LGBTQ+ and allied communities write fan fiction to transform heteronormative texts into more queer texts. For instance, by creating fan fiction in the *Harry Potter* universe featuring gay romantic couples, the stories are more representative of fans' experiences (Binstock, 2016). In fact, these stories are sometimes quite popular, as one such fan fiction novel has over 4 million hits (Hampton,

2021). Queer fan fiction sometimes features real performers, such as Harry Styles, which can impede on the private sexual lives of celebrities. Fan fiction is incredibly diverse, expanding into almost any conceivable direction but often stems from feelings of invisibility and poor representation (see Chapter 4). Some popular culture creators, such as George Lucas (before he sold the rights to *Star Wars* to Disney), are quite territorial with their intellectual property and have sued fans who created movies based on *Star Wars* characters and storylines. As we raise in the final case study of the chapter, fan fiction raises questions: How much control should fans have over their favorite popular culture? How much power do fans have, given the prevailing business logics of popular culture?

Conclusion: Power in fandom, the LGBTQ+ community, and Disney's *Frozen*

In this chapter, we've considered the many ways that communities of ordinary people engage popular culture (sometimes within dominant systems; and other times, through resistant or excessive readings). We conclude the chapter with some examples of how fan communities—and, more specifically, LGBTQ+ fans and allies—can organize in powerful ways through social media. These examples remind us of the power of "organic intellectuals" introduced above. Here, voices from within a community rise up to critique domination. They identify systems of ideas that are taken to be natural and normal, they identify the hegemonic tokens, and they point out their harms to the community. They amplify the voices of community, pushing popular culture creators to build worlds that do not replicate domination—what McKerrow (1989) called the critique of freedom. Fans also take the critique of freedom into their own hands, publishing fan fiction that carries forth excessive storylines into reality.

Disney's *Frozen* earned $64.7 million on its opening weekend in November 2013. A film that cost an estimated $250 million to produce (including marketing budget), the franchise eventually hit $1.27 billion in global box office revenue, which doesn't include revenue from the many branded tie-ins, such as Anna and Elsa dresses, books, *Disney on Ice*, etc. The iconic song from *Frozen*, Elsa's "Let It Go," hit over 1 billion views on YouTube, and stood as the most popular Disney song released until "We Don't Talk about Bruno" from *Encanto* eclipsed it in 2022 (hitting number 5 on the Billboard Hot 100) (Utley, 2022). *Frozen*, in many ways, marks the beginnings of Disney's efforts to reimagine the Disney princess story without replicating White heteropatriarchy. The story follows princesses Anna and Elsa, whose childhood is indelibly shaped by Elsa's magical power to freeze objects around her through her hands, a power which includes projecting ice. Elsa appears as an emotionally intense character who struggles to control her magic, while Anna is a happy-go-lucky kid. The sisters' parents die tragically in a shipwreck, leaving Elsa to be queen of their small kingdom of Arendelle. The fast-paced story sets out from here in a pretty ideological fashion, with Princess Anna getting swept up in a newfound freedom as the palace is open to visitors, including the dashing Prince Hans.

But the story takes unexpected turns, which include Prince Hans eventually turning out to be villainous; Anna questioning her choices to become engaged to him; and the forging of close friendships between Anna, Elsa, their magical snowman Olaf, and a lower-income ice-block hauler with a huge heart, Kristoff, and his reindeer companion, Sven. The film, in other words, presents a White heteropatriarchal story only to knock it down by the ending, which features a "true love" moment—not in the form of a prince kissing Anna following his successful rescue of her, but in the form of sisters defeating the villainous prince and realizing new levels of love and trust in their relationship. Those invested in White heteropatriarchy might still be able to read Anna and Kristoff as hooking up, but Disney mercifully only leaves this as one of many suggestions. The true moral of this story is that the love of family and close friends can win the day. What author Dorian Lynskey (2014) shares as his take on the song "Let It Go" could probably be said for the whole film: they are a kind of equipment for living for children growing up, which can double as feminist and queer anthems.

With this backdrop, we can appreciate why Disney's announcement in 2016 that it was creating a sequel for *Frozen* was met with so much enthusiasm. On May 1, 2016, Alexis Isabel tweeted, "I hope Disney makes Elsa a lesbian princess imagine how iconic that would be." The tweet soon went viral, and the hashtag #GiveElsaAGirlfriend trended on social media, reinforcing a popular interpretation—that Elsa identifies as gay, bi, lesbian, or queer. Disney announced *Frozen 2* with no love interest named for Queen Elsa. The film's writer and co-director, Jennifer Lee, makes public comments that are (fittingly, perhaps, given the representation of Elsa) ambiguous: "We know what we made. But at the same time I feel like once we hand the film over, it belongs to the world, so I don't like to say anything and let the fans talk. I think it's up to them" (Hunt, 2016).

As is often the case, fan fiction and conversation outpace the creativity of major companies like Disney, adapting stories to suit their needs and interests. In the case of Elsa in *Frozen II*, fans imagine an openly gay queen who lives a full romantic life with partners like Honeymaren, a Northuldra woman we meet in the Enchanted Forest. The excessive possibilities of Honeymaren are so apparent that Google suggested (in late December 2022), "Is Honeymaren Elsa's love interest?," as the most asked question that people type when searching "Honeymaren." Put in terms of Hall's theory, *Frozen II* creators did not explicitly encode Elsa as straight, and it would seem introduced so much ambiguity to Elsa's sexuality that it's easy to decode her and Honeymaren as partners (as in one scene where Honeymaren and the queen warmly visit in the glow of a fire; see Figure 5.2).

Figure 5.2 Scene from *Frozen II*.

The hashtag campaign didn't result in Disney explicitly giving Elsa a girlfriend or confirming her queerness (though, Stahler, 2019, unpacks several scenes from *Frozen II* that demonstrate more than ambiguous warmth between Elsa and Honeymaren). Fans of Queen Elsa have continued to write their own stories for her (search "Works in Gay Elsa (Disney), for instance, on *Archive of Our Own* online). And, the images, language, and characters from *Frozen* continues to provide members of social identity groups the means through which to express their identities. Whether or not dominant producers like Disney recognize non-dominant communities, those communities continue to do the work of decoding and even encoding new stories, riffing with the characters and morals of *Frozen*.

Vernacular discourse recognizes that popular culture can not only create a sense of belonging for members of marginalized identity groups, but also interrupt or create friction for dominant ideologies (Calafell & Delgado, 2004; Ono & Sloop, 1995). Excessive readings of Disney's *The Little Mermaid*, for instance, work to reclaim the story as equipment for living for queer identity. As one fan stated, "Ariel's longing to know more about the world and go see it for herself, I think that resonates with the queer community" (Mark Rocks, quoted in Welsh, 2019, November 18). Clearly, even films which are traditionally considered heteropatriarchal leave enough room for queer interpretations and relatability.

However, given the importance of quality representation (see Chapter 4), it is important to remember that just because those in non-dominant identities can read many pop culture artifacts through the lenses of their experiences, it does not mean justice or true representation has been achieved. Even a movie as celebrated for its connections to vernacular communities as *Black Panther*, Griffin and Rossing (2020) remind us, is fraught with tensions, felt in different levels and intensities for audiences of different races and ethnicities, "between jubilation/disappointment, progress/retrogression, and reality/fantasy" (p. 204). Given that popular culture is caught up in systems of representation and reality, how could it be otherwise? It is up to us as interpretive communities to come together to negotiate meaning.

In conclusion, the tools of cultural studies which we have explored in this chapter would lead us to ask: Does Disney replicate domination through *Frozen* and *Frozen II*? As with most matters of popular culture, that's up to interpretation. The decoding power of LBGTQ+ and allied fans suggests that the movies do not replicate the ideology of White heteropatriarchy. But is the ambiguous ending, and a story that centers sisterly love, a small dose of change that maintains an oppressive and profitable system? Do you believe fan voice, such as the ability to publish one's own ending for Elsa and Honeymaren, can represent queer communities well enough (or at all)? Should Disney service fans, manifesting an openly gay relationship for Queen Elsa in *Frozen III*?

Chapter 5 gives you tools to work through these, and related questions, for yourself and with the fan communities of which you are a part. We turn from the tools of cultural studies (especially ideology, hegemony, encoding, decoding) and a discussion of fan negotiation of meaning to focus on a recurring structure endemic to much pop culture in Chapter 6: narrative.

Reflecting on the communities of pop culture in your everyday life

- What fan communities have you participated in either casually or intensely? What do you enjoy about fandom in general, and the fan communities of which you are a part, in particular? Have you ever decided to leave a fan community, and if so, why?
- How do social identities (discussed in Chapter 4) intersect with fan communities in popular culture? How do stories like *Frozen* and *Frozen II* serve as equipment for living for audiences, particularly those in marginalized social identities like girls and women, and folks identifying as LGBTQ+? What challenges does pop culture help people in marginalized identities navigate? How does pop culture provide an opportunity to teach people in dominant and non-dominant identities how to help end oppression and marginalization?
- Chapter 5 introduced the possibility of toxic fandom. Have you ever witnessed toxic fandom in action? What was it like, and how did you respond?
- How much power do fans and consumers of pop culture have, now that you've considered the frameworks from Chapters 1 through 5?

Note

1 Reich (1991) provides a useful framework to define power, beginning with the "classic" definition of power, or the ability to control others' movements and actions (in a liberal democracy, the monopoly of legitimate authority or direct power is owned by the government or law enforcement authorities). It may also refer to agenda setting power, which is the power to tell a community what matters most (which is famously held by journalists, though social media metrics now help determine what we should care about as an engaged community). Power also refers to the power of public symbols, which is widely available to most members of a community—the ability to persuade others through stories and evidence.

Suggested readings

Barker C., & Jane E. A. (2016). *Cultural studies: Theory and practice* (5th ed.). SAGE.

Edgar, A. N., & Toone, A. (2017). "She invited other people to that space": Audience habitus, place, and social justice in Beyoncé's *Lemonade. Feminist Media Studies, 19*(1), 87–101. DOI: 10.1080/14680777.2017.1377276

Fiske, J. (1992). The cultural economy of fandom. In L. Lewis (Ed.), *The adoring audience: Fan culture and popular media* (pp. 30–49). Routledge.

Jenkins H. (1992). *Textual poachers: Television fans and participatory culture.* Routledge.

References

Abad-Santos, A., & Wilkinson, A. (2019, December 27). *Star Wars: The Rise of Skywalker* was designed to be the opposite of The Last Jedi. *Vox.* https://www.vox.com/culture/2019/12/27/21034725/star-wars-the-rise-of-skywalker-last-jedi-j-j-abrams-rian-johnson

Binstock, R. (2016, May 30). Why do queer people write fan fiction? To see themselves in mainstream culture. *Slate.* https://slate.com/human-interest/2016/05/queer-people-write-fan-fiction-to-see-themselves-in-mainstream-culture.html

Calafell, B., & Delgado, F. (2004). Reading Latina/o images: Interrogating *Americanos, Critical Studies in Media Communication, 21*(1), 1–24. DOI: 10.1080/0739318042000184370

Dahl, G. B. (2010), Early teen marriage and future poverty. *Demography, 47*(3), 689–718. DOI: 10.1353/dem.0.0120. PMID: 20879684; PMCID: PMC3000061.

De Certeau, M. (1984). *The practice of everyday life.* University of California Press.

Duke, A. (2011, June 19). Marilyn Monroe's iconic dress sells for $5.6 million at auction. CNN. http://www.cnn.com/2011/SHOWBIZ/celebrity.news.gossip/06/19/hollywood.auction/index.html

Eagleton, T. (1991). *Ideology: An introduction.* Verso.

Fiske, J. (1992). The cultural economy of fandom. In L. Lewis (Ed.), *The adoring audience: Fan culture and popular media* (pp. 30–49). Routledge.

Gitlin, T. (1979). Prime time ideology: The hegemonic process in television entertainment. *Social Problems, 26*(3), 251–266. DOI: 10.2307/800451

Gramsci A. (1976). *Selections from the prison notebooks.* Lawrence & Wishart.

Griffin, R. A., & Rossing, J. P. (2020). *Black Panther* in widescreen: Cross-disciplinary perspectives on a pioneering, paradoxical film. *Review of Communication, 20*(3), 203–219. https://doi.org/10.1080/15358593.2020.1780467

Hall, S. (1980). Encoding/Decoding. In S. Hall, D. Hobson, A. Lowe, & P. Willis (Eds.), *Culture, Media and Language.* Hutchinson.

Hampton, R. (2021, November 27). The next Harry Potter novel isn't written by J.K. Rowling. *Slate.* https://slate.com/culture/2021/11/all-the-young-dudes-harry-potter-fanfic-wolfstar-tiktok.html

Hebdige, D. (1979). *Subculture: The meaning of style.* Routledge.

Hunt, E. 2016, May 2). *Frozen* fans urge Disney to give Elsa a girlfriend in sequel. *The Guardian.* https://www.theguardian.com/film/2016/may/03/frozen-fans-urge-disney-to-give-elsa-girlfriend-lgbt

Jancovich, M. (2002). Cult fictions: Cult movies, subcultural capital and the production of cultural distinctions. *Cultural Studies, 16*(2), 306–321.

Jenkins, H. (2000). *Star Trek* rerun, reread, and rewritten: Fan writing as textual poaching. In H. Newcomb (Ed.), *Television: The critical view* (pp. 470–494). Oxford University Press.

Lanham, R. (1993). *The electronic word: Democracy, technology, and the arts.* University of Chicago Press.

Li, S. (2022, August 9). The powerful, unlikely force shaping modern TV. *The Atlantic.* https://www.theatlantic.com/culture/archive/2022/08/fan-theories-severance-yellowjackets-westworld/671079/

Lynskey, D. (2014, April 10). Why *Frozen*'s "Let It Go" is more than a Disney hit – it's an adolescent aperitif. *The Guardian.* https://www.theguardian.com/music/musicblog/2014/apr/10/frozen-let-it-go-disney-hit-adolescent-lgbt-anthem

Manovich, L. (2001). *The language of new media.* The MIT Press.

Marx, K., & Engels, F. (1947). *The German ideology (Part I).* (C. J. Arthur, Ed.). International Publishers.

McKerrow, R. (1989). Critical rhetoric: Theory and practice. *Communication Monographs, 56*(2), 91–111.

Neilson, S. (2019, May 24). How Disney princesses influence girls around the world. NPR. https://www.npr.org/sections/goatsandsoda/2019/05/24/726129132/how-disney-princesses-influence-girls-around-the-world

Ng, V. (2021). How Disney Princesses became a multi billion dollar brand. Top Ten Social Media. https://www.toptensocialmedia.com/how-disney-princesses-became-a-multi-billion-dollar-brand/

Ono, K. A., & Sloop, J. M. (1995). The critique of vernacular discourse. *Communication Monographs, 62*(1), 19–46.

Paquette, D. (2016, June 22) The unexpected way Disney princesses affect little boys. *Washington Post.* https://www.washingtonpost.com/news/wonk/wp/2016/06/22/what-little-boys-can-learn-from-disney-princesses/

Putnam, R. (2000). *Bowling alone: The collapse and revival of American community.* Simon & Schuster.

Romano, A. (2021, January 2). What we still haven't learned from Gamergate. *Vox.* https://www.vox.com/culture/2020/1/20/20808875/gamergate-lessons-cultural-impact-changes-harassment-laws

Reich, M. (1991). *Toxic politics: Responding to chemical disasters*. Cornell University Press.

Rheingold, H. (1993). *The virtual community: Homesteading on the electronic frontier*. Addison-Wesley.

RT Staff. (2021, January 28). The power of fan service and what it means for the future of movies. *Rotten Tomatoes*. https://editorial.rottentomatoes.com/article/power-of-fan-service/

Saccaro, M. (2015, February 4). America's "free time" problem: Why nearly half of U.S. workers don't get enough of it. *Salon*. https://www.salon.com/2015/02/04/americas_free_time_problem_why_nearly_half_of_u_s_workers_dont_get_enough_of_it/

Setoodeh, R. (2007, November 17). Disney's $4 billion princess brand. *Newsweek*. https://www.newsweek.com/disneys-4b-princess-brand-96993

Sims, D. (2016, May 18). The ongoing outcry against the *Ghostbusters* remake. *The Atlantic*. https://www.theatlantic.com/entertainment/archive/2016/05/the-sexist-outcry-against-the-ghostbusters-remake-gets-louder/483270/

Stahler, K. (2019, November 25). *Frozen II*'s director explains why Elsa doesn't have a girlfriend (& this is the key Word) yet. *Refinery 29*. https://www.refinery29.com/en-us/2019/11/8849966/is-honeymaren-elsa-girlfriend-in-frozen-2-interview

Stebbins, J. (2022, September 16). Michael Jordan's "Last Dance" jersey sells for record breaking $10.1 million. *CNBC*. https://www.cnbc.com/2022/09/16/michael-jordan-jersey-10point1-million-sothebys-record-memorabilia.html

Terray, E., & Serrano, J. (2019). Exploitation and domination in Marx's thought. *Rethinking Marxism: A Journal of Economics, Culture & Society, 31*(4), 412–424. DOI: 10.1080/08935696.2019.1637657

Utley, B. (2022, January 21). *Encanto* song tops *Frozen's* "Let It Go" on the Billboard charts. *Gamerant*. https://gamerant.com/encanto-we-dont-talk-about-bruno-beat-frozen-let-it-go/

Welsh, D. (2019, November 18). How *The Little Mermaid* found a place in the hearts of LGBTQ fans. *Huffington Post (UK Edition)*. https://www.huffingtonpost.co.uk/entry/the-little-mermaid-lgbtq-fans-ursula_uk_5dce8608e4b0d2e79f8adb51

6 Story and popular culture

Introduction

Recall your favorite bedtime story or fairy tale. Why is this a favorite? Do you remember the lessons or moral from the story? When our youngest was in elementary school, the teachers organized an event involving one of our favorite stories, "Goldilocks and the Three Bears." This familiar tale was put to work to teach the kids about how legal arguments work. Goldilocks was on trial, and our kid was on the prosecution team. His contribution focused on evidence that showed Goldilocks was, in fact, in the bears' home, and that circumstantially we could reasonably conclude that she had tasted the bears' porridge, sat in their chair, and slept in their bed. The kids enjoyed the lesson, though we found it a bit odd that Goldilocks was acquitted by some soft-hearted jurors in the classroom—odd not only because the case was well argued, but because of critical attention Goldilocks has received in the 2020s. *Vice* magazine writes in 2017 on a trend from Twitter and Instagram, proclaiming "Goldilocks" as an allegory of White privilege (Barksdale, 2017). Check out Australian comedian Nazeem Hussain, as he riffs with this idea in his stand up (Melbourne International Comedy Festival, 2021). Such a framework may seem silly, insightful, or just plain wrong, depending on your experiences and identities, but this is our point of story: though our kids' prosecution laid out a technically correct legal argument, enough jurors believed that Goldilocks was hungry and afraid, and therefore should be exonerated. Stories work through their own unique standards of reasoning, and therein lies a good deal of their power. As we see in this chapter, stories provide equipment for living, lessons, and points of identification.

"Goldilocks and the Three Bears" is not only appearing across the country to teach kids about court cases, or on social media to educate folks about Whiteness. The story shows up multiple times in *The Simpsons*, has appeared within *Sesame Street*, is featured in the hit movie *Puss in Boots: The Last Wish*, and has been used to anchor car commercials.

DOI: 10.4324/9781003372943-6

In the fall of 2022, Hollywood's marketing machine began reporting that Reese Witherspoon is developing a film version of *Goldilocks*. What is true for *Goldilocks*, though, could be said of countless other children's tales, such as *Hansel and Gretel*, *The Little Mermaid*, and *The Tortoise and the Hare*. As we see in this chapter, the power of story in popular culture is not limited to fairy tales or nursery rhymes (as ubiquitous as they are), or even go-to narrative media like film and television. Story abounds in video games, songs, even social media posts with their truncated character limits, video time parameters, or single images.

How does *Legends of Zelda* (the video game) structure reality? What lessons do we learn in a story like "HUMBLE" by Kendrick Lamar? What identities and morals are invoked as the backstories and resolutions to #HandsUpDontShoot or #MeToo? How do we learn from and act on stories in pop culture? These are but a few of the questions we explore across this chapter. First, we define narrative, and explain why narrative is a unique form of reasoning (this section helps explain why the prosecution lost). We then look to genre to explain the ways stories travel across time, before articulating their power, through the ideas of identification and memory.

Defining story as a sense-making tool

You may recall from our book's introduction that the humanities are unique in what people consider to be useful information, and how people generate knowledge. Narrative, which is a fancy synonym for story, is a common thread across humanistic ways of knowing. Walter Fisher (1984) defines **narrative** as "symbolic actions—word and/or deeds—that have sequence and meaning for those who live, create, or interpret them" (p. 273). In many Western cultures, stories have a consistent structure: they proceed in a linear sequence with exposition, rising action, climax or conflict, ending with a resolution. They take place in a scene, with protagonist characters (often defined as the "good guys") and antagonists (the "bad guys"). Western stories end with a moral, or lesson learned from the story. Other cultures share very different structures, where, for instance, action moves in spirals or circles, resolution is not achieved, and morals are not as explicit.

In spite of this diversity, though, storytelling is so prevalent across time and cultures that some have suggested *homo sapiens* could just as easily be named *homo narrans* (Fisher, 1984), or what Burke (1969) named "the symbol using animal" could be termed "the storytelling animal." Anthropologists and evolutionary biologists believe that "toolmaking, firemaking, and cooperative hunting" in *homo erectus* (the direct ancestor for *homo sapiens*) provided the perfect conditions in which language evolved

(Boyd, 2018, p. 2). Considering longer childhoods for this species, and evidence of play, scholars believe that storytelling (particularly fiction) was a natural outcome. Narrative relates to a number of other abilities, such as "event comprehension, memory, imagination, language," suggesting a competitive advantage over long periods of time for a storytelling species (Boyd, 2018, p. 2). Humans evolved as a cooperative species, "deeply dependent on knowing more about our kind and our risks and opportunities than we could discover through direct experience" (Boyd, 2018, p. 1).

Evidence shows that other primates, like chimpanzees and monkeys, communicate with each other, but this communication is primarily done with body language and different pitches and sounds. Non-human animals seem to lack the syntax (combining sounds into unique words, with meanings) that humans use. If a vervet monkey sounds the alarm for specific predators, the troop will respond in ways unique to the alarm call in anticipation of, say, a python versus a martial eagle (Seyfarth, Cheney, & Marler, 1980). But to our knowledge, vervet monkeys do not share myths about leopards or pythons. Their communication is limited to the "here and now," whereas humans appear to be evolved to weave useful information with fiction and memory, sharing this with each other across time.

In the 1970s and 1980s, communication scholars like Walter Fisher turned to narrative as a tool for reasoning that was available to almost everyone. Fisher contrasted narrative to the "rational world paradigm," which applied the standards of technical reasoning like expertise, rationality, logic, and scientific evidence to public problems. If we viewed narrative as an equally valid, but different, way of knowing, more people could participate in important decisions. Fisher asserted that we used two main standards to evaluate evidence through narrative rationality (his term for the way of knowing through narratives, and particularly an individual's decision to act on the basis of a story): narrative probability and narrative fidelity. **Narrative probability** asks, does a story "hang together" or cohere as a story from beginning to end? **Narrative fidelity** asks, does a story "ring true" to the listener's experience and values?

Let's return to "Goldilocks and the Three Bears" to explain how narrative rationality works—and why it's important to contrast to the rational world paradigm. Applying standards of scientific evidence, and even factual truth, to "Goldilocks" is laughable: bears, of course, do not live in houses, sleep in beds, eat porridge, etc. However, the story provides interesting lessons (or fails to, as we will elaborate below) when viewed from narrative rationality.

Narrative probability, like narrative rationality, does not depend on truth or fiction, but rather the internal structure of a story. "Goldilocks," like other fairy tales, has a strong structure built through repetition. Read the story aloud to a group and you will likely be joined on the chorus of

"Somebody's been eating my food!" as the three bears discover Goldi-locks's antics. The big finale, in which the bears discover Goldilocks sleep-ing in their beds, awakening her to flee, serves as a valuable lesson to lock your home up tight and take care of your belongings (or, from Goldi-locks's perspective, to avoid trespassing … or at least to appreciate what you have). From this vantage, the story passes the test of narrative fidelity.

However, some have questioned just how valuable the moral of "Goldi-locks" is, especially where Goldilocks faces no consequences (beyond a fright) for her actions. In fact, the original tale of the Three Bears posited that the trio (who are not described as a nuclear family) purchase a home in a nice neighborhood. Their neighbor, an elderly woman, calls on them, but the bears refuse to entertain her. As a history of the fairy tale explains, the neighbor "calls the bears 'impertinent,' " and decides to enter anyway, drinking their milk, testing out their furniture and breaking a chair and a bed. The bears react by "first throwing her into a fire and then into water, before finally throwing her on top of the steeple of St. Paul's Cathedral and leaving her there" (Ness, 2017). The original version points out an-other possibility for the story's ending, which might ring more true to the moral of being accountable to one's actions (particularly when one's ac-tions make them cross paths with bears).

The two different endings to "Goldilocks" also underscore that stories change over time. These changes occur as a result of the need for new equipment for living, building on our discussion in Chapter 1. But they also change due to the business of popular culture, per our discussion in Chapter 2. These different endings for "Goldilocks" would appear to be driven by market forces as much or more than narrative fidelity. Victorian authors transformed the Three Bears into the story of Silver-Hair, a young girl, as part of a collection of nursery poems. Later collections morphed the girl to Goldilocks, our infamous heroine who happened upon a bear fam-ily's home (Ness, 2017). Stories can change, too, because they are respon-sive to the need for better representations of social identities (Chapter 4), or to ring true to community (Chapter 5). In the 2022 movie *Puss in Boots: The Last Wish*, Goldilocks and the bears become a blended family work-ing through (and learning to appreciate) their unconventional family ar-rangement. Such a moral has greater fidelity with contemporary audiences, perhaps. Narratives can also change slightly, as long-standing expectations for them shift, as we turn to in the next section.

Narrative and genre

Have you binged a series based on a recommendation from a streaming ser-vice, like Netflix or Hulu? Most likely, the algorithm that suggested your next series used cues from genres to make the recommendation. **Genre** refers to long-standing categories of popular culture content that have consistent features, like style, tone, form, and subject matter. Netflix and other streaming services use standard "genre tags," such as "Comedies," "Dramas," and "Documentaries." Genre, per Burke (1968), is the setting and satisfying of expectation: so a category like "comedy" sets the expectation that one might laugh, or, at least not cry in sorrow, while the term "horror" sets viewers up for content that will shock, scare, and/or gross them out—content that is "horrifying."

As in our definition of narrative above, stories in a genre share consistent structures or features that endure over time. These features can relate to content, such as fiction versus non-fiction. The features also map onto the structure of narratives described above, where "generic" stories consistently share a scene, plot sequence, moral, and/or characters. Here, we point to Westerns to illustrate how a scene of lawlessness, involving a lone stranger who rides into the town and defends justice (and/or weaker individuals) against a "dark" character who is a force of evil. These traits persist whether or not the characters ride horses or wear cowboy hats. So the shows *Yellowstone* and *Breaking Bad*—two of the most popular Westerns in recent memory—share key features. Both series center on the characteristic setting of wide open spaces and sparse population, with cinematography featuring several scenes of mountainous rural Montana and the ruddy desert outside of Albuquerque, New Mexico (see Figure 6.1).

The shows also have archetypal characters, including an older "gunslinger" mentoring an impulsive young outlaw (in the case of Walter White and Jesse); and archetypal conflicts, such as dealing with lawlessness and conflict surrounding homesteads or towns (as in the presence of drugs in both shows). *Yellowstone*, like *Breaking Bad* and other Westerns, dwell

Figure 6.1 Scene from *Breaking Bad*.

on themes of masculinity (particularly dominant straight White masculinity), including aging and toughness. So even though both shows are set in contemporary times, they are undeniably Westerns, which we can track through their classic gun fight scenes, their camera shots that dwell on sunsets and vast landscapes, their casting of strangers or others as threats.

As Burke described, genre repeats the elements of stories like setting, antagonist, protagonist, and conflict. Genres also share similar sequencing of time and the treatment of characters' morality. Burke (1984) famously distinguished comedy from tragedy on the basis of whether or not the ending of a story was foretold in its early stages (think, *Titanic*); or, whether the ending was open-ended and even surprising. Comedies, for Burke, were thus not based on whether or not a story made you laugh—but whether or not the characters in the story had some freedom or flexibility to adjust the story's ending. *High School Musical*, for instance, begins with the "odd" premise of a star athlete (Troy) trying out for the school musical, and falling for a music nerd (Gabriella). We cheer (and perhaps cringe at) the characters' ability to graduate high school and potentially remain a couple, in spite of the obstacles they faced.

Additionally, comedy (from its roots in ancient Greece to today) represents humans as "mistaken, not evil." Burke would link comedy to equipment for living, and judging by the popularity of shows like *The Simpsons* or *Modern Family*, we think he had a point. *Forbes* tracks viewership on *The Simpsons*, which has been in the millions (beginning from 27 million average in 1987) (McCarthy, 2017) and the *Modern Family* finale had 7.47 million in 2020. People are drawn to stories which represent characters in generous or humane ways, like Homer Simpson, the classic fool character who asks for forgiveness and learns from mistakes. People are drawn to stories in which the ending isn't "locked in," in which characters can affect the outcome to some degree, or in which they can adapt themselves to the outcome (which distinguishes comedy from tragedy, all the way from ancient Greece to today). Spoiler: Jay Pritchett, the father/grandfather of *Modern Family*, ends the show's run by becoming a stay-at-home father so his wife, Gloria, can pursue her career in real estate. His character arc is about a 180-degree turnaround from the gruff careerist we meet in season one.

Returning to our discussion of narrative rationality above, we may note that genre helps set expectations on whether or not a story "rings true" to our experience, and whether or not it "coheres." *Breaking Bad* "rang true" to a number of viewers' experiences, in part, because the genre of Westerns had set those expectations: we are somehow not surprised by the gory battles involving such characters as Walter White and Gus Fring, because such scenes are consistent with generic expectations. That a show which spans several years can hang together is a remarkable fete, and the creators of *Breaking Bad* are remarkable storytellers.

But it's also interesting to see how genre is fluid and dynamic. Westerns of the 1950s centered on a "good guy" (wearing a white hat) saving the small town from outside forces that bring peril (outlaws, or, invoking racist stereotypes, Indigenous People). Clint Eastwood helped reinvent the Western genre in the 1960s and 1970s, portraying a grizzled gunslinger who is beaten down by society. The character first appears as though he's a "Robin Hood" type, stealing from the rich to give to the poor; but actually, he is just as selfish as the outlaws are. We see Walter White as being closer to what the reality of Western settlement probably was, with figures like Jesse James who didn't actually help anyone. White creates a pile of money out of hubris and greed, though his original intentions led viewers to believe he would protect his family (Brown, 2017).

Genre is an important link between story and context, where genres provide equipment for living that gives people tools to address the urgent problems (exigencies) they face. *Breaking Bad* is an excellent example— the show came about at the dawn of the Great Recession, the financial crisis of 2007–2008 in which deregulation of the financial industry led to horrendous consequences around housing and employment. Lending companies approved mortgages at low interest rates, with housing prices falling so quickly that homeowners could not keep up with payments. Nearly 9 million jobs were lost, and companies like Lehman Brothers (an investment bank) declared bankruptcy. The financial struggles of a nuclear family (headed by high school chemistry teacher Walter White and stay-at-home mom Skyler, who also participates in the gig economy and a series of odd jobs throughout the show's run) are the focus of the show. When Walter White is diagnosed with cancer, and learns soon that he and Skyler have a second son on the way, this Albuquerque family suddenly moves from the comfort of middle-class privilege to crisis. Like so many other families of the time, the Whites have to figure out how to make ends meet. The show explores themes of moral compromise, gendered/raced hubris, and very real questions of how one family will navigate a series of choices once their income level cannot keep up with their medical and family bills.

Breaking Bad is not only a Western, but also, a tragedy in the classic Greek sense. We feel a foreboding from early in the series, where Walter White is the tragic hero whose fate is sealed through his tragic flaw of pride. Spoiler alert—through the show's second half, White makes a series of horrifying choices, including actions that rip apart his former student (and drug-making and dealing colleague) Jesse. White lies about his actions, to add insult to injury. Walter White begins the series very much as a victim of circumstances beyond his control (cancer, being on the losing end of a business deal), like many middle-class families in the Great Recession. But unlike those folks, Walter White ends the show as an immoral and flawed individual, in a cautionary tale that viewers do *not* want to enact, at least hopefully not, given the deep suffering that White inflicts on the people clos-est to him (like Jesse). Such is the power of the tragic genre: to provide an ex-ample of a hero who is "like me, but better," a sympathetic character (high school teacher diagnosed with cancer) who nonetheless makes fatally flawed choices. This leads to our final section, concerning the power of story.

Understanding the power of story in pop culture

Story promotes identification, which is the ability of people hearing or viewing the story to put themselves in the shoes of a story's characters. Burke (1974) defined **identification** as "one's material and mental ways of placing oneself as a person in the groups and movements," or a way to "see oneself in the social mirror" (p. 227). Identification in popular culture ranges from what feels like a literal "putting oneself in the scene" type of feeling, to a more distanced or "meta" level of questioning: What would *I* do if I were that character's shoes? So we might view a scene from *Break-ing Bad*, and imagine the peril of being chased by local law enforcement when we were only attempting to pay for health care in a system that is so deeply flawed. We might feel the grotesque horror of dissolving a body in a bathtub. Or, from a distance, share certain values with Walter White, an entrepreneur who uses intelligence and perseverance to make a living in very difficult circumstances—particularly against enemies, like Fring or even his brother-in-law, Hank.

Story has a natural relationship to identification, especially in the West-ern world, where stories often end in a moral or meaning that we are meant to take to heart. Stories in a Western tradition often have a clear division in characters, who are defined through an antagonism of "good" (protagonist) versus "evil" (antagonist). Aside—a show like *Breaking Bad* is so intriguing because it really plays with our expectations, and pushes the binary, such that Walter White ends the series more as a representation of the "bad guy." Identification occurs through the power of the negative, or the ability in language to say "I'm *not that*" (Burke, 1974). Othering people through the negative in popular culture has heinous implications. Lechuga (2016), for instance, notes that persistent "filmic constructions of alien Others as monstrous, frightening, and anxiety-inducing, and the subsequent measures often taken by nationalistic US Americans to milita-rize against alien invasions," go hand in hand (p. 226). So many represen-tations of migrant others through frameworks in alien invasion movies, combined with persistent usage of words like "illegal alien" to describe humans crossing the border in the US, paves the way for policies that treat immigration through violence and militarized responses.

Burke believed that the negative (non-A) is peculiar to humans, an abil-ity that only occurs in language. Though monkeys and bees (as described above) seem to have the ability to communicate through symbols, they would appear to lack a language in which to communicate "not that." Bees waggle to show their hive mates where flowers are, and monkeys call out when danger is present—but bees do not dance a "not flower" dance, nor do monkeys call, "just kidding, not prey!" (at least as far as we know). This ability to declare who "we" are, on the basis of who we are *not* ("we are *not them*"), makes language and story very powerful. It provides individuals the ability to declare that they are like "friends" (they share the same values, they agree on the same issues, they might even share the same identity traits), and not like "enemies." Identification occurs through whole stories, fragments of stories, and even in units as small as language or images. So all the laptop stickers you might see with Walter White's profile on them can convey a point of identification, as though the sticker owner wants to adopt the toughness or shrewdness of Walter White.

Given the connection between narrative, identification, and identities (as discussed in Chapter 4), it is especially interesting to see how contemporary audiences are drawn to stories featuring "real people" from the past. The historical biopic is a staple genre of Hollywood, with "greatest" movies of all time lists littered with historical biopics (like *Schindler's List* and *Lawrence of Arabia*). Generally, these movies are designed as inspirational narratives of perseverance and achievement, and as we elaborated in Chapter 3 often denote "quality" cinema. Historic biopics tell the stories of famous figures such as Freddie Mercury (*Bohemian Rapsody*), Aretha Franklin (*Respect*), PT Barnum (*The Greatest Showman*), Johnny Cash (*Walk the Line*), and Abraham Lincoln (*Lincoln*). Why are people drawn to stories of "real" people, including the recent turns to malevolent characters of the past (such as Adolf Hitler and serial killers)? In the final section, we consider nostalgia and memory in the context of narrative.

Conclusion: Memorializing the past through pop culture

We close Chapter 6 through a case study that raises ethical questions for individual users, but also for communities. A powerful source of identification is a collective history. Sports fan communities tell the story of the Lakers, Packers, or Buckeyes with a deep sense of reverence, putting statues of great players and coaches outside the stadium. In fact, all groups of people tell stories about their past. Cultures, countries, and religions have an origin story that details the formation of the group. These stories carry tremendous ideological meaning as well as the foundational values of the group. For most of human life, these histories were shared orally or in foundational texts, taught in schools and reverently shared in families on holidays. These stories gave a sense of meaning and purpose. People fought and died because they believed so deeply in these stories.

For a moment, consider the images that pop into your head when hearing "the 1970s" or "the 1980s." First, you probably have strong mental images associated with these decades. Where did they come from? Chances are, you are recalling images from movies, TV shows, YouTube clips, and advertising that nostalgically paint idealized versions of the past. These images are designed for pleasure, emphasizing the enjoyable recognition of cheesy styles of clothing, iconic pop songs, and silly fads that have come to define how we think about our past. Nonetheless, this is also how we collectively and individually remember wars, civil unrest, and presidential administrations. Whatever the historical event (slavery, World War II, assassinations, etc.) you probably first recall images from popular culture. Today, the stories of the past (in "decades") are much more visually expressed in vague associations with images from popular culture.

Building on the ideas in this chapter, it is clear that popular culture has profoundly changed how human communities tell stories of the past. Frederic Jameson (1991) described how popular culture regularly references the past in terms of decades via stylistic conventions of '1980s-ness' or Y2K-ness (perhaps we are still finding a term for the decades of 2000–2010 and 2010–2020). For instance, the sepia-toned world of the 1930s and 1940s (think of *The Godfather*) with distinctive costumes, dialogue, and music is easily recognizable, even in a few seconds of a TV commercial. Prior to widespread popular media, subcultures may have discussed history in terms of decades (e.g., "the Roaring Twenties," referencing the economic context of the 1920s); but it is remarkable that, from the 1960s onward, popular culture commonly identifies decades as unique time periods with consistent aesthetics and vibes.

The history of the last century is defined by the arbitrary distinctions of decades, which is sometimes awkward when an event like the Vietnam War straddles two decades or an iconic trend like disco was only popular for a few years. Today, the conceptualization of the past through decades is so normalized that clothing trends online are regularly referred to as "'90s looks" or "Y2K fashion" and stations on Spotify, Amazon Music, and Sirius XM refer to decades such as the 1970s and 1980s as "genres" of music.

For Jameson (1991), the "decade-ization" of popular culture is in the form of nostalgia or a "blank parody" of the past. Nostalgic popular culture tends to reference other *images* of the past. Decade-ization, in other words, does not remember actual events or people from 1955 or 1962, but the 1950s or 1960s as seen in movies, TV shows, and advertising. By only referencing the images and styles in older artifacts, nostalgic popular culture can offer idealized, sanitized versions of the past. On many levels, popular culture history is *selling* the idealized version of the decade, e.g., "check out this fun '70s movie." Holiday commercials, too, often evoke nostalgic images of "simpler times."

Nostalgic popular culture comes through in aesthetics (music, editing, cinematography, costumes, etc.), but also in the stories we tell. *Forrest Gump* is perhaps the best example of a pop culture artifact that caters to decade-ization and nostalgia, as the film depicts the lifelong story of Forrest and Jenny by weaving together iconic events and historic figures within each decade from the 1950s to the 1990s such as Elvis Presley, John F. Kennedy, the Vietnam War, Watergate, and disco. Somehow, Forrest is a dim-witted guy from Alabama who stumbled upon the most historically significant moments of the past 50 years, decade-by-decade, scene-by-scene.

The easily recognizable nostalgic images of the film presumably allow generations of audiences to suspend disbelief and fall in love with such an implausible narrative (see Figure 6.2). *Forrest Gump* prominently features images of school desegregation and mass protests that recreate moments featured in montages from movies and TV shows. For most Americans, "civil rights" in the United States is narratively experienced via a series of iconic images from the "'60s" such as Rosa Parks on the bus (which actually happened in 1955), Whites-only water fountains and bathrooms, culminating with Dr. Martin Luther King, Jr., speaking at the March on Washington. These images provide a simple coherence and clear resolution to very complicated and (as the Black Lives Matter movement indicates) quite unresolved racism in the United States. This is what nostalgia offers: brief, uncomplicated, and pleasurable images of the past.

What are the possible consequences of a people's history largely experienced via nostalgic images in movies, TV, and advertising? How does nostalgic popular culture differ from other more complex and ambivalent stories we could tell about our shared past? How do we evaluate today's most popular stories as they serve cultures in the ways that stories have served humans of the past? For instance, would a film or other popular story today inspire you to fight and die for an idea or a group of people? Do today's most popular stories, such as *Avengers End Game* or *Avatar: The Way of Water*, provide equipment for living through complex

Figure 6.2 Scene from *Forrest Gump*.

challenges in your community? Would a story like *Avengers End Game* provide valuable insight into the climate crisis, for instance?

In conclusion, this chapter has made a case for why story continues to matter deeply, across thousands of years and across different communities. We hope to have fostered appreciation for narrative as a way of knowing which is accessible to many people (if not universally available to all, as some have claimed). Narrative contrasts rational and expert forms of evidence, and thus deserves different standards for evaluation compared to statistics or formal logic. A story's ability to cohere and resonate with the experiences and values of listeners matters more than its objective truth. We've seen how genre shapes expectations, carrying story conventions across time and distance, for better and for worse. Story, like other structures within popular culture, provides equipment for living. But as we turn to in Chapter 7, the dizzying practices of referencing other pieces of pop culture (the interconnectedness of pop culture) complicates how stories and other structures of pop culture work.

Reflecting on the stories of pop culture in your everyday life

- Looking back at your pop culture engagement in a day, how do you encounter stories across different platforms? How do you see stories, for instance, on social media, on television and film, in advertising, in music? Do these stories share the fairly linear structure introduced in Chapter 6, sequencing time from beginning to end, with lessons, protagonists, and antagonists? If not, how do they structure time and meaning?
- Building on Chapter 6's discussion of identification, who are the "friends" of the stories you engage, and what issues, ideas, and identities do they represent? Who are the "enemies" in these stories, and what issues, ideas, and identities do they represent? What do friends and enemies tell you about identities and communities in pop culture, to connect the stories of pop culture to Chapters 4 and 5?
- Now, assess the quality of these stories: Do they support you and other members of your community in navigating challenges? If you could revise a story to offer more quality equipment for living—or, perhaps even to avoid replicating ideology or hegemony, as discussed in Chapter 5—how would you go about it?
- How do specific pieces of popular culture shape our public memory of events, particularly those which are now out of lived experience for many people? For instance, what does it mean to teach civil rights and desegregation through the popular film *Remember the Titans*?

Suggested readings

Brown, J. A. (2017). *The modern superhero in film and television: Popular genre and American culture*. Routledge.

Hoerl, K. (2018). *The Bad Sixties: Hollywood memories of the counterculture, antiwar, and Black Power movements*. University Press of Mississippi.

Murphy, P. D. (2018). Lessons from the zombie apocalypse in global popular culture: An environmental discourse approach to the walking dead. *Environmental Communication, 12*(1), 44–57. 10.1080/17524032.2017.1346518

References

Barksdale, A. (2017, August 11). The Internet is convinced that Goldilocks is a story about gentrification. *Vice*. https://www.vice.com/en/article/vbbm5x/the-internet-is-convinced-that-goldilocks-is-a-story-about-gentrification

Boyd, B. (2018). The evolution of stories: From mimesis to language, from fact to fiction. *Wiley interdisciplinary reviews. Cognitive Science, 9*(1), e1444. https://doi.org/10.1002/wcs.1444

Brown, P. (2017). The American Western mythology of "Breaking Bad." *Studies in Popular Culture, 40*(1), 78–101. http://www.jstor.org/stable/44779944

Burke, K. (1968). *Counter-statement*. University of California Press.

Burke K. (1969). *A rhetoric of motives*. University of California Press.

Burke, K. (1974). *The philosophy of literary form*. University of California Press.

Burke, K. (1984). *Attitudes toward history* (3rd ed.). University of California Press.

Fisher, W. (1984) Narration as a human communication paradigm: The case of public moral argument, *Communication Monographs, 51*(1), 1–22, DOI: 10.1080/03637758409390180

Jameson, F. (1991). *Postmodernism or the cultural logic of late capitalism*. Duke University Press.

Lechuga, M. (2016). Battling identity warfare on the imagined US/Mexico border: Performing migrant alien in *Independence Day* and *Battle: Los Angeles*. In E. J. Hartelius (Ed.), *The rhetorics of US immigration: Identity, community, otherness* (pp. 225–246). Pennsylvania State University.

McCarthy, N. (2017, April 20). 30 years on, *The Simpsons* isn't aging well. *Forbes*. https://www.forbes.com/sites/niallmccarthy/2017/04/20/30-years-on-and-the-simpsons-isnt-aging-well-infographic/?sh=a39b26726967

Melbourne International Comedy Festival [@melbcomedyfestival]. (2021, May 20). *Goldilocks and the Three Bears is a story about White privilege. #NazeemHussain #standup #standupcomedy #comedy #whiteprivilege* [Video.] TikTok. https://www.tiktok.com/@melbcomedyfestival/video/6964537489394502913?is_from_webapp=v1&lang=en

Ness, M. (2017, May 11). She doesn't always get away: Goldilocks and the Three Bears. TOR. https://www.tor.com/2017/05/11/she-doesnt-always-get-away-goldilocks-and-the-three-bears/

Seyfarth, R. M., Cheney, D. L., & Marler, P. (1980). Monkey responses to three different alarm calls: Evidence of predator classification and semantic communication. *Science, 210*(4471), 801–803. https://doi.org/10.1126/science.7433999

7 The interconnectedness of popular culture

Introduction

The Simpsons is utterly unique in the history of television. No television show has had the longevity (34 years and counting), cultural impact, and global popularity of *The Simpsons*. That *The Simpsons* airs in over 200 countries worldwide is especially interesting, since every episode of the show has specific, and sometimes obscure, American popular culture references. For instance, just focusing on American musical theater, *The Simpsons* has parodied *Mary Poppins*, *The Music Man*, *The Best Little Whorehouse in Texas*, and *Evita*. The show's rapid-fire references to TV, movies, sports, video games, etc. has influenced subsequent popular culture in very obvious ways, including series like *Family Guy* and *Southpark* (which share stylistic conventions). *The Simpsons* style and characters have left their mark in more subtle ways, including rap lyrics that drop references, as in Drake's "Good Girls Go Bad," "I love ya ... like Milhouse love Lisa."

The vast majority of American popular culture styles now knowingly reference other popular culture. Think about what it is like to watch movies, TV shows, and advertisements (and listen to music), as a kid today. A TV commercial for Mountain Dew recreates a scene from *The Shining*. *Sesame Street* and *The Muppets* parody *Mad Men*, *Game of Thrones*, and *Downton Abbey*. The biggest pop songs of today sample the music of decades past, artists like Rick Astley, Donna Summer, and Notorious B.I.G. In each of these cases, the references are intended to be a big part of the meaning of the popular culture text. Yet, it is hard to imagine the average little kid has watched *Game of Thrones*, *Mad Men*, or *The Shining*. Sometimes, if they are like our kids (or their friends), they will look at you perplexed and ask, who is Hannibal Lector? What is *Deadpool*? Other times, kids apparently just let the references wash over them, unconcerned about their meaning. A lot of this stuff must seem weirdly uninteresting without meaningful references. These same strange experiences likely apply to people

DOI: 10.4324/9781003372943-7

migrating to the United States from other cultures or even anyone over 70 years old. Welcome to the world of intertextual media, where rapid and continual references to old popular culture are essential to making sense of TV, movies, music, and even games.

When confronted by a show like *The Simpsons* early in its emergence (way back in 1989), academics turned to the study of literature to make sense of how popular culture was referencing itself, and to what ends. Building off the discussion of narrative in Chapter 6, Chapter 7 focuses on how the study of intertextuality helps explain the various connections between pieces of popular culture. But as we explore, the relationality between and across popular culture has only become more complex between broadcast and digital media logics—and not always for the better. By looking at the sophistication of signs between and across bits of popular culture (or "texts"), we sort out the meaning of intertextuality.

The first section defines text and context, introducing the idea of semiotics or study of signs as a useful tool to make sense of intertextual references. We then elaborate on parody and pastiche as two long-standing practices of intertextual reference in pop culture; as well as "drillable" texts, which are a relatively new phenomenon. Finally, the conclusion looks to several cases in which intertextual play crosses boundaries of fiction and truth, many times without permission: transforming an individual into a brand, or "memeing" someone or their actions shows how quickly pleasurable play can turn into dehumanization. We conclude with questions to help pop culture enthusiasts sort the quality parody from vapid references and texts designed to keep you "stuck" to a show in the contemporary branding economy.

Intertextuality: Text and context

The word intertextuality is a mouthful and requires a bit of background to understand. Literary and rhetorical critics often draw a distinction between the text, which is the thing being analyzed such as a book or a movie, and its context, which is all the meaningful stuff outside the text. The text begins and ends within the boundaries set up by the author—between page one and page 322 (if the book is 322 pages long) or during the run time of the movie. In order to make sense of a movie or book, though, a critic (the one doing interpretation and evaluation) has to look outside the text's boundaries. Critics might explore the historical moment in which the text was made, relevant political, economic, and social circumstances. Critics might also look at the medium or media in which a text appears, the content creator's other work, and what audiences said about the work.

As noted above, many texts reference or allude to other texts, making these outside texts important contextual dimensions for analysis. Hip-hop artists frequently reference other rappers, often as a rivalry or "beef" in a "diss track" that belittles the other rapper. In order to understand these songs, an audience needs to explore these outside texts (songs) and artists as references. **Intertextuality** is simply this process: texts referring to other texts, a practice as old as literature itself as all stories are building upon the conventions of stories of the past (see Chapter 6). For instance, writers love to rework classic stories in new historical moments such as Homer's the *Odyssey* or Shakespeare's *Hamlet*. Intertextuality becomes especially interesting when it adds new layers of meaning to a text. In this regard, intertextuality is similar to genre (recall the categories of stories from Chapter 6) but even more general, involving any form of referential comparison between texts (not just generic qualities).

However, in popular culture, the intertextual references are often not linguistic. Rather, intertextuality within popular culture occurs with visual images or auditory allusions to other "texts" of popular culture. Still, we make meaning of these images and hooks (think sampling in pop music here), in much the same way that we make sense of words. To appreciate how, we turn to semiotics. **Semiotics** is a fairly large and complex area of study, but at its heart it is the study of signs. A sign is composed of the signifier (image) and the signified (concept). Familiar logos illustrate the ubiquity and power of visual signs, as we easily recognize the "golden arches" of McDonald's or the "swoosh" of Nike. College mascot re-designs have stripped away language, as in the case of the Kansas State Wildcat, which adopted the sleek signifier of a "power cat" in 1989. In each of these cases, the sign combines image and concept, such as power cat and Kansas State University students or alumni.

Semiotics suggests that just as people go about their everyday life talking and texting with words that have meanings, they also interpret the endless parade of images and sounds surrounding us every day on social media, advertising, television, movies, etc. Intertextuality makes semiotics more complicated (sometimes for better, sometimes for worse). To appreciate the complexity of today's intertextual pop culture, we walk through the semiotics of memes.

Memes are anything that is imitated and spread quickly across a culture (Shifman, 2013). For most of us, memes are simply those silly images, usually with a few words of text in that familiar meme font, that spread on social media (although memes can take other forms such as sounds and phrases). Whenever we encounter a meme on social media, we engage in a kind of semiotic decoding process. Below, the two memes feature screenshots of Willy Wonka and Tony Stark (Iron Man). When encountering these popular memes on social media, the consumer recognizes the dry ironic style of the characters, decoding the words "new year new you" as achingly sarcastic (see Figure 7.1). Further, memes are often intertextual as the images are referencing meaning in other texts (movies, politics, etc.)

such as the characters Willy Wonka and Tony Stark (both arrogant and sarcastic) (see Figure 7.1).

Iconic images, such as the painting the *Mona Lisa*, are especially compelling signs, particularly in digital culture. As a brief exercise, search "mona lisa meme" on Google Images. You will find an endless sea of photoshopped images that add mustaches, turn the *Mona Lisa* into cartoons such as Sonic the Hedgehog or The Joker, and make Mona Lisa dab, smoke marijuana, or gesture the peace sign.

The image of the *Mona Lisa* is closely attached to the concept of "great art" allowing for playful and irreverent intertextual references to popular culture. The broader concept of "great art" is ideological in nature as it frequently reinforces the prestige and status of historical European (White) artists. For scholars of semiotics, signs are not benign but communicate ideology (see Chapter 4). When we see the image of an American flag on the back of a pickup truck, on someone's t-shirt or tattoo, etc., it expresses a complex set of meanings that are highly politically and emotionally charged. This is the distinction between **denotation**, just the literal meaning—"this is the American flag"—and **connotation**, deeper, often ideological meaning—freedom, sacrifice of soldiers, democracy, etc. A red ball cap with the words "Make America Great Again" on a denotative level is simply decoded as: I support Donald Trump. Of course, the connotation is complexly associated with Trump himself and his statements and policies concerning immigration, the media, women, etc. The sign is so powerful it might compel others to gravitate toward the wearer of the hat, cross the street, or even angrily threaten them. Comedian Larry David,

Figure 7.1 Memes featuring Willy Wonka and Tony Stark.

using this principle of connotation, on a 2020 episode of his show *Curb Your Enthusiasm* wore a red MAGA hat as a way to avoid talking with people he didn't like using it as a kind of social "repellent."

A lot of advertising works as a semiotic process, especially a product or company's logo. For instance, over decades of expensive advertising campaigns, the Nike swoosh and the Apple logo (with a silhouette of an apple with a small bite removed) have become ubiquitous and easily identifiable. On a denotative level, we are simply identifying these shoes or this computer as a Nike or Apple product. On a connotative level, these companies spend millions every year to reinforce the sign's (logo's) deeper connotative meaning: Nike represents athletic excellence while Apple represents simple design and technological innovation. Similarly, graphic t-shirts function as a simple meme-like sign to others to quickly communicate fandom (see Chapter 5). Many of these t-shirts might remain on a denotative level simply expressing an identification with an NFL team or musical artist. Nonetheless, a number of logo-like t-shirt designs can express broader cultural or connotative meanings: Rage Against the Machine represents anti-corporation and anti-political corruption, Wu Tang Clan represents an appreciation for the values of early "authentic" hip hop, Bob Marley represents the values of peace and love as well as the broader marijuana culture.

As discussed in Chapter 1 and 6, reality is socially constructed—that is to say, for humans, reality is not limited to our direct experience of the world as animals. Reality also includes complex worlds of meanings built through language, images, and other symbols. I. A. Richards, a famous linguist, theorized that a symbol (like the word "cat") represents a referent (the actual, handsome tabby who wakes you at 4am to play), and, for humans, indexes a reference, or thought(s), perceptions, and feelings ("Archie, please go make your own fun, I'm tired!"). Symbols are abstract (meaning that they represent or "stand in" for material reality but are not themselves material); arbitrary (meaning there is no necessary or essential connection to what they stand for); and ambiguous (meaning that they are open to interpretation). They are the building blocks of meaning.

In fact, the stylistic conventions of television and film are often dependent on the audience's understanding of previous media texts. In a simple example, the television show *Modern Family*, involved a "mockumentary" style with characters speaking directly to the camera in an interview format, similar to *The Office*. But, unlike *The Office*, there was never any reference to a camera crew or any sense that the characters on *Modern Family* were in a reality show. Stylistically, the show simply expected the audience to recognize the stylistic convention of the mockumentary based on other TV shows they had seen. Further, a few notes of a song are quickly decoded by an audience, such as the opening notes of Marvin Gaye's "Let's Get It On" referencing an anticipated sexual encounter or Kenny G's "Songbird" as referencing a mellow, easy-going vibe (or simply lame soft jazz).

In many ways, the semiotic project entails understanding texts intertextually, or in relation to one another as a "semiological chain" (Barthes, 1972, p. 114). While all images in one way or another reference other images, intertextuality was pretty limited in popular culture before the last 20 years or so. For a TV viewer, the genre of a show would offer a clear set of expectations such as a sitcom is 30 minutes, set in a family or workplace (or both), have a studio audience and laugh track, and would resolve the story at the end of each episode (see Chapter 6 for more on genre). These "common textual knowledges" (Ott & Walter, 2000, p. 432) were important but rarely extended beyond such generic expectations. In other words, people would sit down to watch a TV show or a movie and not need any additional information beyond the conventions of the medium (TV, movie, novel, etc.). Some of this was due to the limitations of the medium itself. Because television could only be viewed when scheduled, writers avoided too much complexity for the ongoing storyline in case a viewer missed the previous week's episode (remember, before streaming and DVRs viewers could not easily rewatch an episode and, of course, could not find recaps on the Internet). In order to make sense of a show such as *Severance* or *Stranger Things*, with a complex ongoing narrative, the episodes much be watched in order, in their entirety.

Increasingly, especially over the last decade, audiences enlist an extensive reservoir of specialized knowledge to make sense of popular culture texts. Intertextuality is about the complex relationship between audience, text, and author (Ott & Walter, 2000). Audiences sometimes erroneously presume an author determines meaning. For instance, in order to determine the meaning of a song, someone might be inclined to search for interviews with the songwriter to find the *intended* meaning or "real" meaning of the song. From an intertextual perspective, meaning is fluidly negotiated between audience, text, and author. For instance, the chorus of Bruce Springsteen's song "Born in the USA" functions as a kind of auditory sign, evoking the concept of patriotism and pride, especially at a July 4th event. When Ronald Reagan, a strong conservative, ran for president in 1984, he played Springsteen's song to evoke working-class patriotism. If you have a moment, listen to "Born in the USA" with the lyrics on YouTube. The song's verses tell depressing stories of soldiers returning from the Vietnam War facing suffering and trauma due to loneliness, unemployment, and alienation. The song is intended to be a powerful anti-war anthem and a harsh critique of the jingoistic patriotism that politicians like Reagan have used to escalate military spending. Yet, the next July 4th, you will almost certainly hear the song and most people will simply hear pride and patriotism. These various meanings are not wrong or right as meaning is always evolving in the negotiation between text, author, and audience.

Visual signs surround us in every direction, every day on billboards, on our phones and computer, on television, and on our clothing. The connotative meaning of these signs is always changing. For instance, the iconic McDonald's "M" logo in the 1980s represented (to the vast majority of consumers) a beloved, nostalgic American family-friendly restaurant experience. Over time, this M has evolved for many people to represent unhealthy cheap fast food or unsustainable corporate farming and plastic waste. These evolving meanings compel companies to "rebrand" by changing logos and pivoting their advertising campaigns. Kentucky Fried Chicken replaced its name and logo with "KFC" shifting from a traditional Southern family restaurant chain to a meaning tied more loosely to playful ironic pleasure. By hiring a series of unexpected and oddball celebrities such as Reba McEntire, George Hamilton, Ray Liotta, and Rob Lowe to play "the Colonel" in a series television commercials, the fast-food chain embraced an ironic, fun, viral experience better suited to a younger audience.

Pastiche, parody, and remediation

Frederick Jameson referred to **pastiche** as a blank parody of past forms. Frequently, a TV show, advertisement, or music video will faithfully recreate a scene from a beloved movie such as Ariana Grande recreating scenes from *Mean Girls* in her video for "thank u, next." In these moments, the audience is invited to simply recognize the old movie, and derive pleasure from the recognition. Intertextuality (here in the form of pastiche) leads to an "aha" moment for viewers in the know. Recently, television commercials have similarly recreated scenes from *E.T.*, *Austin Powers*, and *Groundhog Day*, among many, many others. TikTok and YouTube are filled with these sorts of recreations by fans such as mimicking the dance moves of a pop star. Country music star Walker Hayes had a massive hit, "Fancy Like," that largely referenced his favorite menu items from the chain restaurant Applebees. In many ways, social media is the perfect venue for these empty intertextual references as they offer a brief spark of recognition, then are quickly forgotten as the user scrolls through images and videos on their phone. Digital media affordances are well suited to pastiche, including the ability to share small bits of audio on TikTok, intertextually spliced with any number of visual images like dance moves and conversations with one's pet.

Intertextuality becomes more complex when woven into the narratives of television, film, and music videos. In some cases, the parody exaggerates or offers a "caricature" of a previous text (Ott & Walter, 2000). Rather than a faithful recreation, there is a bit more bite to the parody by exaggerating some aspect of the old text. Often, this is still a gentle parody, especially Mel Brooks's classic and highly influential spoofs of Westerns (*Blazing Saddles*), classic horror movies (*Young Frankenstein*), and science fiction blockbusters (*Space Balls*) that use exaggeration to highlight silly conventions of each genre such as dramatic styles of dialogue, stereotypical characters, and cinematography. Following Brooks's lead, animated series such as *The Simpsons*, *Rick and Morty*, and *Family Guy* routinely offer similar exaggerated versions of classic movies. Specifically, *Family Guy* reproduced *Star Wars* with jokes mocking some of the more melodramatic elements or exaggerating plot holes in the film. Both Taco Bell and Geico have produced a series of commercials parodying horror films that make fun of the dumb choices of characters such as running into a shed filled with chainsaws or making over-the-top paranoid conspiratorial speeches.

When a parody crosses into critique, it is evaluating deeper ideological dimensions of the production of the text. In other words, this is a kind of political critique addressing the broader social or cultural forces creating the referenced text(s). In the film *Tropic Thunder*, Ben Stiller not only makes fun of the over-the-top acting and melodramatic directing style of war films (especially Vietnam films), he critiques the shameless commercial interests of the actors and filmmakers who basically follow a formula of previous Oscar-winning films (recall the discussion of quality in Chapter 3). In the film, between scenes of the actors filming incredibly violent war footage, the characters casually discuss their career aspirations. Similarly, the television show *The Boys* uses exaggeration and excess to critique the comic book franchises produced by giant media corporations with propaganda-like celebrations of American superheroes that audiences continue to blindly support. On the show, superheroes have a giant corporate marketing machine including theme parks, big-budget movies, and TV specials (eerily similar to Disney) that masks their power-hungry narcissism, excessive violence, and pathetic insecurities.

Parodies often work on multiple levels simultaneously. On the animated television show *Rick and Morty*, the writers often make complex references to science fiction and fantasy films, specifically *Mad Max: Fury Road*, *Inception*, and *The Purge*, among many others (see Figure 7.2). Nonetheless, the show features plenty of bodily noises, cursing, and sex jokes, so an adolescent may easily giggle along to the show without any understanding of the deeper references. Missing the deeper meaning can radically change the interpretation of a text.

As these examples demonstrate, there is often a bit of irreverence involved with intertextuality. In particular, intertextual references usually tear down the author's original work, placing it in a new context and fundamentally altering the intended meaning. In recent years, the revered works of William Shakespeare and Jane Austen have been playfully and irreverently intertextually altered in animated movies (*Gnomeo and Juliet*), teen comedies (*Clueless*), broad romantic comedies (*Fire Island*) and even zombie horror movies (*Pride, Prejudice, and Zombies*). Banking on the familiarity of the classic texts, filmmakers radically alter the original literary

Figure 7.2 Scene from *Rick and Morty.*

work with little reverence for the author's original intentions. As Roland Barthes famously stated, in this regard, the author is dead as "producers" are just cobbling together other people's work in ways that shift interpretation to the inferences of the audience.

Further, all this borrowing and repurposing is within the logic of digital media's "remediation" (Bolter and Grusen, 2000). **Remediation** is simply "the representation of one medium in another." As stated previously, types of media (TV, newspapers, movies, etc.) in the past tended to remain relatively separate. In a digital environment, though, types of media are integrated, repurposed, refashioned, and reformed. For instance, on social media or on a Website, video, text, music, photography, etc. blend together effortlessly moving from one medium to another for the user. For the purposes of popular culture experiences, today, audiences tend to prefer texts that have interplay between media allowing the user to enlist understandings from many sources. A hastily created TikTok might integrate 10 seconds of a Lil Nas X song, clips from *The Office* and *Toy Story*, and a quote from Gandhi. What would have been a jarring and nonsensical video clip 20 years ago (and still might be to folks over 65) fits effortlessly into the present culture. Remediation is not only in the form of media woven seamlessly into new technologies such as social media but also old technologies that integrate digital technological forms to fit with users' new expectations. Today, movies increasingly integrate the computer graphics and editing style of video games. Further, television is experienced as a digital interface via Netflix or Hulu that features algorithms and interactivity comparable to social media. If people read any content produced by newspapers, it is likely via their social media feed on their phones. In other words, the dominant aesthetic (or media logic) of digital technology is an intertextual play between old and new media.

The weaving together of old and new media is also a kind of bricolage allowing people to experiment and tinker with popular culture. TikTok represents a form of **bricolage** (De Certeau, 1984) in which users cobble together bits and pieces of popular culture into new and interesting texts. In many ways, this is the collages kids still sometimes make in elementary school gluing together photos from magazines. Now, of course, these bits of sound, video, imagery, text, etc. are strewn together with relatively little effort for a single social media post. In a world dominated by social media and other forms of digital technology, these brief, yet complex, collages are a common, even the dominant, aesthetic. In pop music, the integration of musical styles with the visual aesthetics of the past creates a kind of bricolage for intertextual interpretation. When pop star Dua Lipa evokes 1970s and 1980s dance music styles with overt disco guitar riffs and drum tracks it is coupled with music videos featuring dress and choreography also in a 1970s and 1980s aesthetic. Similarly, Silk Sonic deliberately modelled their songs, live performances, and music videos on 1970s soul stars such as Al Green, Earth Wind and Fire, and Stevie Wonder. TikTok star Yung Gravy raps over a sampled Rick Astley song and wears clothes in garish 1970s and 1980s styles walking a line between parody and homage. In other words, pop stars are now the embodiment of bricolage and remediation with elaborate intertextual references in their vocal and musical style, samples, dress, dance, and music videos.

Digital affordances carry remediation and bricolage quickly, offering what appear to be "new" trends, dances, and memes that leap across platforms. It's interesting to consider some of the more popular trends and memes from early social media days (from the start of Facebook around 2004 to the start of Instagram around 2011), and see them still circulating today, such as the T-pose, rickroll, keyboard cat, and peanut butter and jelly time. Similarly, memes from Vine (circa 2011–2013) hop onto TikTok (from 2016 on), including Baby Shark, grumpy cat, and Big Chungus. Content mutations provide enough novelty and play to make such pop culture "stick" in the network economy.

Advertising campaigns are now creating their own sort of cinematic universe of ads. Old Spice has created an extended advertising campaign, "The Man Your Man Could Smell Like," with dozens of commercials spanning over a decade that references previous actors and commercials. Dos Equis has continued its "Most Interesting Man in the World" campaign for many years, also with knowing nods to old ads. Bud Light has produced a series of "Dilly Dilly" ads set in medieval times (similar to *Game of Thrones*) that build on the details of previous commercials. In each of these cases, the producers of the advertisements are counting on the audience's familiarity with previous commercials in the series.

Perhaps the greatest champion of popular culture intertextuality over the past 40 years is Weird Al Yankovic. Weird Al came to fame on MTV in the 1980s by altering the lyrics of pop songs from artists like Michael Jackson and Madonna, frequently into food-oriented themes, and then creating parodied versions of the music videos with lots of intertextual pop cultural references. Through the 1990s and 2000s, with only occasional minor hit songs, Weird Al was largely a likeable oddball who occasionally popped up in a sitcom or movie for a quick and easy laugh or some nostalgia. Yet, in the last decade, Weird Al has seen a renaissance with sold-out concert tours and growing appreciation from A-list celebrity fans (and friends) such as Lin-Manuel Miranda and Jack Black. Today, Weird Al seems unexpectedly relevant, a trailblazer who understood the power of intertextuality years before it came into fashion. In fact, in 2022, a zany Weird Al biopic starring Daniel Radcliffe is receiving rave reviews (Murphy, 2022).

The aesthetics of intertextuality are in every aspect of contemporary popular culture. Celebrated filmmaker Quentin Tarantino cobbles together bits of old TV shows, B movies, and classic Hollywood cinema into a filmmaking style uniquely his own. Whether integrating bits of martial arts movies from across the world in *Kill Bill*, or TV Western iconography in *Once Upon a Time in Hollywood*, Tarantino invites the audience to identify his many influences. As Disney makes numerous TV shows within the *Star Wars* and Marvel universes, the platform has increasingly experimented with unexpected intertextual styles by integrating elements of courtroom dramas (*She Hulk, Attorney at Law*) and classic sitcoms (*Wanda Vision*) into superhero narratives. In short, once associated with weirdos and outsiders like Weird Al, intertextuality has gone mainstream.

Digital media logics and intertextuality

The layering of meaning within popular culture texts has placed greater demands on audiences to make sense of these many layers. Before the blockbuster *Avengers: Endgame* was released, bloggers and YouTubers produced extensive "tutorials" to prepare moviegoers to make sense of the movie. Because the film built off the narratives and iconography of 21 movies, many moviegoers expressed feeling overwhelmed, fearing some key detail from a movie ten years old would be forgotten. Today, it seems that many movies now require homework. This investigative process associated with popular culture is referred to as "drillable texts" or "a mode of forensic fandom that invites viewers to dig deeper, probing beneath the surface to understand the complexity of a story and its telling" (Mittell, 2015). As the term "forensic fandom" indicates, **drillable texts** require audiences to be like a detective searching for clues to make sense of a complex, highly intertextual popular culture text. The clearest examples of drillable texts are in narratively complex television series. Perhaps the most influential drillable text was the show *Lost* whose narrative about a group of people stranded on an island was so mystifying that fans would gather online after each episode to analyze tiny details as clues. *Lost* became a bit of a cultural sensation and has inspired a wide range of drillable TV series such as *Mr. Robot*, *Westworld*, and *Severance*. Each of these shows teased the audience with the nature of its basic reality yet had deeply loyal fans who scoured episodes for possible theories concerning the uncertain storylines. Specifically, *Mr. Robot* was told from the subjective perspective of the main character, Elliot, who struggles with both mental illness and drug addiction. As Elliot sometimes experienced irrational delusions as a coping mechanism, the audience needed to spot small details in the dialogue and imagery to try to determine what was real and what was fantasy on the show. Even shows with relatively straightforward plots, such as *Game of Thrones*, have grown so complicated (with a sprawling list of characters and ongoing narrative universe) week after week that after five or six seasons they require a bit of research just to follow along.

The logic of drillable texts has spread in some unexpected directions suggesting a new set of expectations and even preferences for popular culture consumption. Taylor Swift places extensive "Easter eggs" (hidden, ambiguous, or brief references with words or images) throughout her songs and music videos referencing older music and details from her personal life. Artists such as Beyoncé (with *Lemonade*) have produced dense music videos filled with "hidden" symbols that are designed to invite discussions online about possible interpretations. As these videos are typically watched on YouTube with a lively comments section, fan interpretation fits seamlessly into the viewing experience—and can build community amongst fans (see Chapter 5). As we will see in Chapter 11, video games are probably the best example of these drillable texts with both game problem-solving and complicated narrative details shared extensively online between players.

In the discussion of narrative in Chapter 6, we described how history has become nostalgia in the form of decade-ization. In similar ways, a show such as *Stranger Things* is on one level pure intertextual nostalgia for the 1980s with images of arcade games, sounds of pop songs, and a wardrobe of vintage t-shirts. On another level, *Stranger Things* features complex aesthetic intertextuality with stylistic references to specific movies, especially a number of blockbusters from the 1980s. The cinematic style of *Stranger Things* makes direct references to movies such as *E.T.*, *Jaws*, *Stand by Me*, *Alien*, *Goonies*, *Poltergeist*, and *Carrie* with composition, cinematography, editing, and sound design. For those of us old enough to remember these movies, we have an immediate spark of recognition from movies of our youth. For the core audience of *Stranger Things* who are far too young to remember these movies, it invites them to drill into the text discovering these references through online discussions. Social media posts feature screen shots of scenes from *Stranger Things* and a referenced movie placed side by side, such as the image of an egg opening from *Alien* or kids walking along a railroad track from *Stand by Me*.

A culmination of these intertextual aesthetic forms came in the highest-grossing movie of 2021, *Spiderman: No Way Home*. In many ways, *Spiderman: No Way Home* was even more intertextually complex than *Avengers: Endgame* as it bridged two franchises and dozens of movies and TV shows in both the Avengers and Spiderman universes. With multiple characters from both the Avengers and Spiderman franchises dating back over 20 years, images and lines of dialogue required an astonishing reservoir of knowledge for sense-making. Most notably, in *Spiderman: No Way Home*, by opening a portal to different universes, former characters are summoned such as two previous versions of Spiderman (Tobey Maguire and Andrew Garfield) and the villains from the previous films (Green Goblin, Octavius, etc.), making numerous specific references to details from the franchise's nine movies over the last two decades. Yet, based on the $1.9 billion in box office, such audience demands were an advantage not a disadvantage.

Even the growing emphasis on reboots and remakes is inherently built on a familiarity with the previous texts. Of course, a huge blockbuster from 2022, *Top Gun: Maverick*, demands some familiarly with the original 1980s blockbuster making numerous direct recreations of specific scenes. Similarly, the successful and critically beloved TV series *Better Call Saul* is a prequel to the massive hit show *Breaking Bad*. *Better Call Saul* includes routine references to specific details such as locations and obscure characters, even single scenes, from *Breaking Bad*, which are intended to be enjoyed with a detailed knowledge of the entire *Breaking Bad* universe.

The growth of intertextuality is also emerging from the giant corporations producing popular culture. Recalling the discussion of business in Chapter 2, the logic of convergence is also a logic of intertextuality. By building these elaborate cinematic universes, media companies keep consumers in their platform going from property to property in an endless loop. In many respects, giant media conglomerates have found ways to profit tremendously from the growth of intertextuality. Intertextuality can be the active, thoughtful, and creative process of audiences producing unique and interesting meanings, especially as equipment for living. Unfortunately, at its simplest, intertextuality is a dutiful process of following the prompts of media corporations endlessly directing us to their next property.

The most shameless corporate strategy associated with intertextuality is the crossover. Back in the 1980s and 1990s, TV networks would bring a character from a popular TV show, such as *Seinfeld* or *Cheers*, into a new (and less popular) show to try to attract more viewers. This strategy continued to be effective through the 2000s enlisted by the Disney Channel by bringing Hannah Montana onto less successful Disney shows. This simple intertextual strategy has expanded in scale with Marvel and DC both adding new superhero characters to movies and TV shows to pull in viewers, sometimes for a single scene or episode. In *Ralph Breaks the Internet*, for instance, the filmmakers added a gratuitous scene featuring an argument between iconic Disney princesses that attracted a lot of attention for the movie and other Disney content. Such scenes are easily "meme-able" or capable of being circulated by users on social media platforms. This is the challenge of intertextuality. Media corporations and advertisers emphasize a form of intertextual popular culture that is largely just promoting name recognition for the corporation's brands and products in the logic of advertising.

Why do audiences today like intertextuality so much? First, the pleasures of intertextuality are closely associated with fandom. As you recall from Chapter 5, fans demonstrate their authenticity via cultural capital. The ability to effortlessly identify Easter eggs and other intertextual references is valuable currency in fan communities. In many ways, intertextuality gives the knowing audience a sense of superiority, a feeling that "I'm smarter than all the people who missed this Easter egg." Nonetheless, a lot of intertextual experiences occur outside of fan communities. For an individual consumer watching a TV show or movie, as we noted above, intertextuality provides the "aha" moment of recognition. Movies based on old TV shows such as *Baywatch* and *The Brady Bunch* are filled with such empty moments. Memes sometimes function purely at this level when someone on social media recognizes a few notes of "Africa" by Toto, an image from the TV show *Full House*, or a GIF from *Minions*. Trending topics on social media are often simply collective intertextual references. Of course, this spark of recognition is remarkably devoid of depth and therefore offers little in terms of meaning-making, compelling users to scroll passed them in a matter of seconds.

On the other hand, intertextuality can be incredibly deep and meaningful offering audience's opportunities to actively engage a complex text. Childish Gambino (the alter ego of actor and musician Donald Glover) produced a music video for his song "This Is America" that featured complex intertextuality. In the dense four-minute video, Childish Gambino's dancing and singing (in a conventional music-video style) is interrupted by moments of shocking gun violence as well as unsettling images of a horseback rider, children in school uniforms, police cars, and a choir. The ambiguous, haunting imagery of the video is widely discussed and, according to most interpretations, includes references to the White supremacist violence of Charlottesville, Virginia; icons of the Jim Crow era; and recent racially motivated violence. Childish Gambino shows how intertextuality can demand viewers enlist sense-making beyond the simple recognition of familiar images and nostalgic pastiche.

Additionally, as "This Is America" demonstrates, intertextuality can build community, where a complex text with many allusions invites people to make sense together. Interestingly, the cult hit *Community* (also featuring Donald Glover) was a wild hodgepodge of intertextual references to such artifacts as *Star Wars*, *Reading Rainbow*, *The Godfather*, and the Barenaked Ladies. A few times each season, an entire episode would become a full-on spoof of a specific popular cultural form such as the movie *Die Hard*, the TV show *Law & Order*, Claymation Christmas specials, and a Ken Burns-style PBS documentary. The show grappled with the pleasures and meanings of this intertextuality, particularly through the character of Abed and his obsession with old movies and TV shows. Over the course of the series, Abed used popular culture intertextuality as a coping mechanism (particularly his feelings of loneliness and alienation) as well as a way of building friendship and community with his peers. Perhaps we can take a page from Abed's storyline, and reflect together on how intertextuality affects our lives. This leads to our closing case study, which considers what happens when we read ordinary people and their lives in an intertextual sea of popular culture.

Conclusion: Treating people as signs

In a world dominated by social media, it is increasingly imperative to challenge ourselves to thoughtfully interpret the intertextual imagery in our everyday lives. Platforms such as Instagram are becoming more dominated by influencers and celebrities promoting themselves as brands.

In the logic of advertising, these "people as brands" are encouraging users to view people as a choice between Coke and Pepsi. The Instagram experience is a superficial intertextual process of evaluating images of people (as signs) as simply "awesome" or "crap" via likes (or withholding likes). Celebrities have felt the immediate and severe judgment of social media users with cruel body shaming and other knee-jerk reactions to celebrity photographs. Of course, mixed in with Britney Spears, Tom Brady, and Ed Sheeran are regular people, even our friends and family. Yet, flipping through images, humans can become just another intertextual sign used for a brief moment of pleasure via split second evaluations. Dating apps such as Tinder are perhaps the ultimate realization of this dehumanization when individuals are reduced to instantaneous judgments of visual signs by swiping left or right. When we intertextually play with images, we rarely stop and think about the people represented in these images—people who (like all living things) exceed the ability of signifiers to represent them.

Random people have become the objects of memes, with the joke directed at their physical appearance or embarrassing facial expression. We all have seen these memes: the school picture of the guy with braces in a plaid vest, the "ermahgerd" girl, scumbag Steve, etc. They were not celebrities, just regular people whose awkward photographs were turned into memes for the endless judgmental pleasures of the Internet. One of the first occurrences, "Star Wars Kid," featured a video of a 14-year-old named

Ghyslain Raza enthusiastically imitating a character in a lightsaber battle from *Star Wars: Episode One* (Rowe, 2022). Versions, usually modified to make him look especially ridiculous, have been viewed hundreds of millions of times and parodied by TV shows like *Southpark* and *Arrested Development*. The video was shared by a classmate without the boy's permission, leading to intense harassment and a lawsuit over the unauthorized use of his image. What is remarkable is that the millions of people laughing at these images never seemed to stop and think about impact on the *child* represented in these memes. It appears that intertextuality distances us from the popular culture we consume, at least in some cases, encouraging a kind of callous indifference to the people represented.

Reflecting on the interconnectedness of pop culture in your everyday life

- View an episode of *The Simpsons* or other highly intertextual pop culture artifact. Track the number and types of references made in the episode. Did you "get" all the references? How did you feel when you knew the connections being made? How did you feel when you did not know the connections being made (if you noticed it)? What does this tell you about the pleasures and pitfalls of intertextuality?
- Are you a fan of intertextual popular culture? Why and why not? What are the "best practices" for intertextuality in pop culture?
- Would you consider intertextuality as a kind of equipment for living, or reading practice, for today's pop culture world? Why or why not? Do you see drillable texts and Easter eggs as more within the logic of communities of popular culture, or the business of popular culture?
- Do we still value originality in popular culture? If so, how do you see people around you or yourself valuing originality? If not, do you think originality still matters?
- When you are on the Internet or social media, do you stop to consider the people represented in intertextual references, as in memes, or other "viral" trends, like "Star Wars Kid"? What is our ethical responsibility to the images, experiences, and identities of people (or the people producing these images) we reference and judge on social media?
- Has someone you know ever been "memed" or subject to the type of dehumanizing treatment described in the case study? How did that person respond?

For audiences, intertextuality can offer unique opportunities for meaning-making that extends beyond the limitations of sometimes simplistic texts and social media interfaces. Self-reflexivity, addressed further in the final chapter of the book, provides a technique to be more mindful and conscious of the choices we make with intertextual signs. Like so many dimensions of popular culture, intertextuality holds tremendous promise and tremendous potential hazards. For instance, in the discussion of globalization (Chapter 9), we will also address how a kind of intertextual hybridity is occurring across cultures creating interesting popular cultural forms while bringing together people from all over the world. By learning the basics of semiotics, and exploring the many ways today's popular culture is interconnected to its present and past (e.g., pastiche, parody), as well as the ways today's producers invite intertextuality via memes, bricolage, remediation and drillable texts, you are hopefully able to engage in a more mindful experience in social media and elsewhere. In the following chapter, we will shift toward the embodied experiences and sensations engaged by popular culture.

Suggested readings

Barthes, R. (1977). *Image-music-text*. (S. Hill, Trans.). Hill & Wang.

Bolter, J., & Grusin, R. (2000). *Remediation: Understanding new media*. MIT Press.

Davisson, A. (2018). "Hallelujah": Parody, political catharsis, and grieving the 2016 election with *Saturday Night Live*. *Communication Quarterly, 66*(2), 196–213. 10.1080/01463373.2018.1438489

Durham, M. G. (2017). Resignifying Alan Kurdi: News photographs, memes, and the ethics of embodied vulnerability. *Critical Studies in Media Communication, 35*(3), 240–258. https://doi.org/10.1080/15295036.2017.1408958

Harriss, C. (2017). The producer as fan: Forensic fandom and *The Good Wife. Journal of Communication Inquiry, 41*(4), 368–381. https://doi.org/10.1177/0196859917712233

Winslow, L. (2010). Rhetorical homology and the caveman mythos: An(Other) way to ridicule the aggrieved. *Communication Studies, 61*(3), 257–271. https://doi.org.aurarialibrary.idm.oclc.org/10.1080/10510971003797036

References

Barthes, R. (1972). *Mythologies* (A. Lavers, Trans.). Hill & Wang.

Chandler D. (2022). *Semiotics: The basics* (4th ed.). Routledge. https://doi.org/10.4324/9781003155744

De Certeau, M. (1984). *The practice of everyday life*. University of California Press.

Langer S. K. (1957). *Philosophy in a new key: A study in the symbolism of reason rite and art* (3rd ed.). Harvard University Press.

Mittell, J. (2015). *Complex television: The poetics of contemporary television storytelling.* New York University Press.

Murphy, C. (2022, November 2) The Weird Al movie is weirding people out in a good way. *Vanity Fair.* https://www.vanityfair.com/hollywood/2022/11/the-weird-al-movie-is-weirding-people-out-in-a-good-way

Ott, B., & Walter, C. (2000). Intertextuality: Interpretive practice and textual strategy. *Critical Studies in Media Communication, 17*(4), 429–446. https://doi.org/10.1080/15295030009388412

Richards I. A. (1936). *The philosophy of rhetoric.* Oxford University Press.

Rowe, D. (2022, March 30). "Star Wars Kid" reflects on his 2003 viral video, the media circus and human nature. CTV News. https://montreal.cTVnews.ca/star-wars-kid-reflects-on-his-2003-viral-video-the-media-circus-and-human-nature-1.5841434

Shifman, L. (2013). Memes in a digital world: Reconciling with a conceptual troublemaker. *Journal of Computer-Mediated Communication, 18*(3), 362–377. https://doi.org/10.1111/jcc4.12013

8 The sensations of popular culture

Introduction

In full disclosure, we didn't have a lot of experience with children prior to the arrival of our firstborn. Being a dual-career couple who live a healthy distance away from the help of extended family, much of our parenting has been trial and error. And having become attached to Apple technology from the early days of the iPod, it is no surprise that when the iPad was first released, we were early adopters. We are suspicious of claims concerning the "addictive" qualities of any pop culture modality or media technology (particularly since, as we've already stated in prior chapters, each new modality and technology in US history has been accompanied by dystopian public outcry). But even we weren't prepared for the lure of unboxing videos.

We had set limits for iPad use, following guidance from experts (whom we'd consulted through, no surprise, Internet searches): limit screen time to one hour per day, do not use it as a replacement for interaction (in other words, try to be present with your child while they experience pop culture), set clear expectations on who owns the iPad and where it can be used (e.g., this device cannot be brought near water) (Simone, 2012). We downloaded and used a special search engine designed for young children to filter out inappropriate content (particularly since we had welcomed a second child to our family, we knew we did not have as much bandwidth to guard media use). One day, our oldest approached us requesting Shopkins toys for her birthday. The cute plastic collectibles in the shape of various grocery store products were popular in our kiddo's kindergarten class, and they appeared on a YouTube video that she shared with us of someone who called herself the "Toy Genie." Christina's inner Marxist lost it—how could this have entered our home? Not only ridiculous collectibles that made shopping seem "cute," but a video only depicting hands opening toys, with a mild-mannered maternal voice reacting with surprise, "Oooh, it's Stapler!" "Oh, here comes the Blender!" and "Look at this case to put them in!"

DOI: 10.4324/9781003372943-8

Our oldest wasn't the only human enthralled by the Toy Genie's unboxing videos. As of this writing, the Toy Genie has 6.38 million subscribers on YouTube. Other popular unboxing videos (like Mommy and Grace, a mother/daughter team who primarily unbox dolls) yield 17 million views per month and 295 million views overall (Basu, 2015). If we look at this genre of video—not from the eyes of our inner Marxist, but from the eyes of the user who becomes entranced by them—we might understand why. The soft voice shares the happiness and surprise of a birthday or holiday opening, capturing the moment in which we first encountered the bright object of our desire. There is no face in the frame, just a set of small, pale hands positioned close to the camera, close enough to be extensions of our body, from the vantage of our eyes (see Figure 8.1). The only sounds in the video, save the Toy Genie's voice, are the squeaks of plastic wrapping being pulled away, the quick swish of a box lid.

It is as though we are alone in the room of our experience, opening new toys. It's any wonder, really, that folks leave their home when unboxing videos are available for free to them to view all day. This is the experience we want to feature in Chapter 8, which dilates on the parts of popular culture that draw us without reliance on words or symbolic action (alone). We experience popular culture through our body, our emotions and even the ephemeral "vibe" shared with others around us. In this chapter, we explore the sensations of popular culture with a quick tour through embodiment and the senses, with special attention to emotion and pleasure. We then expand our focus to collective bodies, with an extended example of electronic dance music (EDM) as a genre, which includes EDM as a live and

Figure 8.1 Unboxing video from the Toy Genie.

virtual experience. Our chapter then engages the potential of pop culture as support and equipment for living through challenging times, before ending with a case study on horror. Horror invites questions on ethics. It demonstrates that people are nervous about the immediate power of popular culture, its ability to arouse us; but perhaps this capacity (which is present in other aspects of communication) is working for the collective good?

The body, senses, emotion, and pleasure

Readers who use digital technologies such as smartphones and tablets can appreciate how contemporary popular culture enlists our bodies frequently as part of its experience. We likely take for granted how intuitively our fingers move across a smartphone or tablet touch interface, but much of this technology appeals precisely because of how seamlessly it fits into our embodied experience. Smartphones can be pulled out of pockets and engaged by fingers instantly, tablets manifest writing from a stylus or fingers. To those who were not born into this technology, there is something magical about it. Scrolling and swiping left are but two easy examples of the digital's dominant media logic when it comes to embodiment (see Chapter 1).

It should go without saying that individuals are "embodied beings," but much of Western philosophy has separated mind and body. Perhaps you've heard the famous phrase *cogito ergo sum*, "I think therefore I am," famous from Descartes' writings in the 1640s. Descartes responded to questions of existence, the reliability of sensory input and experience, by stating that because he thinks, he is not merely dreaming, nor the projection of an alternative (demonic?) reality. Unfortunately, in establishing firm ground for existence in the mind—and, a brain separated from its vital connections in a body, in relation to other bodies, in a world—Western philosophers set the conditions for us to forget or diminish the human condition of embodiment. Not surprisingly, other critical theorists reject the "Cartesian dualism" of body versus mind. And science has provided ample evidence of the mind's complex embodiment, including recent headlines concerning the links between brain health and the micro-organisms of our intestines, as well as research that touts the benefits of physical activity for supporting aging/staving off memory loss.

Communication and cultural studies became increasingly influenced by critical theories that pushed against the Cartesian dualism through the turn of the 21st century through theories that centered emotion, the body, and **affect**. As Harold (2009) summarizes, affect refers to "the response we have to things before we label that response with feelings or emotions. It is a visceral sensation that precedes cognition" (p. 613). Affect scholarship tends toward the obtuse (like many other concepts introduced in this book, there is much writing and debate devoted to the word affect). But what matters for our understanding of popular culture here is that affect, emotion, and sensation give us the ability to name experiences that slip away from our ability to name them. Like the different "vibes" that register in our bodies when we move from the street to the club to the train to our apartment, affect provides us opportunities to reflect together on human experiences that are not just symbolic.

Further, as Sas (2022) describes, affect gives us the ability to perceive and process together different scales of the human experience: The concept raises "new questions and new approaches, taking place around and between larger structures (language, capitalism) and the smaller, seemingly individual but also highly structured and overdetermined worlds ('my' self, my body, sounds and words resonating inside my mind ...)" (p. 2). Like the atmosphere or air, affects circulate in macro, mezzo, and micro scales, and hit us individually and collectively. Pop culture provides another medium through which affective energies circulate, and it is perhaps easier to track such circulation beginning with the body and senses than it is with the mental, symbolic representations that made up our focus in prior chapters.

Contemporary popular culture regularly plays with and off the embodied nature of the human condition. Touch, hearing, taste, smell, and sight are the basic senses, but proprioception (which is our ability to sense movement in our bodies as a whole or parts) allows for safe navigation of the daily world as bodies (Tuthill & Azim, 2018). Media hardware creators, as well as popular culture content developers, regularly enlist the human senses. Consider, for instance, the touchpad interface Apple created for the iPhone (building from its predecessors, the iPod and the iPad). Users are able to navigate this interface seamlessly, where the surface of the device responds almost like skin to the touch of a user. When Apple marketed the first (very expensive) personal computer, it added a rudimentary mouse to the hardware to allow users to point and click rather than typing in all commands (Montag, 2018). Apple continued to include a mouse in its Macintosh computer. As discussed in Chapter 1, affordances like the mouse give way to related affordances, like the touchpad and touchscreen, and one can see the importance of "swiping left," "scrolling," and other ways the senses are engaged by communication technology. For those readers who have lived through this transition, what do you recall about the shift from mouse-based computing to touchpad computing? Or a flip phone to a touch-screen phone? Perhaps you recall the ease of navigating when touch interfaces were widely adopted. Steve Jobs once shared in an interview that the mouse and touch interface were brilliant for their attention to nonverbal (embodied) communication over linguistic expression alone: "If I want to tell you there is a spot on your shirt, I'm not going to do it linguistically: 'There's a spot on your shirt 14 centimeters down from the collar and three centimeters to the left of your button ...'" Instead, Jobs pointed to his shirt, stating, "If you have a spot—'There!' I'll point to it. Pointing is a metaphor we all know" (quoted in Montag, 2018).

But not only does hardware enlist the body; content, too, engages the senses at the level of sensation and embodiment. Unboxing videos, like the ones described above, aren't that revolutionary when we consider beer commercials. The sound of a can, dripping with water, opening ("crsssssh!") and then getting poured slowly into a glass, to foam at the top, became a best practice in the beer industry some time ago. Visual and sound cues within content, in other words, often are as good at enlisting the body and senses as is hardware. And these can certainly be amplified by stories. For instance, Wrigley's Extra gum created a sensation in 2015 when it released the "Cant' Help Falling in Love" ad, set to the popular tune (from Elvis, but recorded by *American Idol* winner Haley Reinhart). The ad (viewed 78 million times on Facebook shortly after its release, and shared 1.1 million times) shows several moments in the individual and romantic life of the couple Sara and Juan, who continue to find each other and write messages of love and support on gum wrappers—including the climactic moment, in which Juan proposes marriage to Sara. The soft color palette and the song's swelling emotion map perfectly onto the love story. Here, the logical person may ask: What does gum have anything to do with falling in love? And the answer is, it doesn't really matter—the sound and visual cues, combined powerfully with a narrative referent, are more than enough to make this ad quite memorable in our experience.

But outside of story, it's important to consider the ways that contemporary social media call out an embodied, sensory experience. Today's TikTok and Instagram users have developed a sophisticated vocabulary around sensations, perhaps owing to the increased awareness of sensory differences (such as kids who seek or avoid touch, seek movement, or avoid sound), neurodiversity and differences in mental health. We regularly hear young people stating "that's satisfying" or viewing TikToks and Instagrams that represent a certain *feeling* in one's hands or body—the slow turn of a wooden spoon stirring cake batter, freshly sharpened graphite whisking lines on textured sketch paper, a warm, purring ball of fur resting on a lap. Though the immediacy of new media may make it seem like sensational content is new, one need only look to horror and suspense genres to understand the tension-release qualities of popular culture. Though Gen Z may reflect on "jump scares," their ability to do so derives from the manipulation of sensation and embodiment in horror films. As with Jobs's justification for developing a mouse to "point" on a computer screen, horror scenes typically do their work without language. Even outside the horror genre, films have become increasingly sophisticated in their use of special effects, where productions often showcase technology or technical achievement (over and sometimes against the story of a film).

Lighting, music, visual imagery, and camera angles manipulate the viewers' physiological responses to popular culture, as much, if not more, than language. We joke about how you shouldn't look in a mirror or shower in a horror film because such scenes have been used many times to build tension, only to see it released in a violent attack from the masked maniac. We believe that one of the reasons social media is so alluring is because it is close, intimate even, to the viewer (recall parasocial relationships from Chapter 3). Watch many TikToks and Instagrams, and you will find they are filmed or photographed within inches of the photographer's body. This relates to theories of proxemics in nonverbal communication, whereby the closer we place our bodies to another, the more intimate we are with them (Hall, 1968). The same might hold true for screens, as well as the angles filmed and then recast on screens.

Much of social media appears inside a cocoon of intimacy that is only enhanced by "earbud" technology—not only privatizing the sound experience (which can register a whisper of sound), but quite literally putting the technology inside the body (the ear) of the user. Is it any wonder that many who spend time scrolling social media feel intense emotional connections to influencers, as photography and hardware court intimacy?

The human sensorium relates closely to physical states that are, again, manipulated for good and ill through popular culture—notably, arousal and pleasure. Though we typically associate arousal with sex, it refers more generally to the awakening of the body, or priming the senses to get to work. It's a state of excitement, where blood pressure and respiration (breathing) increase. The American Psychological Association (Berridge, 2004) describes pleasure as a kind of "gloss" or "value added" to sensation—neural associations that color a sweet taste as "nice" instead of "nasty." Certainly, popular culture plays into what individual neural networks (aka, brains in bodies) color as pleasurable. Pop culture circulates arousing images and sometimes reinforces stories about what is nice versus nasty.

As Sut Jhally (1987) and other researchers have demonstrated (recall Chapter 2's discussion of branding), not so subtle imagery has been associated with products as diverse as cologne, cars, and even hamburgers, cueing the physiological arousal of consumers with the presence of commodities. What is even more dystopic and alarming, perhaps, are the ways marketers are leveraging involuntary and unconscious responses, particularly in social media. The 30-second ad from the television days is shifting to the 5–10-second condensation in social media spaces. You may view an ad for, let's say, peanut butter cups. The ad has very sparse text, such as "Chocolatey" or "Boost!" The ad contains mostly visual imagery, quick cuts, and music, with the message driven home in the form of a sensation—"this peanut butter cup provides you pleasure." Marketers derive such effective techniques from the use of brain scans, attempting to light up the neural networks for pleasure in certain individuals (see Lindstrom, 2011).

Historically, much of dominant US culture has reacted to popular culture's power to arouse us—especially sexually. It may seem, with the ubiquity of pornographic material on the Internet, concerns over sexual imagery are new. One survey of US high school students in 2021 found that over half had viewed pornography in the previous year, with a second study showing a higher percentage—80.3%—had accessed it (Giordano, 2022). Experts share concern that online arousal may affect offline arousal experience, leading to sexual dysfunction. Teens themselves worry about how pornography influences attitudes about violence and attraction, along with dictating scripts for how sex should go (to be exact, 68.4% in the study reported above).

Concerns about digital affordances and sex notwithstanding, explicit imagery in films in the 1930s inspired the Hays Code, which was replaced in 1968 by the Motion Picture Association of America (MPAA) standards with which we're familiar today. The Hays Code sought to enforce morality into film content, specifically banning nudity, profanity, and interracial relationships, while also encouraging "wholesome" family values. The ability of popular culture to arouse our bodies has been a subject of concern that has included fears around addiction and immorality for some time. As Roland Barthes (1975) notes of the erotic, though, it is not what is seen, but what is hidden, that creates arousal—where a sleeve parts before a glove covers the hand, in Barthes' original analogy, the seam where a blouse parts and the teasing possibility of nudity are what creates arousal. Sex isn't only an experience of arousal and pleasure; for most folks, it is entangled in, creating, and amplifying *emotions*.

An emotion is a social construction that is shared across members of a culture, which names individual and physiological experiences. Psychologists note that all emotions have three components: "a subjective experience, a physiological response, and a behavioral or expressive response" (Hockenbury & Hockenbury, 2007, cited in Cherry, 2022). A working mom laughs at *Late Night with Seth Meyers* before crashing, friends boo a call that goes against their team at the basketball game. These popular culture experiences combine the bodily response (raising heart rates) with individual experience (viewing comedy, being present at the game) with their response (laughter, yelling and angry facial expressions). The mom and the friends might name their feelings with words, happy or frustrated. A lifetime of sharing such emotions helps name the experience of physiology with individual script with expression; and, as we've discussed in prior chapters (and even more in Chapter 10), popular culture is like a machine of reality creation and representation, whose effects are profound at collective levels.

The collective body: Shaping sensation via affect, technology, and content

In 2019, an IMS Business Report survey found electronic dance music (EDM) is the third most popular genre of music, behind only pop and rock (Swanberg, 2019). Globally, an estimated 1.5 billion people regularly listen to EDM. The Electric Daisy Carnival, a three-night EDM festival held regularly in Las Vegas, drew an estimated 100,000 people each night in 2022. That is like an entire US city descending on Las Vegas for the outdoor festival, which, like most EDM festivals, combines electronically generated, rhythmic percussion (with few lyrics) with complex, vibrant lighting displays and set pieces, concert-goers in costume and fireworks. As the *Las Vegas Weekly* describes, the theme of "Kinetic Bloom" included "a sunburst flower blooming at the center with cathedral-like glass panes alight and glowing" (Miller, 2022). Tiësto ran a 1.5-hour set and DJ Snake also headlined, emanating songs that are continuous, hypnotic and almost trance-like with their driving beats and sparse lyrics. Part of EDM's appeal, in fact, is its skewing toward a language-free music (some fans resist characterizing Tiësto's "Let's Get Down to Business" as EDM, because of its use of more than five words). EDM as a genre tends to deflect attention not only from language, but also from celebrity or identity, as a DJ appears sometimes shrouded in darkness, sometimes wearing costume or mask, to hide their faces and names. The focus in EDM is on the fans' experience, which really isolates their bodies and senses (to avoid distraction from storytelling and identity). People dance, sometimes developing impromptu and complex routines using LED lights (included in gloves).

EDM festivals also are famous for their circulation of drugs to enhance the experience. Certainly, the EDM community grapples with its reputation for taking ecstasy (with Adam Posner's revered song "I Took a Pill in Ibiza" demonstrating some reflection on how depression and grappling with expectations potentially intertwine with substance use and abuse). Here, we want to note that EDM joins other popular culture communities in norming the use of certain substances to help promote the affect possible in its subcultures. Gamers drink Mountain Dew or caffeinated energy drinks for energetic play, country music fans share beer to promote a laid-back vibe. Such choices are individual, but often shared by those who experience the popular culture together (we elaborate on this in Chapter 12, with an eye toward rituals in popular culture spaces).

EDM demonstrates how the sensations of popular culture aren't just individual, and relate to a theory that humanities scholars introduced in the 2000s to try to explain why collections of people sometimes move in unpredictable, irrational ways. Affect, as we introduced above, is a key term to describe feeling pre-, non-, or "extra-" linguistic senses; without splitting hairs too much (as academics sometimes seem to enjoy doing), affect is the energy or sensation prior to the emotion that is named. But a benefit to the affective perspective in popular culture is the ability to connect sensations to shared experiences. As Ahmed (2004) theorizes (pushing back a bit on the definition of emotions from psychology), emotions are a name that connects sensation with objects. They are not possessed by individuals, but instead are a shared, cultural experience, particularly in the effects they have. Some political discourse and popular culture, for instance, repeats stereotypes telling groups of people who is an enemy based on defining others in terms of fear and hate.

On the other hand, popular culture can escalate and direct affect that registers in more positive ways. The popularity of EDM demonstrates, for instance, how a whole space pulses with energy. People *move* because it feels right, or for no good reason at all, and they gather together to do so. Concerts and sporting events further show the ways that a contagion of feeling, a "vibe," can be created or enhanced, channeled, and moved through groups of people and popular culture. And as with EDM, football fans regularly enhance their experience with beer, while others turn to caffeine for a visceral boost. Such rituals (Chapter 12) may make us believe that affect most appears or is felt in immediate ways. But trends from social media—remember the Renegade, flossing, and Savage from TikTok?—demonstrate the viral circulation of bodily movements and joy between immediate and mediated spaces. Other social media trends, such as "challenges" (two of our favorites, the Chubby Bunny, in which people try to fit as many marshmallows into their mouth as they can until they can't say "chubby bunny" anymore; and the Harlem Shake challenge, in which one person acts casually while another nearby does the Harlem Shake, until everyone starts dancing like mad) further illustrate how affects of joy and affinity are not limited to immediate pop culture.

Similarly, we might look at the expansion of EDM into virtual reality. Marshmello joined forces with the game *Fortnite* in 2019, performing a ten-minute concert for over 10.7 million players (Baker, 2020). Marshmello appears as a white figure with trademark large cylindrical marshmallow head and black eyes, as a field of avatars dance surrounded by a brightly colored laser light show (see Figure 8.2). Virtual reality (VR) refers to a computer-generated environment in which avatars (simulated people or other characters) can interact with the environment and each other. VR relates to immersion, which is the sense in which one is physically present in the virtual world, often an outcome of the sensory engagement between sight, sound, touch, proprioception, and other senses as engaged through media.

People in the EDM community joke about their fandom, with articles offering tips on "educating parents about EDM 101" or sharing studies to

Figure 8.2 Marshmello performing in *Fortnite*.

demonstrate EDM's connection to youth (Bain, 2015). Though we don't personally follow EDM (save for the occasional pop-crossover from Zedd or Tiësto), we also respect the sensations popular culture provides. Rather than giving into some of the dystopian views on any type of popular culture (e.g., EDM is a "guilty pleasure"), we encourage folks to own the pleasure they get from popular culture. Put simply, it's okay to enjoy and experience something because you like how it makes you feel. Obviously, there are limits to this statement (e.g., your pleasure cannot derive from actively harming or excluding another, and your pleasure should not harm you). We will unpack the edges of acceptability for popular culture sensation later in this chapter with the genre of horror; but first, we want to also recognize the emotional support and comfort popular culture provides.

Pop culture as support: Equipment for living with emotion, adversity

In Chapter 1, we considered how popular culture provides equipment for living—tools which communities turn to and make use of to navigate challenging times. In Chapter 3, we followed work on domesticity and parasocial relationships in television, which suggests that the need for intimacy is satisfied through popular culture. Building on these two observations, we consider here how popular culture provides a resource for coping through dark times, perhaps even trauma, for groups of people.

Much literature exists on the power of social media and digital spaces to organize social support, which professionals basically define as a network of people (family, friends, and neighbors) who give emotional, mental, spiritual help, along with financial and physical resources, during times of need (Rains & Wright, 2016). As interpersonal and health communication scholars have noted, for instance, once someone gets diagnosed with a disease, there is often stigma attached that requires processing, a processing that demands support. The COVID-19 pandemic (which began in November 2019, but forced widespread lockdowns in the US in March, 2020) shined a light on the potential for not only new communication technology, but of popular culture, to provide social support resources as face-to-face communication in schools, spaces of worship, businesses, and civic spaces, shut down.

The pop music sensation, Billie Eilish, shared in September 2020, that she has watched the entire series of *The Office* 14 times (mostly on her phone), and that she "finds comfort in being familiar with every episode" (Lee, 2020). Some might consider Eilish's fandom as a "guilty pleasure," a source of distraction; but as every routine individuals experienced was disrupted, we'd suggest that Eilish and others turned to popular culture to provide comfort and support.

What popular culture forms do you regularly turn to in order to feel better individually? What types of popular culture do you share with others, in the hopes of supporting them, perhaps through a time of crisis or mourning? It's interesting to note the different affective and emotional registers of comforting popular culture, from the very big, loud spectacles which allow folks to scream or dance out their emotions; to voices (like those of Billie Eilish) that really "get into the head" of the listener, quite literally, through earbud headphones.

Popular culture can help collectivities of people survive or persevere, make sense of, and perhaps even lessen shared fears and uncertainties. We remember during the late spring of 2020 turning to John Krasinski (who played Jim in *The Office*), a dad showing up in the intimacy of YouTube, on the iPad at our kitchen table, for *Some Good News*. As our day-to-day life changed with emergency remote learning for us as teachers, and our kids as students (and we count ourselves both privileged and fortunate to have made it through the pandemic), for a few weeks in late spring 2020 we regularly pulled out the iPad for *SGN* each night with dinner. It was comforting to see so many faces from around the country coming together with the help of the Krasinski family, who culled social media feeds for #SomeGoodNews following widespread lockdowns. With a hand-drawn, colorful "SGN" backdrop (and cheesy DIY special effects, such as a hand making a globe spin), Krasinski anchored news stories such as a grandfather seeing his newborn grandson (held by his son, near an open window) and a couple who had cancelled their trip to Paris getting engaged with chalk drawings of the Eiffel Tower behind them.

The YouTube sensation (with over 18 million views and nearly 2.54 million subscribers) shared acts of kindness, generosity, support, and creativity, between family members and neighbors, as well as strangers. Popular culture provided an important means of coping and social support directly (and as a point of conversation between folks, too). As introduced in Chapter 1, popular culture provides equipment for living. It has long provided stories to help individuals navigate challenging situations, as when a beloved character dies in a story or experiences trauma in their life. Popular culture like *Harry Potter, Euphoria,* and *Star Wars* have served as equipment for living in these ways. *Black Panther* and *Wakanda Forever* have earned a reputation for demonstrating how intergenerational trauma affects the Black community, providing possibilities for healing.

This public grieving and support became even more pronounced when *Black Panther* star, the incomparable Chadwick Boseman, died of colon cancer in 2020. Boseman and his family did not disclose that Boseman had been dealing with the diagnosis for four years prior to his death, and so the news that Boseman was gone—during the midst of a global pandemic disproportionately affecting the Black community—shook many. Artist Courtney Lovett created a comic to help support grieving, featuring a young Black boy with a panther next to him, and an angelic Boseman speaking from the clouds. The first panel states "Always remember," with the conclusion in the second panel, "You are a king!" Popular culture, it would seem, provides an outlet for grieving, whether that be intergenerational grieving, the loss of a beloved actor, or the intensity of loss to COVID-19. In Lovett's words to PBS, "the outpouring after Boseman's death felt like a 'collective release'" (Barajas, 2020, September 9). Along with points of identification within the stories themselves, conversations on Twitter and around homes and workplaces show the ways popular culture can promote support and healing.

Conclusion: Horror and the ethics of sensation in popular culture

In this chapter, we have focused on popular culture's effects and relationship to embodiment, more specifically its capacity to engage human senses, emotions, and affects. As in other chapters of this book, we consider the sensations of popular culture in a neutral capacity, which can be activated toward the good and just (such as popular culture to support coping, and as a collective equipment for living), or the harmful and unjust (including the ability to reinforce marginalization, or even encourage self-destruction or pain for others). We end the chapter with an extended case study in popular culture, to allow you to sort out such complexities for yourself: the genre of horror.

Like other genres, horror books, films, TV series, and video games rely on a consistent set of characteristics and plots. Horror is distinguished mostly by the intensity of the emotional response it elicits in participants, an emotional response we often associate with the darkest parts of humanity: fear, dread, terror, and repulsion, or commonly evoked emotions that accompany horror texts. Horror represents and activates in audiences these emotional responses in both content and method. For instance, in the *Rolling Stone* 101 Best Horror Films list, we see plots that include serial killers, mental illness, graphic violence, monsters or aliens that threaten large groups of people, and haunting ghosts or demons. Death, murder, unmanageable psychosis, and evil set the stage for eliciting emotions in audiences. But horror, especially in audiovisual media like film, doesn't stop the sensational engagement there. Camera techniques and lighting, sound and special effects stoke the physiological engagement in horror. You may recall here your own reactions to films on the *Rolling Stone* Top 101 Horror Films, including *The Ring, Friday the 13th* or *Get Out*: scenes of bloody dismemberment and torture, dark rooms in which the threatening figure appears with a sudden high-pitched minor chord, or even a "found footage" aesthetic (using different lenses or a "jittery" filming technique to make it look as though what one is seeing on the screen really happened) are all techniques to heighten horror.

Horror tends to be dismissed as a "lower" form of film, particularly "slasher" and "monster" movies which earned their reputations as campy "B" movies at the start of film history. However, horror is predictably profitable. For instance, *Texas Chainsaw Massacre*, it was reported in 2021, earned $247 million over the franchise's eight-movie run (Mendelson, 2021). One study suggests that horror has the greatest likelihood of generating profit (between the years 1996 and 2016), compared to other genres, even adventure and romantic comedy (Follows, 2017). The popularity of horror film begs a question: Why do people love these films so much?

Unsurprisingly, given their content and technical devices, some suggest that horror appeals to "sick" people. One psychologist (Scrivner, 2021) responded to a film critic's assertion that fans of the *Saw* franchise are "depraved lunatics who should not be allowed near animals or most other living things," given the film's horrifying story and images (Scrivner, 2021). Scrivner shares an interesting take, built on his research. If we measure cold-heartedness (which is the "disregard for others' feelings or a lack of concern for them") amongst horror fans, we see a negative relationship. In other words, if someone shares a higher appreciation for horror, they have a lower tendency toward cold-heartedness. Scrivner finds that the same holds true for morbid curiosity, that is an interest in "violent people, death, ghosts … gore or body disgust." So the psychological profile of individuals who enjoy horror does not fit with the stereotype that they are mentally ill or unstable. In fact, it's quite the opposite.

Some argue that horror speaks to an evolutionary need for humans to experience, in a very visceral way, threats to their lives so that they might master threatening situations (Vinney, 2022). Horror provides humans a kind of rehearsal for the worst-case scenario, a sensory/emotional "test run" if you will. Other psychologists suggest that horror increases arousal, which then leads to an increased sense of relief—like a post-scare "high" in the body. Finally, from more of a collective perspective, horror experts argue that this genre allows us to peer into the darkest parts of the human experience, but not only to *contemplate* them with the mind. Horror really brings the body and sensorium into the experience of grotesque violence and terror. So, horror fans might get closer to experiencing safely some of humanity's worst, which is far outside of our control. At the very least, psychologists suggest, horror viewers exhibited less psychological distress from the COVID-19 pandemic (Vinney, 2022).

Yet, as in past chapters, we think it wise to ask critical questions. The popularity of Netflix's *Monster: The Jeffrey Dahmer Story* represents well some of the ethical stakes involved in the popularity of "true crime" stories, podcasts, and even tourism, as a play on horror. The Dahmer series is based on an absolutely shocking and gruesome case, in which a man living in Milwaukee killed, dismembered, and cannibalized victims (Whiting, 2022). Netflix developed this real-life horror into a record-setting series, with over 701.37 million hours viewed between its release date of September 21, 2022 and October 15, 2022 (Havermale, 2022). This made *Monster: The Jeffrey Dahmer Story* the 13th most viewed series of all time for the streaming platform.

As the *Independent* reports, *Monster* producer Ryan Murphy claims that he attempted to consult with victims' families in the show's run-up, but no one agreed to consult. Rita Isbell, sister of Errol Lindsey (who was murdered by Dahmer), discussed how she felt when she became aware of Netflix's series, "just like everyone else" because the company did not notify victims' families of the release: "When I saw some of the show, it bothered me … I was never contacted about the show. I feel like Netflix should've asked if we mind or how we felt about making it. They didn't ask me anything. They just did it." After stating that she was "comfortable" (and thus not criticizing Murphy or Netflix over money), Isbell stated that the descendants of Dahmer's victims should be compensated: "If the show benefited [descendants of Dahmer's victims] in some way, it wouldn't feel so harsh and careless. It's sad that they're [*Monster* creators] just making money off of this tragedy. That's just greed" (Vlamis, 2022).

In conclusion, Chapter 8 encourages us to critically reflect upon the ways that popular culture enlists the body and sensorium. While it may seem that the immersive qualities of digital media affordances make the sensations of popular culture "new," a media ecology perspective encourages us to see how pop culture has involved the body and senses for a long time. Further, a media ecology approach asks us to carefully look to how people make use of popular culture in organic ways, leading to more careful evaluations. Many illustrations in Chapter 8, like horror and EDM, have been criticized as morally repugnant or mindlessly bad. Rather than give into such "common sense" interpretations, by unpacking the ways popular culture engages the body and senses we can sort out the harmful consequences of popular culture (such as profiting from "true crime" stories without being in reciprocity to victims and families) from the banal or even positive consequences (people having fun together). The ability to sort out and navigate this complexity will be amplified as we introduce globalization and popular culture in the next chapter.

Reflecting on popular culture and sensation in your everyday life

- Chapter 8 introduced the ways that content (such as horror and EDM), production style (like camera angles in an unboxing video), and digital affordances (like earbuds or the touchscreen interface) engage us as embodied, sensory beings. What popular culture do you regularly consume that engages your body and senses? Do your choices tend to feature sensational popular culture content, style, or digital affordances more? How might this awareness lead to better choices for pop culture consumption?
- What are the risks involved in connecting senses and embodiment to popular culture, especially given the potential for others to profit from enlisting our bodies and senses in the experience? At what age is it appropriate to invite children into the sensory and visceral world of popular culture? Why, and how would you suggest regulating this?
- What popular culture do you individually or with immediate family turn to as a "comfort food?" What are the benefits and drawbacks to finding comfort from pop culture?
- Chapter 8 suggested that popular culture can be equipment for living with collective difficulty, and even trauma. What does it mean for groups of people to turn to popular culture as equipment for living? How might this differ from an individual uses and gratifications approach as introduced in Chapter 3?
- Are all "true crime" stories worthy of consumption? Why would you draw a line and "cancel" a true crime show (see Chapter 4)?
- Are you a fan of horror? Why or why not? Do the potential positive effects of horror mean that we should all expose ourselves to such films?

Suggested readings

Chávez, K. R. (2018). The body: An abstract and actual rhetorical concept. *Rhetoric Society Quarterly*, 48(3), 242–250. DOI: 10.1080/02773945.2018.1454182

Eguchi, S., & Baig, N. (2018). Examining embodied struggles in cultural reentry through intersectional reflexivity. *Howard Journal of Communications*, 29(1), 33–48. 10.1080/10646175.2017.1315692

Lechuga, M. (2023). *Visions of invasion: Alien affects, cinema, and citizenship in settler colonies*. University of Mississippi Press.

Moscowitz, D. (2018). Affect, cruelty, and the engagement of visual intimacy. *Communication & Critical/Cultural Studies*, 15(1), 90–95. 10.1080/14791420.2018.1435081

Phillips, K. R. (2018). *A place of darkness: The rhetoric of horror in early American cinema*. University of Texas Press.

References

Ahmed, S. (2004). *The cultural politics of emotion*. Edinburgh University Press.

Bain, K. (2015, May 11). There's a scientific reason why old people don't like EDM. *Insomniac*. https://www.insomniac.com/magazine/theres-a-scientific-reason-why-old-people-dont-like-edm/

Baker, B. (2020, March 16). Six ways EDM has crossed over into virtual reality. *EDM*. https://edm.com/features/edm-in-vr

Barajas, J. (2020, September 9). What Chadwick Boseman's death means in a year marked by grief. *PBS News Hour*. https://www.pbs.org/newshour/arts/what-chadwick-bosemans-death-means-in-a-year-marked-by-grief

Barthes, R. (1975). *The Pleasure of the Text*. (R. Miller, Trans.). Hill & Wang.

Basu, T. (2015, December 16). Why are we obsessed with "unboxing" videos? *Mental Floss*. https://www.mentalfloss.com/article/72336/why-are-we-obsessed-unboxing-videos

Berridge, K. (2004, November 1). Simple pleasures. *Psychological Science Agenda*. https://www.apa.org/science/about/psa/2004/11/berridge

Cherry, K. (2022, February 25). Emotions and types of emotional responses. *Very Well Mind*. https://www.verywellmind.com/what-are-emotions-2795178

Follows, S. (2017, November 13). How profitable are horror movies. Stephen Follows. https://stephenfollows.com/profitable-horror-movies/

Giordano, A. (2022, February 27). What to know about adolescent pornography exposure? *Psychology Today*. https://www.psychologytoday.com/us/blog/understandingaddiction/202202/what-know-about-adolescent-pornography-exposure

Hall, E.T. (1968). "Proxemics." *Current Anthropology*, 9(2/3), 83–95.

Harold, C. (2009). On Target: Aura, affect, and the rhetoric of "design democracy." *Public Culture*, 21(3), 599–618. DOI 10.1215/08992363-2009-010

Havermale, A. (2022, October 15). "Monster: The Jeffrey Dahmer Story" bumped out of top spot at Netflix. *Collider*. https://collider.com/the-watcher-replaces-monster-the-jeffrey-dahmer-story-netflix-top-spot/

Hockenberry, D. H., & Hockenbury, S. E. (2007). *Discovering psychology*. Worth Publishers.

Jhally S. (1987). *The codes of advertising: Fetishism and the political economy of meaning in the consumer society.* F. Pinter.

Lee, J. (2020, September 15). Billie Eilish talks to Steve Carell and Brian Baumgartner on why *The Office* is her "safe space." *Variety.* https://variety.com/2020/music/news/billie-eilish-the-office-fan-steve-carell-brian-baumgartner-1234770670/

Lindstrom M. (2011). *Brandwashed: Tricks companies use to manipulate our minds and persuade us to buy* (1st ed.). Crown Business.

Mendelson, S. 2021 Why Netflix is buying the new Texas Chainsaw Massacre. Forbes. https://www.forbes.com/sites/scottmendelson/2021/09/01/why-netflix-buying-the-new-texas-chainsaw-massacre-may-be-a-big-mistake/?sh=3db6a06f39e4

Miller, S. (2022, May 24). Wrapping up Electric Daisy Carnival. *Las Vegas Weekly.* https://lasvegasweekly.com/ae/music/2022/may/24/wrapping-up-electric-daisy-carnival-las-vegas-2022/#/0).

Montag, A. (2018, May 21). Here's why your computer has a mouse, according to Steve Jobs in 1985. CNBC. https://www.cnbc.com/2018/05/21/why-your-computer-has-a-mouse-according-to-steve-jobs.html

Rains, S., & Wright. K. (2016) Social support and computer-mediated communication: A state-of-the-art review and agenda for future research. *Annals of the International Communication Association, 40*(1), 175–211, DOI: 10.1080/23808985. 2015.11735260

Sas, M. (2022). *Feeling media: Potentiality and the afterlife of art.* Duke University Press. DOI: https://doi.org.aurarialibrary.idm.oclc.org/10.1215/9781478023098

Scrivner, C. (2021, May 30). A film critic claims *Saw* fans are depraved. Is he right? *Psychology Today.* https://www.psychologytoday.com/us/blog/morbid-minds/202105/film-critic-claims-saw-fans-are-depraved-is-he-right

Simone, I. (2012, May 12). My kid's first iPad. *Common Sense Media.* https://www.commonsensemedia.org/articles/my-kids-first-ipad

Swanberg, J. (2019, May 30). EDM ranked third most popular music genre. *Dance Music Northwest.* https://www.dancemusicnw.com/edm-3rd-ims-business-report/

Tuthill, J. C., & Azim, E. (2018). Proprioception. *Current Biology, 28*(5), R194–R203. https://doi.org/10.1016/j.cub.2018.01.064

Vinney, C. (2022, April 8). Why do we enjoy horror movies? *Very Well Mind.* https://www.verywellmind.com/why-do-people-like-horror-movies-5224447#:~:text=Horror%20is%20one%20of%20the,The%20Silence%20of%20the%20Lambs

Vlamis, K. (2022, September 25). My brother was murdered by Jeffrey Dahmer. Here's what it was like watching the *Netflix* show that recreated the emotional statement I gave in court. *Insider.* https://www.insider.com/rita-isbell-sister-jeffrey-dahmer-victim-talks-about-netflix-show-2022-9

Whiting, A. (2022, October 28). "Netflix receives the gain, the Dahmer victim families the pain:" Attorney calls on Ryan Murphy to share TV profits. *Independent.* https://www.independent.co.uk/arts-entertainment/tv/news/dahmer-ryan-murphy-backlash-b2213175.html

9 Globalization and popular culture

Introduction

The history of rap music, and hip-hop culture more generally, is absolutely fascinating. Back in the late 1970s. a handful of DJs were playing music on turntables at parties in their neighborhoods in New York and had "MCs" talk over the music to get the partygoers excited. The MCs began to creatively rap funny lines, often in rhyme, and became more and more popular. At the start of the 1980s, a few of these early rappers boldly recorded their songs and slowly a fan base started to grow. Mostly by word of mouth, the music spread and finally started to get radio play in a few local markets. Eventually, radio and MTV (the music television channel on basic cable) started to broadcast these records and videos nationally, and hip-hop culture steadily grew, eventually spreading across American popular culture (in advertising, sports, movies, etc.) in the late 1990s. Since 2000, hip hop and rap, both in performance and production style, has dominated pop music.

Now, there is rap music all over the world. Truly, *all* over the world. Search on YouTube "rapper" and *any* country (e.g., Sweden, Ethiopia, New Zealand), and you will find that a uniquely American art form is now a global phenomenon. While you watch these YouTube clips of rap from all across the globe, it is immediately evident that in each case the rappers are infusing their music and lyrics, as well as their clothing and dancing, with unique elements of their own culture. Many of these styles are then integrated back in hip hop in the US (think of Bad Bunny's collaboration with Cardi B). The global rap examples from YouTube demonstrate the astonishing reach of the Internet and social media, which has produced a wide range of unintended consequences. On one level, globalizing hip hop illustrates how members of cultures integrate new artistic forms to express their unique cultural experiences. On another level, the globalization of rap is yet another example of American styles and values replacing a local cultural history or tradition, which, as we raised in Chapter 2,

DOI: 10.4324/9781003372943-9

raises questions of who gets compensated, and how much, for their creative labor.

Hip hop demonstrates that all popular culture is now, in innumerable ways, globalized. Globalization, as we address in the first section, refers to both the economic expansion of capitalism around the world and the increased circulation of popular culture and other forms of contact around the world. Among the reasons that convergence is the prevailing logic in which popular culture business operates (see Chapter 2) are the loosening of regulations and increased markets around the world. Proponents argued that this system would increase development and standards of living, along with wealth—but as we discuss in the second section, critics argue that globalization is a form of cultural imperialism. As in the rap example above, local culture and art are replaced by popular culture often originating in the US, leading to the term "Americanization." The flip side of this coin is cultural hybridity, whereby local creators around the world infuse different ideas into their own work. Cultural hybridity differs from cultural appropriation, the latter of which continues to funnel profits into those who already have privilege. The chapter concludes by raising some ethical issues concerning the global production of popular culture and overconsumption, the environmental effects of globalized popular culture, and the spread of American political values around the world via social media and celebrity.

Economic globalization and popular culture

Many books, some of which are quite long, have been written about the complexities of economic globalization, so boiling it down to a few simple points is challenging. Of course, trade between peoples and countries has occurred for centuries: not only does trade include European explorers circumnavigating the world, but also Indigenous nations trading across geographic boundaries (see Deverell & Hyde, 2018). While global trade grew over the centuries—aided, as critical scholars point out, by violent practices, such as colonization and enslavement—for the most part, national borders were still quite significant as most country's economies were still relatively separated (certainly by today's standards).

Accelerating in the 1980s and 1990s, a worldwide political movement grew (sometimes referred to as neoliberal globalization) that championed the value of global free markets. The basic principle was that whatever company, no matter where they are in the world, that produces the best, cheapest, newest, etc. product or service to meet consumer demand should be most successful. Led by the United States, governments began loosening (or ending entirely) regulations, such as restrictions on how companies could pollute as they manufactured, for instance, plastics that go into most pop culture products today; or, the minimum wage they were required to pay the workers that assembled the smartphones, toys, and clothing that would meet consumer demand around the world. You may read headlines concerning Apple's ethics, for instance, after former employees went public with evidence that the tech giant's supply chain in China included computer components manufactured by underage workers (as young as 14); and that workers who manufacture iPhone screen glass were placed in unsafe conditions (Sonnemaker, 2020). Workers at Foxconn, an Apple supplier, protested in Zhengzhou, China, due to failed promises for increased wages and benefits (Liu, 2022). Foxconn paid workers $1400 (the equivalent of about two months of pay) to simply leave their jobs and vacate the premises.

Again led by the US and Western European countries, governments brokered trade partnerships to allow companies to easily do business globally, even creating incentives, such as tax breaks and an end to tariffs or fees that were often passed along to consumers for buying goods outside of their home economies. Simultaneously, technologies, especially transportation and digital networks, further enabled global business to thrive as people could travel and communicate across the world with remarkable ease. Building on the famous "blue marble" photo (the first widely circulated photograph of our home planet taken by NASA astronauts while orbiting above Africa), consciousness began to change. As media scholars state, journalism doesn't tell us what to think, but tells us what to think about. This type of power, known as agenda-setting power, isn't limited to journalism, and is shaped by public conversations in popular culture. Seeing our planet suspended in the blackness of space, along with other economic and cultural flows, people began to see matters that affected the globe, as well as local matters from all over the world, as important. Business took advantage of such increased circulation, developing new markets for products, such as bringing fast food to new countries, as we elaborate below. Developing and increasing new markets, ending tariffs on goods made outside the home economy, and loosening the environmental and labor restrictions that made business cost more, led to unprecedented business across national borders, and a host of other consequences for workers, the environment, and local cultures, as we explore in the pages to come.

Companies sold products in new markets around the world. Manufacturing could be outsourced to whatever country had the cheapest labor. From a US consumer's perspective, it is now incredibly hard to find products manufactured in the United States, especially at large big box retailers such as Walmart. Further, a behemoth global company such as Amazon could not exist without these complex worldwide transformations. The relative cost of everyday consumer goods has dropped (pandemic and post-pandemic inflation notwithstanding), many people's homes (especially in the Global North) are overflowing with *stuff*. As we set forth in Chapter 3, the options for consumers in everyday life is paralyzing, and often follows the dominant media logic of digital media: whatever options will promote the most people to "stick" to a site for the longest amount of time (or repeated visits) get rewarded with monetary (and attention) investments. Such is the state of the **network economy**.

For popular culture, globalization has meant a wide variety of significant changes. First, new markets emerged to sell movies, TV shows, music, and video games. For instance, big budget Hollywood movies, especially action blockbusters with little dialogue, increasingly made much more money outside the United States, than inside the US. Further, American popular culture producers were increasingly dependent on foreign markets for revenue, especially China, the largest film market in the world. In fact, US film studios regularly conform to the constraints imposed by the Chinese government in order to export their movies to Chinese movie theaters, even enlisting Chinese regulators on set. Chinese censors have even demanded scenes removed from American films for depicting same-sex relationships (*Bohemian Rhapsody*) and ghosts (*Pirates of the Caribbean: Dead Man's Chest*) (Li, 2021), even changing the ending of *Minions: Rise of Gru.*

Like other industries, American television producers increasingly outsource aspects of production, especially animation for shows such as *Family Guy* and *Bob's Burgers*, to companies in Asia. Much like other globalized industries, these animated shows sometimes faced challenges collaborating across cultures between writers in the US and animators in Korea or India. For instance, the American writers of the TV show *Bob's Burgers* sometimes confused Korean animators with uniquely American references to dance moves, everyday expressions, or gestures (May, 2016). In other words, there are subtle movements in a character's animation that can make a twerking Gene Belcher, an 11-year-old boy on *Bob's Burgers*, either hilarious or creepy to an American audience.

Second, with manufacturing now outsourced to countries outside the United States, knowledge work such as producing entertainment media has become much more central to the overall American economy. The US media and entertainment industry is the largest in the world at $660 billion of the overall $2 trillion global market. In other words, as Richard Lanham stated, fewer and fewer Americans make "stuff" (automobiles, appliances, etc.) and more and more Americans make "fluff" (software, TV shows, YouTube content, etc.). Twenty years ago, the biggest American companies such as Ford, General Electric, and Exxon produced stuff (cars, oil, ovens, etc.). Today, the biggest American companies (which are also some of the biggest global companies), such as Google, Microsoft, and Facebook, don't really make anything physical, just ephemeral (or weightless) data, information, software, etc. These shifts were especially startling in the late 1990s when "cultural-industry sales" (of film, music, television, software, journalism, and books) grew rapidly becoming America's largest export surpassing aerospace, defense, agriculture, and automobiles (Miller, Aksikas, & Harney, 2012).

As this brief primer on economic globalization suggests, changes to doing business at this scale are very complex. Though global circulation of goods and ideas has occurred for centuries, the speed and scale of economics since the 1990s feels quite intense. For many living in the US, we've witnessed a shift from trading in an economy of goods to an economy of goods, services, and, as social theorists Michael Hardt and Antonio Negri (2000) write, affects (see Chapter 8). While US capitalism was once driven by the efficient and uniform manufacturing of consumer goods (like the toothpaste discussed in Chapter 2), today's capitalism often looks like the circulation and sale of *experiences* and *emotions* that go along with products, connected to the familiar brands (recall Chapter 2).

As you might imagine, these developments in the global production and distribution of popular culture have some big implications. Back in the early 2000s when we were first understanding economic globalization (and the protest movements against it), we encountered a book that distinguished "globalization from above" and "globalization from below" (Brecher & Costello, 2000). **Globalization from above** is driven by incredibly powerful elites (multinational corporations and their allies in governments), and refers to the changes in policy and practice that increased profits for those entities. **Globalization from below** is driven by cultural exchange and networking, often done by ordinary people (including the poor and lower income) who use new communication technologies to build knowledge and solidarity—especially in response to urgent problems they face. Globalization from above and below are useful to understand the complex practices involved, and make evaluations on them, relative to popular culture. We consider two sides to the globalization coin, both of which are quite evident in the daily popular culture experience of most of us today: cultural imperialism and cultural hybridity.

Popular cultural imperialism

Back in the 1960s, scholars such as Marshall McLuhan began writing about a "global village" of mass media. The observation was simple but significant: people all over the world were increasingly sharing common experiences due to media's instantaneous communication that transcends space. For instance, TV shows such as *Dallas* and *Baywatch* were watched in dozens of countries. Specifically, at its peak around 1996, *Baywatch*, with its beautiful lifeguards in red swimsuits, was broadcast in over 100 countries and had over a billion viewers each week. As noted above, the United States still dominates popular culture production. Further, streaming services based in the United States, such as Netflix, are popular all around the world. Most people outside the United States, especially young people, prefer American movies to locally produced films (Wike, 2013). So, a lot of people all around the globe are enjoying TV, movies, and music produced by Americans.

The growing influence of American popular culture has been described as a kind of cultural imperialism or "**Americanization**" of the world. When we hear the word "imperialism," we often think of colonizing powers centered in Western Europe sailing to Africa, Asia, and the Americas, planting the flag of Spain or Great Britain, and claiming the land as a colony. The horrors of this imperialism are well chronicled, as colonization frequently required genocidal violence and physical domination to erase the language, religion, and way of life of an entire culture, people (many of whom are indigenous to the lands) who had lived there for centuries prior to European "discovery." For critics of Americanization and globalization, the exporting of popular culture represents a variation on imperialism that does not always require the violent suppression of another culture.

Using a kind of "soft power," the United States can ship its TV, movies, and advertising to Africa, Asia, etc. erasing a local culture and imposing a new way of life. As Miller (2008) writes, "the broad sweep of American culture," in the form of "Hollywood movies, television, advertising, business practices, and fast-food chains from the United States" (p. 24), is compelling a kind of anti-American backlash (which we elaborate on in just a moment). Popular culture that many people in the US regularly take for granted includes representations that violate the norms and ethics of some religions: open sexuality, violence, and displays of disrespect from characters. Interestingly, as Pew Research Center (2012) reports, people living in predominantly Muslim countries like Pakistan, report negative attitudes toward American popular culture. Additionally, popular culture from the US represents other perceived threats, including American economic and political power, a blind embrace of greed and capitalism, and even freedom to live different types of lifestyles.

"Americanization" has been happening for some time now. In the early days of film in the 20th century, movies often portrayed glamorous American lives in lavish musicals and heroic cowboys in romantic Westerns. Embedded in these early films were themes of American economic opportunity and rugged individualism set against a wide open landscape. People all over the world clamored for American popular culture and Hollywood was eager to export their products to every corner of the globe. Some commentators have even suggested that the desire for American consumer products and popular culture helped spur the protests that brought down the Berlin Wall and helped end Soviet communism (Crothers, 2021). Protestors in Eastern Europe were demanding freedom, but a freedom to buy Levi's jeans and Nike sneakers as well as listen to Michael Jackson and David Bowie records, among other possible outlets for freedom.

Today, Americanization happens with the sheer ubiquity of US popular culture exports, some of which occurs through the networked pathways of global media companies as we laid out in Chapter 2. As Gray (2007) observed, "turning on television in Sri Lanka or Costa Rica, one is just as likely to find CNN Headline News or NBC sitcoms as in Louisville or Tucson" (p. 130). Disney has opened theme parks, with their unique American small town nostalgia, in Tokyo, Paris, Shanghai, and Hong Kong.

Americanization is also evident in the dominance of English in popular culture (Salomone, 2022). It has been widely reported that the second most recognized word in the world, after OK (incidentally, also an American idiom), is Coke. More generally, English is the most spoken language in the world, often as a second language, and its massive growth is, at least in part, due to the fact that English dominates content on the Internet (about 60% of the Internet is in English), and is the language of pop music lyrics as well as the dialogue in TV shows and movies exported from the United States.

As American television, movies, and advertising spreads into new cultures, American beauty standards also seem to become the new cultural norm. For instance, with the expansion of Western advertising in China, Chinese women reported similar body image issues as American women (Parker, Haytko, & Hermans, 2008). Skin-lightening products promoted by American cosmetics companies are a multi-billion-dollar industry in India and other parts of Asia (Arora, 2020). Spending a few moments looking through the most popular fashion magazine in India (e.g., *Vogue: India*) the cover models look astonishingly similar to the models on the covers of American fashion magazines. Further, Mattel sells Barbie dolls in over 150 countries around the world. While they have elements of dress, skin tone, and style specific to the culture, these dolls have the body shape and facial features that are unmistakably Barbie (see Figure 9.1). For proponents of a cultural imperialism perspective, the conventions of American advertising, with thin, light-skinned models, are spreading all over the world dramatically altering beauty standards, and more generally gender norms, of other cultures.

Americanization also occurs as the values and methods of US-based business practices displace local traditions. Perhaps the most iconic examples of American popular cultural imperialism are associated with fast food. There are over 35,000 McDonald's restaurants in 120 countries around the world (see Figure 9.2). Fast food carries with it a whole set of American values, sometimes referred to as "McDonaldization," such

Figure 9.1 Barbie "Dolls of the World" collection.

Figure 9.2 McDonald's and KFC in China. Victor Jiang/Shutterstock.

as capitalistic efficiency, rationality, uniformity, and predictability (Ritzer, 2021). Kentucky Fried Chicken (KFC) is now the traditional food to eat on Christmas Day in Japan (Smith, 2012). Replacing local cafes for assembly-line hamburgers and fried chicken, as well as displacing cultural history represented by food, is a pretty awful consequence of globalization (joined by other environmental and human costs). But the global circulation of popular culture has an upside, too, in the form of cultural exchange and hybridity, as we also elaborate below.

For now, we consider the backlash against Americanization via popular culture, which has been dramatic at times: in 1999, for instance, a French sheep farmer became an icon of anti-globalization by ransacking a McDonald's (Wike, 2013). When volatile heads of state use their power, anti-Americanism and popular culture have intersected in surprising, and even shocking, ways. In 2014, comedian Seth Rogen directed and starred in *The Interview*, a movie about an American celebrity journalist (played by James Franco) who travels to North Korea for an interview with Kim Jong-Un and is recruited by the US Central Intelligence Agency (CIA) for an attempted assassination. The movie (produced by Sony Pictures) so angered the North Korean leader he ordered a hack of Sony Pictures emails. The emails were released to the public as part of the hack, revealing many embarrassing and incriminating private details about executives of the company. When American Women's National Basketball Association (WNBA) star Brittney Griner was arrested in Russia for possession of cannabis, she was given the excessive sentence of nine years as a response to American criticism of Russia's policies, particularly in Ukraine.

Other countries have tried slowing Americanization through policy, beginning with bans on pop culture artifacts or artists. *Fifty Shades of Grey*, for instance, was deemed obscene due to sexual content and banned in Indonesia, Kenya, and Cambodia. *South Park: Bigger, Longer, and Uncut* was banned in *a lot* of countries, interpreted as some combination of subversive and offensive. Miley Cyrus's songs were forbidden in the Dominican Republic because she "undertakes acts that go against morals and customs" of the country (Lawson, 2014). Because musicians from the US continue to dominate airplay all over the world, some countries limit how much American music can be played on the radio. For example, in France, national law requires that 40% of the songs played on radio must be from French artists, and in Zimbabwe 75% of radio airplay must be by local artists (Okapi, 2016). Such policies are joined by a kind of cultural backlash to Americanization, which we elaborate more when evaluating the ethics of globalization.

The Americanization argument, per Gray (2007), goes in and out of fashion in academia and public policy circles. The incredible power of a few media companies headquartered in the United States is undeniable (recall Chapter 2). On the other hand, local cultures continue to maintain unique languages, traditions, rituals, and storytelling, despite importing American popular culture for decades. Critics of the Americanization argument point out that pop culture does not just flow from the US to other parts of the world. For instance, the last few years has seen South Korean popular culture exploding in popularity in the US. K-pop groups such as Black Pink and BTS are topping the music charts. *Parasite* is a blockbuster movie winning the Best Picture Oscar. *Squid Game* is the biggest new show on Netflix in years. While some may view this as a "South Korean-ization of pop culture" in the US, it illustrates the other side of the coin when it comes to globalization: popular culture is flowing in all directions across the globe, all the time. While this fact doesn't refute cultural imperialism, it does complicate things. By looking at global popular culture more from the ground up, we see how popular culture can increase connection and solidarity—while also inviting appropriation and profit in global business logics.

Popular cultural hybridization and hybridity

As we saw in the prior section, food is caught in the crossfire of economic globalization. Food is so intimately connected to local cultures, expressing powerful meanings in rituals and family traditions. But, food also circulates globally, along with people and ideas. If you walk down a street in any American city's downtown, you will likely see Japanese, Brazilian, Thai, German, and Indian restaurants, among others. If you walk down a street in most urban centers around the world, you will see American fast-food companies that have taken advantage of economic globalization. These companies have learned the importance of adapting the menu of their restaurants to the unique palate of the local culture. Fast-food chains even alter their marketing characters in other countries such as Ronald McDonald, who is replaced in France with a comic-book character named Asterix and Colonel Sanders who is replaced in China with the mascot Chicky the Chicken (Pavlova, 2019). Whether or not such adaptations are hegemonic (as discussed in Chapter 5, offering a small dose of local culture, to pave the way for fast food) is open to debate. The point here is that cultural exchange is multidirectional, food included. Sushi, for instance, is a food indigenous to Japan (there is even folklore about the origins of sushi, which involves a woman hiding rice pots in an osprey nest, and discovering fish scraps mixing with fermented rice—delicious, and a great way to preserve the seafood) (Avey, 2012). Historians believe sushi spread alongside Buddhism, and preparation changed over time, expanding globally in the 1970s with refrigeration and transportation networks. Today, of course, sushi is popular all over the world (and has its own life in pop culture, in iconography of Hello Kitty and Pusheen, in songs, etc.). Additionally, as with our opening example of hip hop, new styles of sushi emerge around the world (think California rolls). The other side to globalization is a blending of traditions and practices that results in new aesthetics, new values, and new connections between people. Such connections can result in profits (for ordinary people, though admittedly, often for multinational corporations and investors), but they can also result in social relationships (including solidarity) between people around the world.

The intermixing of cultural forms, what sociologists call "cultural hybridization" (Martell, 2010), occurs with intercultural contact, and may not result in dramatic transformation of the original popular culture. At other times, cultural hybridization can result in cultural hybridity, a term which scholars critical of colonization use to recognize the ways that most marginalized people living under colonial regimes (the subaltern) persevered through oppression (Bhabha, 1994). For instance, subaltern writers used "ideology, aesthetics, and identity" of the colonizing power or empire to write their own stories, resulting in a new hybrid creation (Kraidy, 2005, p. 58). As with most concepts, then, **cultural hybridization** and **hybridity** exist on a continuum. Cross-cultural contact ranges from simple co-existence or hegemonic adaptation, such as a "Sheroes" Barbie inspired by Olympic fencer Ibtijah Muhammad, its first Barbie wearing a hijab (Khoja-Moolji, 2017); to more authentically local creations, as in the hip-hop, funk, Indigenous flute fusion of Brazilian artist Essa Rua E Minha, profiled as part of Brazilian Indigenous art and activism (Miranda, 2020).

Cultural hybridization, certainly, relates to marketing, where music, film, and television are blended across cultures to best reach new consumers. Stories about *Hallyu*, the Korean wave of pop culture (including South Korea's $5 billion music industry), include the systematic efforts by South Korean business and government elites to cultivate pop culture for export (see Romano, 2018). Americans dancing to Black Pink and BTS videos likely note the similar clothing, choreography, and vocal styles of US-based girl pop and boy bands, especially from the 1990s and early 2000s.

Television is another example of cultural hybridization, where formats like game shows, talk shows, and soap operas are popular all over the world. Likewise, popular franchises or brands of programs in one country get rebooted in others, including US favorites *The Office* (originally a British show), *The Voice* (originally a Dutch show), and *The Good Doctor* (originally a South Korean show). Of course, American shows are sometimes adapted to other cultures and languages such as *Modern Family* (with versions in Chile and Greece), *It's Always Sunny in Philadelphia* (with a Russian version), and *Friends* (with a Chinese version called *Planet Homebodies*).

American film has been exported across the world for decades, and has often been incorporated into new genres and styles in other parts of the world, which then influence filmmakers in the US. In the 1960s and 1970s, Italian filmmakers incorporated elements of US Western movies into their own dark sensibility creating the genre known as "spaghetti Westerns." These Italian Westerns then influenced a new generation of American filmmakers, such as Quentin Tarantino, who used their stylistic conventions in movies in the 2000s. Similarly, American horror films have been quite influential globally with new, often stranger and darker, horror styles and themes developing in countries such as Japan and China. Finally, Bollywood musicals, produced in India with distinctive Indian songs, have elements of classic Hollywood musicals with specific new generic qualities (styles of dance, music, dress, editing, etc.), many of which have subsequently influenced American filmmakers.

In fact, American movies often integrate elements of other cultures, especially Asian cultures, to appeal to audiences in other parts of the world. *The Matrix* franchise was heavily influenced by anime and appealed to the huge global fan base of this animation style developed in Japan. More shamelessly, the *Transformers* franchise consciously (and often clumsily) integrates Chinese characters and locations as these films are wildly popular in China (Langfitt, 2014). Disney has recently prominently featured Asian characters in movies such as *Shang-Chi and the Legend of the Ten Rings* and *Raya and The Last Dragon*. These films blend together the production style and narrative conventions of classic Disney animation and superhero films with Asian traditions, symbols, icons, and characters, putting cultural hybridization to work in popular culture production.

Digital affordances put the potential for cultural hybridization into the hands of ordinary people, too. Social media, such as TikTok and YouTube, permits a kind of cobbling together (or *bricolage*, as defined in Chapter 7) of various popular cultural forms. While the *digital divide*, the unequal access/use of the Internet, still affects people all over the world, in the last decade, Internet use, and especially social media use, has expanded tremendously across the world. For instance, Facebook has almost 3 billion users worldwide and is incredibly popular in Brazil, Indonesia, and India. Over 2.5 billion people use YouTube worldwide and the video sharing site is quite popular in India, Russia, Japan, Mexico, and Germany. It's interesting that two of the most viewed music videos of all time are "Gangham Style" and "Despacito." Homegrown musical artists, PSY (South Korea) and Luis Fonsi (Puerto Rico) produced songs and videos primarily for their local communities, in their native languages, only to see them spread virally on the Internet.

The algorithmic logic of "trending" topics has also created some unintended consequences in cultural hybridization. For instance, the idea of "wokeness," as a shorthand for an awareness of the institutional processes of racism, has spread from American artists, activists, and academics to become a trending topic globally. The idea of being woke, by most accounts, began in the United States emerging from the African-American community in blues recordings and literature dating back to the 1930s but gained popularity in last decade by artists such as Erykah Badu and Childish Gambino and a wide variety of social media activists (Romano, 2020). As in our discussion of cancel culture in Chapter 4, though, the original idea of wokeness (which refers to staying awake, bearing witness to and testifying to injustices such as racism—injustices which the mainstream will want you to forget as it marches on) has come to mean many different things, including an "enemy" for certain political figures and movements.

Right-wing populist movements around the world, for instance, consider wokeness a kind of "Americanization 2.0," where Hollywood values are too influential in local politics. Authoritarian regimes carefully monitor and control Internet traffic, while anti-immigration and nationalist movements (stoked in conservative media echo chambers in the US, as discussed in other chapters) circulate to other countries.

As cultures blend popular cultural forms, issues of power invariably complicate matters. Back in the 1960s, young British musicians such as the Rolling Stones and the Beatles blended the styles of African-American blues musicians with a catchy, Brit pop sensibility and became global superstars. Of course, the Black blues musicians who invented these guitar riffs and vocal styles lived in relative obscurity, and sometimes in poverty. **Cultural appropriation** occurs when a member of a privileged group takes an aspect of a marginalized group's culture (stories, identities, practices, styles) without acknowledging it or doing so inappropriately. Cultural appropriation seems readily available as popular culture artifacts from around the world pop up in the "FYP" (TikTok's "For You Page"). Claims of cultural appropriation have taken on a life of their own on social media, where collectives call out celebrities like Katy Perry (who has dressed as a Japanese geisha) and Selena Gomez (who performed Bollywood choreography while wearing traditional Indian clothes and accessories). Social media call-outs, of course, make cultural appropriation seem like it's always 100% clear and 100% heinous. But today's popular culture hybridization is actually pretty grey: when Paul Simon tours with the same African musicians with whom he collaborated on his classic album *Graceland*, is this cultural appropriation? When a White celebrity chef like Bobby Flay uses Asian or Latin fusion cooking, is it cultural appropriation? When Rihanna wears a dress on the red carpet made specifically for her by a Chinese designer, is it cultural appropriation?

Like many other marginalizing and oppressive practices, cultural appropriation has a long history. Scholars critique orientalism, a style that spread from literature to many different forms of popular culture, emerging from a binary between the West-as-"civilized" and East-as-"exotic other." From the perspective of European colonizers, the "Far East" or "'Orient' became synonymous with romance, mystery, and barbarism" (Rosenblatt, 2009, p. 51). Orientalist images pervaded novels, movies, and TV throughout the 20th century and still pop up today (often intertextually). The *Indiana Jones* film franchise offers some clear examples of this stereotypical exoticism still associated with Asian cultures. Stereotyping Asian and Asian-American cultures and people as sensual, exotic, and mysterious, like other stereotypes (Chapter 4) dehumanizes people and paves the way for violence. Given the uptick in violent attacks on Asian Americans (as in the mass shooting in a massage parlor outside Atlanta in 2021 or the mass shooting at a Lunar New Year celebration in Monterey Park, California, in

January 2023), advocates continue to call for greater, and higher-quality, representations (Kai-Hwa Wang, 2022).

How do we sort out, and respond, to different types of cultural hybridization? Given the vast amounts of inmixing in clothing, music, visual imagery, and other signs (see Chapter 7), it can be challenging. Furthermore, content creators have responded to the need for greater representation of diversity by sharing stories from marginalized communities. We may appreciate a film like *Moana*, for instance, because it centers a girl of color as protagonist—not only avoiding stereotypes from prior Disney films, but also telling a story where one girl's perseverance and wit heals the relationship between the land and its people. However, Disney has faced criticism for portraying the Polynesian demigod Maui (voiced by Dwayne Johnson) as "a big and goofy Disney character" (Higson, 2016).

In contrast, as ethics blogger Rachel Higson (2016) notes, "to many Pacific people, he is very real—a hero, ancestor ... and spiritual guide." Though the line between appropriation and borrowing or being influenced by another culture's work can be gray, one way to think of it is in the material benefits of representation. So, if Disney profits from their use of Maui in Moana, while the Polynesian people do not, we would consider this appropriation. Cultural appropriation that relies on economic exploitation and stereotypes (like orientalism) appear to be particularly egregious.

On the other hand, cultural hybridization can bring about hybridity, with the potential for solidarity within and across national borders. The story of "Love Nwantiti" by Nigerian singer Chukwuka Ekweani (who performs as CKay), and other Afrobeat songs (like "Calm Down," by Rema, remixed with Selena Gomez), is an interesting example. CKay dropped the song in 2019 when it circulated around Africa, remixed by a singer from Ghana (Kuami Eugene) and Nigerian singer (Joeboy) in 2020. CKay collaborated with many other local artists to remix "Love Nwantiti," including versions with Moroccan rapper ElGrandeToto, French rapper Franglish, and De La Ghetto (a Puerto Rican reggaeton artist), and the song made nightclub circuits around Africa and Europe. CKay notes that the iconic chorus, which serves as the alternate title of the song ("Ah, Ah, Ah"), started as a placeholder that he had put into the song before finally going to bed. The next morning, he realized the song was perfect. In September 2021, a friend surprised CKay with a TikTok clip of the song, and over the next few weeks, a version of it went viral on the platform, including a dance routine. CKay eventually released an acoustic clip on TikTok, affirming that he was the original creator of "Love Nwantiti." To be sure, CKay is benefiting from cultural hybridization, as "Love Nwantiti" is helping make him a millionaire in US dollars (Ezebuiro, 2022). With its blending of Igbo (a language spoken in Nigeria) and English, its inmixing of West African beats with American funk, soul, and jazz, this Afrobeat song also shows the power of digital affordances and pop culture to connect people from around the world. In CKay's words: "One person cannot speak all the languages in the world so for a song like 'Love Nwantiti' it just made sense to have remixes," he says. "To be fair, artists were reaching out to us and people are *still* reaching out for remixes. It's just a situation of music bringing the world together and I happen to be the vessel for this to happen" (Esomnofu, n.d.).

Popular culture hybridity has even more potential impacts. Global popular culture opens unique opportunities for political action organized around the world. Think of Bob Marley. While American college students might see this important artist as a symbol of marijuana culture, to members of the African diaspora around the world, he has inspired cultural pride and resistance to colonial power. The BTS Army, fans of the K-pop group from all around the world, have helped support a wide range of political causes, raising millions of dollars and flooding social media with hashtags for such causes as Black Lives Matter. BTS fans even falsely ordered tickets to a campaign rally for President Trump in Tulsa, Oklahoma, so only a few thousand people showed up to the event planned for hundreds of thousands (Bruner, 2020).

A transnational movement to support Indigenous People, particularly in South America, is infused with and by popular culture. Indigenous futurism is a style of art, typically popular culture in its presentation (that is, designed as populist, not elite or folk), that centers Indigenous People's experiences, against colonizing stereotypes, and policies that are currently destroying Indigenous lands in countries like Brazil and Peru. Through digital pop-art pieces, as well as music that blends Indigenous traditions and urban culture, Indigenous creators are forging connections across identity and geography (see Miranda, 2020).

Though it is unclear whether Indigenous futurism will translate into policy impacts, the point here is that cultural hybridization is not only a means for globalization from above to achieve greater profit. This leads to our closing case study, on the environmental impacts of economic globalization.

Conclusion: Disposability of popular culture on a global scale

Globalization has raised some complicated questions for consumers of popular culture. The scale of the issues associated with globalization are enormous and well outside the brief discussion of this chapter. We are hoping to reveal some the workings and consequences of these complex systems. To try to raise as many questions as possible, we want to point your attention toward a remarkably banal popular cultural artifact: the t-shirt. Chances are, you have drawers filled with t-shirts that have sports logos, pictures of music artists, silly phrases, Nike swooshes, maybe even free corporate swag that you received at some event. Spend a moment looking at the label of these t-shirts: they were likely made in a country outside the US, perhaps far away from where you live. A generation or two ago, people in the US knew where their clothing came from and how it was made—they may have even known the factory workers who made it. Now, many people living in the US don't think about Honduras, China, or Pakistan, and the workers that produce our favorite team's or rock band's t-shirts. We don't consider the low wages and oppressive conditions of these factories. We also don't consider the natural resources needed to make a single t-shirt: the cotton to grow a t-shirt uses the equivalent of 1849 gallons of water, and all the production to get cotton from its plant stage to yarn to sewn into a t-shirt emits air pollution and greenhouse gases (Sumner, 2020) doesn't even account for the pollution of transporting goods from areas with lower labor costs and regulations (like Honduras, China, and Pakistan), to the US. Part of the trick of global capitalism is to mask the process of production with the pleasures of consumption, which we discussed in Chapter 2 in terms of advertising fetishes. For many living in the US, logging onto Amazon, choosing a cool t-shirt, finding the best price, and getting the package at your door in a day or two is an ethically simple act. The entire system is designed to hide how our products are made, and to maximize returns to investors and business owners.

The pleasures of consumption are really the pleasures of overconsumption. If you are like most Americans, you have *way* more t-shirts than you need. In fact, the World Bank's (2019) report on fast fashion asserts that 40% of clothing in the average closet in the US goes unworn. Every couple of years, you likely take a pile to GoodWill or the Salvation Army, never thinking about them again. A lot of this donated clothing ends up in poorer countries (Minter, 2019). The US regularly produces so much stuff that even brand new clothing is donated. In fact, because the NFL produces boxes of swag for both Super Bowl teams so the players can wear them immediately after the big game ends (to show off for cameras, of course), the losing team's t-shirts and ball caps are sent to countries in Africa and South America where people wear a Cincinnati Bengals 2022 Super Bowl Champ t-shirt. Unfortunately, though, most of our discarded clothing does not go to people in need or is recycled to make new clothes. At the other end of the overconsumption cycle are impossibly large piles of discarded clothing in landfills. In fact, 85% of discarded textiles in the US end up in landfills or incinerated (Beall, 2020). And given the amount of clothing now regularly produced with cheap (low-cost and lacking in durability) synthetic fabrics like polyester, microplastic pollution is growing worldwide—to the point that scientific studies showed microplastics in the bloodstream of 17 out of 22 participants in a 2022 study (Osborne, 2022).

The waste of popular culture has some unexpected effects. For instance, no one seems to know what to do with old televisions, cell phones, computers, and other electronics with hazardous materials (also known as e-waste). The poorest countries become the "digital dumping grounds" for all this e-waste produced from the devices used to consume popular culture, creating tremendous health risks to some of the poorest and most vulnerable people in the world. The problem of e-waste is exacerbated by planned obsolescence. Slade (2006) explains that lightbulb and car manufacturing led the way in planned obsolescence—a "catch-all phrase used to describe the assortment of techniques used to artificially limit the durability of a manufactured good in order to stimulate repetitive consumption" (p. 5). Designers may, for instance, build imperfections into a television, setting its useful life to, say, 15 years. They may also make it very difficult (or even a violation of intellectual property) to repair goods, leaving consumers to take the easier route and buy new goods.

Planned obsolescence, as Slade concludes, is not only the result of design. It is also habitually (perhaps ritualistically, in the words of Chapter 12) reinforced through marketing, advertising, and consumer routines, whereby we become numbed to anything but single-use, disposable products. Recall the discussion of mindless social media scrolling from Chapter 3, and we see that disposability isn't limited to the devices that we engage, but also the content we consume. As social media companies continue to grow globally, the basic business model of social media demands further scrutiny. People from all over the world now produce content for YouTube, Facebook, and Instagram essentially serving as cheap labor for the platform's content. Further, this content is not simply silly videos and fun memes but also users' private information that is stored, organized, and sold for enormous profits, largely for the purpose of targeted advertising.

Fortunately, we believe, consumer advocates and small businesses are starting to hold multinational corporations accountable for the waste they produce. For instance, Apple paid $500 million in settlements in the US, and was issued a 25 million euro fine (roughly $27 million dollars) in France, after iPhone software updates caused older phones to perform slowly (Harris, 2020). A "Right to Repair" law was introduced, though not passed, in California state government in 2022. Such legislation would allow consumers to repair their technology with greater ease, either themselves or with the help of local repair shops. Secondhand influencers (like @ThriftQueenLola or @saint.thrifty) use their social media platforms to show how fashionable thrifting and vintage looks can be. And, extending our discussion of "globalization from below" above, many people are turning to digital affordances to gather ideas for repairing clothes, including over 162,000 instances of #VisibleMending on Instagram. Whether people can normalize repair over consumption, while also adapting to the global climate crisis and continued environmental injustice, remains to be seen.

In conclusion, Chapter 9 starts to navigate the globalization of popular culture, beginning with a primer on economic globalization. We considered two sides of the globalization coin, with arguments that popular culture exports are "Americanizing" local cultures around the world, while cultural hybridization can lead to unique hybrid forms of culture. Our closing case study extends the work of Chapters 2 and 3, asking each of us to consider what is in our own sphere of influence to support the carrying capacity of the Earth, which includes pop culture's role in polluting or disseminating new habits while we attempt to hold powerful entities accountable. As we turn to in Chapter 10, this is particularly important, since some popular culture producers turn to a simulated reality that may be distracting from the urgency of overconsumption.

Reflecting on globalization and popular culture in your everyday life

- Do you enjoy popular culture from outside your home country? What do you like about this popular culture? Reflect on the path that some of your favorite pop culture artifacts from outside your home country took to make its way to you. What does this path say about the networked economy described in Chapter 9?
- What concerns or interests you about American companies selling popular culture all over the world? What might make American popular culture desirable to people living in other cultures? What might make it repugnant to people living in other cultures?
- Review the distinctions between cultural hybridization, cultural hybridity, and cultural appropriation. Then, locate an example of cultural appropriation criticism on social media (e.g., posts hashtagged #CulturalAppropriation on Instagram). Do users seem to follow scholars' understanding of cultural appropriation? How so, and how do they differ?
- Find one example of cultural appropriation and one example of cultural hybridity in popular culture. What do each of these say about how pop culture producers can blend artistic forms from different parts of the world without unethically appropriating others' work?
- Chapter 9 encourages visibility to the production of popular culture, including the labor and environmental practices through which smartphones and t-shirts arrive. View Annie Leonard's *The Story of Stuff* (available as a feature-length film, or a 21-minute YouTube video from *The Story of Stuff Project*). Do you believe *The Story of Stuff* is effective equipment for living in response to the climate crisis or plastic pollution crisis? Why or why not? How might popular culture, and even you personally, be more responsive to global environmental injustices?

Suggested readings

Kang, J. (2019). Call for civil inattention: "RaceFail '09" and counterpublics on the internet. *Quarterly Journal of Speech*, *105*(2), 133–155. doi.org/10.1080/00335630. 2019.1595100

Malik, S. I. (2019). The Korean wave (Hallyu) and its cultural translation by fans in Qatar. *International Journal of Communication*, *13*, 5734–5751. https://ijoc. org/index.php/ijoc/article/view/9591/2877

Onanuga, P. A. (2020). When hip hop meets CMC: Digital discourse in Nigerian hip-hop. *Continuum: Journal of Media & Cultural Studies*, *34*(4), 590–600. 10.1080/10304312.2020.1757038

Shome, R. (2014). *Diana and beyond: White femininity, national identity, and contemporary media culture*. University of Illinois Press.

References

Arora, P. (2020, June 25). Criticism of skin lighteners brings retreat by Unilever and Johnson & Johnson. *The New York Times*. https://www.nytimes.com/2020/ 06/25/business/unilever-jj-skin-care-lightening.html

Avey, T. (2012, September 5). Discover the history of sushi. PBS. https://www.pbs. org/food/the-history-kitchen/history-of-sushi/#:~:text=In%201970%2C%20 the%20first%20sushi, dish%20spread%20throughout%20the%20U.S

Beall, A. (2020, July 12). Why clothes are so hard to recycle. BBC News. https:// www.bbc.com/future/article/20200710-why-clothes-are-so-hard-to-recycle

Bhabha, H. K. (1994). *The location of culture*. Routledge.

Brecher, J., Costello, T., & Smith, B. (2000). *Globalization from below: The power of solidarity*. South End Press.

Bruner, R. (2020, July 25). How K-pop fans actually work as a force for political activism in 2020. *Time*. https://time.com/5866955/k-pop-political/

Crothers, L. (2021). *Globalization and American popular culture* (5th ed.). Rowman & Littlefield.

Deverell, W. & Hyde, A. F. (2018). *Shaped by the west: A history of North America to 1877*. University of California Press. https://doi.org/10.1525/9780520964372

Esomnofu, E. (n.d.). How CKay's "Love Nwantiti" became the world's song. *Okay Africa*. https://www.okayafrica.com/ckay-love-nwantiti-trending-tiktok/

Ezebuiro, G. (2022, July 18). CKay Net worth, best songs, and music albums. *Buzz Nigeria*. https://buzznigeria.com/ckay-net-worth-best-songs-and-music-albums-including-love-nwantinti/

Gray, J. (2007). Imagining America: *The Simpsons* go global. *Popular Communication*, *5*(2), 129148, DOI:10.1080/15405700701294111

Hardt, M., and Negri, A. (2000). *Empire*. Harvard University Press.

Harris, J. (2020, April 15). Planned obsolescence: The outrage of our electronic waste mountain. *The Guardian*. https://www.theguardian.com/technology/2020/ apr/15/the-right-to-repair-planned-obsolescence-electronic-waste-mountain

Higson, R. (2016, October 1). Disney's *Moana* and cultural appropriation. Prindle Institute. https://www.prindleinstitute.org/2016/10/disney-moana-cultural-appropriation/

Kai-Hwa Wang, F. (2022, April 11). How violence against Asian Americans has grown and how to stop it, according to activists. PBS News. https://www.pbs.org/newshour/nation/a-year-after-atlanta-and-indianapolis-shootings-targeting-asian-americans-activists-say-we-cant-lose-momentum

Khoja-Moolji, S. (2017, November 26). Don't be quick to celebrate the hijab-wearing Barbie. Aljazeera. https://www.aljazeera.com/opinions/2017/11/26/dont-be-quick-to-celebrate-the-hijab-wearing-barbie

Kraidy, M. M. (2005). *Hybridity, or the cultural logic of globalization*. Temple University Press.

Langfitt, F. (2014, August 11) Autobot$ rule: Why *Transformers 4* is China's box office champ. *NPR*. https://www.npr.org/sections/parallels/2014/08/11/339485807/autobot-rule-why-transformers-4-is-chinas-box-office-champ

Lawson, R. (2014, October 22). Miley Cyrus has been banned in the Dominican Republic. *Vanity Fair*. https://www.vanityfair.com/hollywood/2014/08/miley-cyrus-banned-dominican-republic

Li, S. (2021, September 10). How Hollywood sold out to China. *The Atlantic*. https://www.theatlantic.com/culture/archive/2021/09/how-hollywood-sold-out-to-china/620021/

Liu, J. (2022, November 26). Apple has a huge problem with an iPhone factory in China. *CNN*. https://www.cnn.com/2022/11/25/tech/apple-foxconn-iphone-supply-china-covid-intl-hnk/index.html

May, K. (2016, May 20). A new age of animation. *The Atlantic*. https://www.theatlantic.com/entertainment/archive/2016/05/a-new-age-of-animation/483342/

Martell, L. (2010). *The sociology of globalization*. Polity Press.

Miller, T. (2008). Anti-Americanism and popular culture. In R. Higgott, R. & I. Malbasic (eds.), *The political consequences of anti-Americanism* (1st ed.) (pp. 58–73). Routledge. https://doi.org/10.4324/9780203926543

Miller, T., Aksikas, J., & Harney, S. (2012). Culture industries: Critical interventions. *Lateral: Journal of the Cultural Studies Association*, 1, https://csalateral.org/section/culture-industries/culture-industries-critical-interventions-miller-aksikas-harney/

Minter, A. (2019). *Secondhand: Travels in the new global garage sale*. Bloomsbury.

Miranda, B. (2020, October 26). "The way I am is an outrage": The Indigenous Brazilian musicians taking back a burning country. *The Guardian*. https://www.theguardian.com/music/2020/oct/26/brazil-music-indigenous-tribes-environment-bolsonaro

Okapi, D. (2016, February 26). South African artists fume over lack of radio airplay. *Music in Africa*. https://www.musicinafrica.net/magazine/south-african-artists-fume-over-lack-radio-airplay

Osborne, M. (2022, March 28). Microplastics detected in human blood in new study. *Smithsonian Magazine*. https://www.smithsonianmag.com/smart-news/microplastics-detected-in-human-blood-180979826/

Parker, R. S., Haytko, D. L., & Hermans, C. M. (2008). The marketing of body image: A cross-cultural comparison of gender effects in the U.S. and China. *Journal of Business & Economics Research*, 6(5), 55–66. https://doi.org/10.19030/jber.v6i5.2418

Pavlova, R. (2019, April 8). Globalization of American fast-food chains: The pinnacle of effective management and adaptability. *Haze*. https://globalist.yale.edu/

in-the-magazine/globalization-of-american-fast-food-chains-the-pinnacle-of-effective-management-and-adaptability/

Pew Research Center. (2012, June 13). Attitudes toward American culture and ideas. *Pew Research.* https://www.pewresearch.org/global/2012/06/13/chapter-2-attitudes-toward-american-culture-and-ideas/

Ritzer, G. (2021). *The McDonaldization of society: Into the digital age* (10th ed.). SAGE Publishers.

Romano, A. (2018, February 26). How K-pop became a global phenomenon. *Vox.* https://www.vox.com/culture/2018/2/16/16915672/what-is-kpop-history-explained).

Romano, A. (2020, October 9). A history of "wokeness." *Vox.* https://www.vox.com/culture/21437879/stay-woke-wokeness-history-origin-evolution-controversy

Rosenblatt, N. (2009). Orientalism in American popular culture. *Penn History Review*, 16(2), 51–63. https://repository.upenn.edu/cgi/viewcontent.cgi?article=1005&context=phr

Salomone, R. C. (2022). *The rise of English: Global politics and the power of language.* Oxford University Press.

Slade, G. (2006). *Made to break: Technology and obsolescence in America.* Harvard University Press.

Smith, A. (2012, December 14). Why Japan is obsessed with Kentucky Fried Chicken on Christmas. *Smithsonian Magazine.* https://www.smithsonianmag.com/arts-culture/why-japan-is-obsessed-with-kentucky-fried-chicken-on-christmas-1-161666960/

Sonnemaker, T. (2020, December 31). Apple knew a supplier was using child labor but took 3 years to fully cut ties, despite the company's promises to hold itself to the "highest standards," report says. *Business Insider.* https://www.businessinsider.com/apple-knowingly-used-child-labor-supplier-3-years-cut-costs-2020-12

Sumner, M (2020, November 30). Following a t-shirt from cotton field to landfill shows the true cost of fast fashion. *The Conversation.* https://theconversation.com/following-a-t-shirt-from-cotton-field-to-landfill-shows-the-true-cost-of-fast-fashion-127363

Wike, R. (2013, February 22) American star power still rules the globe. *Pew Research.* https://www.pewresearch.org/global/2013/02/22/american-star-power-still-rules-the-globe/

World Bank. (2019, September 23). How much do our wardrobes cost to the environment? *World Bank.* https://www.worldbank.org/en/news/feature/2019/09/23/costo-moda-medio-ambiente

10 The simulation of popular culture

Introduction

Over the last 25 or so years, popular culture seems a bit obsessed with the notion of a "false reality." In 1999, *The Matrix* became a box-office sensation with its portrayal of a dark world in which humanity exists in a computer simulation created by sinister artificial intelligence. Most famously, Neo is asked to choose between the blue pill (which represents living in the simulation) and the red pill, by which he will face the stark and brutal reality. Since then, the idea of living in a simulated or false reality seems to be everywhere in cinema (including a 2021 *Matrix* reboot), in movies ranging from compelling to cheesy: *Inception, The Adjustment Bureau, Source Code, Ready Player One, Total Recall, Serenity,* and *Vanilla Sky,* to name a few. Similarly, on TV, shows such as *Black Mirror, Upload, Made for Love, Westworld,* and *WandaVision* continue the theme of characters grappling with a false reality. Simulated realities also appear frequently in video games, comic books, advertising, and music videos, often intertextually referencing these movies and TV shows. Of course, this trend is quite unsurprising. In the 21st century, people experience simulation in many, many forms, as detailed in this chapter. Our lives are now filled with fantastic, spectacular images on screens truly everywhere we look. The "false reality" movies and TV shows listed above are ostensibly critiques of simulation, with scenes portraying characters fighting against the forces creating the fake world. Nonetheless, quite ironically, the best parts of many of these movies, video games, and TV shows (e.g., *The Matrix, Ready Player One*) are the computer-generated special effects and the amazing action sequences that occur *inside the simulation.* In other words, the simulation is actually really, really cool. This encapsulates the contemporary feelings about simulation within popular culture—we both fear it and love it.

As Jean Baudrillard (1988) argues, popular culture creates illusions compelling us to desire and appreciate images more than "real" material reality. Put differently, we willingly suspend disbelief to live in a spectacular,

DOI: 10.4324/9781003372943-10

simulated reality. In this chapter, we are offering tools to navigate a culture dominated by simulation.

We first explore the concept of simulation, looking at how digital logics, affordances, and practices work in a wide range of simulated forms. We consider the pleasures (and even psychological benefits) of simulated realities, before turning to the many concerns associated with a culture filled with simulation. Notably, Chapter 10 presents more of the "dark side" of the business of popular culture (Chapter 2), as people are regularly invited into simulated realities to deflect the harm that consuming popular culture creates in the material world. We close the chapter with a look at the growing backlash to simulation, as people trade in consuming ordinary people on social media for authentic experiences in pop culture.

Hyperreality and simulation

To help understand the idea of simulation, we want you think about the tomatoes you see in advertising. Yes, you read that correctly, *tomatoes*. In fact, take a minute and search "tomato ad" on Google. You will see an endless series of images and videos of bright red, symmetrically round tomatoes (see Figure 10.1). Of course, these tomatoes look nothing like the tomatoes (or any other vegetables) you might see in a real backyard garden. Real tomatoes have spots, are usually greenish red, and can be a lot of different shapes. Nonetheless, the next time you are at a giant supermarket, look at the pile of tomatoes in the produce section. They are probably bright red and symmetrically round.

Figure 10.1 Whole Foods commercial.

How is this possible? Literally tons of greenish, misshapen (but perfectly delicious) tomatoes are thrown out each year because they do not match the images in advertising. Further, the massive corporations that produce most of our food on huge industrial farms now genetically modify tomato plants doused in pesticides so they are bright red and spotless. In fact, these bright red tomatoes are actually significantly less flavorful without the natural sugars in the "blotchy" ones (Nguyen & Ginovannoni, 2012). Why do supermarkets usually stock these visually attractive but largely flavorless tomatoes? The popular culture representation of tomatoes is hyperreal simulation that has altered consumer's expectations of food. Our reality of a fundamental part of our lives, our food, has been radically skewed. As consumers, we now expect, even demand, photographically perfect food. In other words, consumers desire a "false" reality in which fruits and vegetables are blemish-free and visually match the illusions of advertising.

The idea of **hyperreal simulation** is primarily attributed to Jean Baudrillard. For Baudrillard, when we buy and sell the essential parts of our daily lives based on images in media such as advertising, we start to live in a kind of false or substitute reality. Think about the essential aspects of your everyday life: food, shelter, medicine, education, transportation, etc. An elaborate image-based system constructs meaning for every facet of everyday life—as noted in Chapter 2, meanings (sign-value) disconnected from the actual function (use-value) of these products and services and closely attached to the consumer's identity. The image system extends into both advertising and other forms of entertainment products such as television and social media. For instance, the image-system for homes, both the houses people purchase and home décor such as furniture and appliances, is experienced via advertising, reality TV shows (such as *Home Town*, as discussed in Chapter 3), magazines (like *Better Homes and Gardens*), and social media influencers who record videos in their impeccably decorated houses. When a viewer watches a show on the Food Network, the entire kitchen set is filled with product placements for appliances and cookware creating an image of an idealized kitchen space. Similarly, health images circulate around prescription drug advertising, medical Websites, magazines such as *Shape*, social media diet trends, etc. In both cases, people internalize this false reality and reproduce it in their own life. People work long hours in order to earn enough income to have the tasteful kitchen appliances, dishes, cookware, and countertops they see on the Food Network and reality TV. People follow fad diets and rigorous exercise routines to reproduce the photoshopped bodies they see in magazines, advertising, and in social media—not to follow fitness advice from medical experts (in fact, social media fad diets are virtually always quite unhealthy) but to *appear* healthy in photographs and videos. We then put our perfect kitchen and toned body on Instagram for others to see, in a sort of endless cycle.

From the perspective of hyperreality, most consumers no longer care about physical reality (e.g., the actual function of products such as furniture or even food and prescription drugs), what Baudrillard calls the "desert of the real," they only desire the images representing the false reality. For instance, many people would rather visit Disney's version of Paris with impeccably clean streets, predictable schedule, and English-speaking employees than visit the more historically complicated, occasionally dirty, unpredictable, and diverse *real* Paris (today, this might also be "the Las Vegas version" or virtual reality version of Paris or New York). Following Baudrillard's reasoning, when consumers think of tomatoes, they don't think of the physical produce they can hold in their hand, chew, and provide sustenance; instead they think of the *images* of tomatoes they have seen over and over, across a variety of media platforms. Most people only want the evocative, visually "perfect" tomatoes. As U2 once sang back in the 1990s (sorry to quote a bit of dad rock), it's "even better than the real thing."

The world we now inhabit involves images referencing images referencing images (what Baudrillard calls simulacrum)—endlessly. The more images reference other images, the further their meanings drift from physical reality becoming pure stimulation and desire. A search on Google for images provides both an example and a kind of practical representation of this simulation process. The search could be anything of random fleeting interest: a celebrity's new hairstyle, a basketball player's latest dunk, a fancy new sports car, etc. As a user clicks on images of interest, each image references other images, which reference other images, ad infinitum. Of course, clicking on images offers a remarkably superficial, surface-level orientation to the world. In many regards, all imagery on our screens (social media, TV shows, pop songs, news media, etc.) function in similar ways. On social media platforms such as Instagram, people post carefully selected and airbrushed selfies of themselves in idealized environments. Social media users often remove blemishes from their skin and always have a good hair day. Increasingly, in a practice that likely would have terrified Baudrillard, everyday people describe "branding" themselves on social media. Acting as an advertiser of their own lives, social media users feature their most compelling and enviable experiences such as eating at the hippest restaurants, traveling to far-away destinations, or attending the big play-off game (intended to provoke an ever-present "fear of missing out" in their peers). We have internalized simulations to such an extent we now have created a hyperreal life for ourselves filled with images of our fashionable clothing, tasteful home décor, and extravagant vacations that we circulate on social media.

Most importantly, hyperreal simulation subsumes all facets of everyday life including our social relationships and identities. In this regard, the ecology of digital media plays a role in this ubiquitous simulation. As Manovich (2001) has described, the numerical representation of digital media (i.e., the ones and zeros of binary code) allows for endless variability and alteration. We do this so frequently, it hardly seems like a big deal. We cut and paste a photo into a PowerPoint slide in seconds, stretching it out to fit the slide or cropping out the part irrelevant to the presentation. But, for people who study photography as representation of reality, this effortless manipulation of images is a *huge* deal. Many of us remember a time when a photograph or video represented a definitive reality. In the past, for generations, a photograph represented factual information and was treated as the truth. Historians carefully analyzed images of historical events and lawyers referenced surveillance photographs in legal cases. Experts carefully analyzed the photographs or filmed recordings of an event in order to discover the truth, such as the famous Zapruder film of the Kennedy assassination. We "witnessed" the terrorist attacks of September 11, 2001 as they unfolded on television.

Of course, in our post-truth world, photographs and videos are far from definitive truth. Today, people can continually tinker with a photograph (or song, movie, etc.) pixel by pixel until they get the perfect version they desire (e.g., altering an image of a magazine cover model to fit an idealized notion of beauty). Anyone can easily manipulate a photograph to create whatever reality they prefer—you broke up with your boyfriend, just remove him from the family photos of the holidays. Utilizing software powered by artificial intelligence, deep fakes, or doctored images that are convincingly real can alter videos of anyone to get them to say or do almost anything (Appel & Prietzel, 2022). A deep fake can depict a famous pop star engaged in a sex act, the president provoking a nuclear war, or a prominent politician appearing intoxicated in public (as occurred with a widely circulated video of Nancy Pelosi in 2019). A world of simulation, untethered to reality, has endless possibilities for better and for worse.

The pleasures of simulation

Unlike Baudrillard's dystopian view (it probably comes as no surprise that *The Matrix* franchise was heavily influenced by his writings), in everyday life simulated reality can provide a wonderful escape and opportunities for genuine social connection. For instance, movies and video games are more pleasurable when capable of immersive simulation. As we argued through the turn to uses and gratifications theory, as well as cultural studies, in Chapters 3 and 5, people are not "dupes" tricked into living a false reality through popular culture. There are some very good reasons to enjoy simulation.

The fear of experiencing the unreal or fantastical is, in some contexts, unwarranted. Fantasy and make-believe are truly fundamental to human life.

Cultures all over the world role-play by wearing masks and costumes. Theatre has existed for thousands of years, across the globe, transporting people into fantastical worlds. Reality, much like identity (see Chapter 4), is actually not a unitary absolute but socially constructed, malleable, and context-specific. Perhaps more fundamentally, psychologists believe children need make-believe play for healthy development of language, identity, emotional expression, empathy, and divergent thinking, among many other benefits (Kaufman, 2012). If you spend any time with children between two and nine years old engaging in open-ended pretend play, you will likely see them role-playing as Disney princesses, NFL quarterbacks, superheroes, or some other form of popular culture. Not only does this play not deserve great concern, psychologists are imploring parents to give contemporary "over-scheduled" children more time for open-ended pretend play with peers.

Further, simulation in popular culture is not especially new. Classic stories such as *Alice in Wonderland* and *The Wizard of Oz* involve a kind of simulated reality. All film and television, and video games for that matter, are a kind of illusion, a sort of magic trick (Duncum, 2021). From the earliest movies shown in nickelodeons, viewers watched films with a sense of wonder and magic. From the earliest days of film around 1900, filmmakers were experimenting with special effects such as stop-motion animation to create images of spaceships and Cinderella's pumpkin transformed into a carriage. In other words, as long as film has existed, audiences have flocked to see a false reality.

Over time, special effects evolved allowing for new types of immersive illusion (Duncum, 2021). 3D movies, which create the illusion of three dimensionality, became quite popular in the early 1950s but were quickly relegated to a kind of niche novelty associated with cheesy horror movies, until relatively recently. The massive 2009 blockbuster *Avatar*, which has grossed nearly three billion dollars worldwide, offered a more immersive form of 3D that dazzled audiences. Immediately after *Avatar*'s historic success, a wave of 3D movies were released. In short, when a movie presents are truly great magic trick, such as *Avatar*, it becomes a sensation. In fact, looking over the top grossing movies of all time, adjusted for inflation, the list is filled with movies that offered fantastic images with cutting-edge special effects bringing the audience into exciting new worlds such as the parting of the Red Sea (*The Ten Commandments*), children flying on bikes (*E.T.*), an ancient chariot race (*Ben Hur*), and a violent shark attack (*Jaws*). In fact, throughout film history, for the biggest blockbusters, audiences have often flocked to see a movie's spectacular special effects, even more so than the story, characters, or other cinematic qualities (calling back to Chapter 8).

Simulation can also offer unique forms of communal experiences. On some level, simulation offers a form of pretend play, not unlike how children can imagine being star basketball players or heroic Jedis with their friends.

Elaborate virtual worlds in games such as *Second Life* offer players opportunities to create new identities and live in fantastic environments with others (not unlike the psychological benefits to children). Psychologist Sherry Turkle found that computer simulation games offer opportunities for role playing with tremendous psychological benefits for understanding one's self and reflecting upon personal issues (Turkle, 1994). Similarly, cosplay, or costume play, in which fans can dress and act as their favorite movie or TV character, also can improve body image and self-esteem and even diminish anxiety and depression for the cosplay performer (Muller, 2021). In short, participating in a simulated reality can be both an entertaining escape filled with wonder and magic, as well as an opportunity for self-exploration. Yet, as noted in the introduction, people still feel uneasy about living in a culture filled with simulation. Next, we explore how the production techniques of digital technology may account for some of this uneasiness.

Digital affordances and popular culture production: From simulated perfection to spectacle

The production of popular culture has changed radically, particularly in the transition from analogue recording techniques to digital recording techniques. For example, for most of recorded music history, the goal was to create a recording that captured the best live performance of the musicians. Equipment was expensive and required specialized engineers. Only the most successful artists, such as the Beach Boys, Beatles, or Pink Floyd, could afford the time-consuming and expensive process of experimenting with sounds via new recording techniques or extensively recording take after take to finally get a "perfect" version. Digital recording techniques offered opportunities to easily and cheaply splice many performances together as well as create more synthetic, experimental, or artificial sounds. More specifically, versions of autotune software are routinely used in the recording and performing of popular music (Tyrangiel, 2009). Autotune uses digital technology's ease of automation, which allows users to quickly apply a template to a new document, video, image, or, in this case, song. Every time we create a new Microsoft Word document or PowerPoint presentation, we are working within templates of automation. Using automation, the software corrects "errors" in the singer's pitch to remain "perfectly" in tune. Some creative musicians such as Bon Iver and T-Pain have used autotune in explicitly obvious ways to create a very robotic, synthetic sounding song. More commonly, producers use autotune in subtle ways that are invisible to the listener. Now, virtually all pop songs carefully adjust the singer's voice to remove moments that are even slightly out of tune.

The use of autotune in the recording industry has been compared to the use of photoshop by advertisers and magazine publishers as it is ubiquitous and has created an expectation of "perfection" (Tyrangiel, 2009). Much like the uniformly attractive models on fashion magazine covers, the consumer simply gets used to only hearing impeccably pitched singing voices. Listening to pop radio today, all the autotuned voices sound quite similar with uniformly perfect pitch. It seems hard to imagine the unique and idiosyncratic voices of previous eras such as Neil Young, Joni Mitchell, Kurt Cobain, Axl Rose, and Alanis Morissette on pop radio today. The unintended consequence is that singers literally cannot sound perfect like their studio recordings (much like models cannot look their images) in their live concerts. Because audiences now expect perfect vocal performances, the vast majority of pop music performers use a combination of backing tracks and live autotune software to also sound perfect in their live concerts (Kachka, Milzoff, & Reilly, 2016). In this regard, many live concerts are a simulation (prerecorded tracks or autotuned live vocal) of a simulation (and autotuned studio recording). In some cases, such as Ashley Simpson on *Saturday Night Live* or Mariah Carey on New Year's Eve 2016, singers have struggled to lip sync along with the backing track and faced public embarrassment and ridicule on social media. Interestingly, people seemed most offended by their inability to maintain the *illusion* of the perfect live vocal performance, rather than revolting against the revelation of the common practice of lip syncing/ backing vocal tracks in live performances. In other words, people seemed largely bothered by the singer's poor effort at *simulating* a live performance.

Digital techniques have also radically altered the movie industry. When the technicians at Industrial Light and Magic (ILM) developed computer software to create photorealistic dinosaurs for the movie *Jurassic Park* in 1993, everything changed. Specifically, ILM, who were to technical wizards behind the special effects for pretty much all the major 1970s and 1980s blockbusters such as the *Stars Wars* franchise, the *Indiana Jones* franchise, *E.T.*, the *Back to the Future* franchise, and *The Goonies* completely overhauled their operation (as detailed in the documentary *Light & Magic*). Instead of a warehouse filled with plastic models and stop-motion animators, they shifted to offices filled with computers. Of course, these computer-generated effects were often dazzling, creating walking and talking photorealistic bears (*Paddington*) and apes (*Planet of the Apes*), and even alternate dimensions (*Dr. Strange*) and worlds (*Avatar*). Further, computer-generated imagery (CGI)— which is used in almost all studio movies to some extent—is often used in much more subtle and seamless ways, adding tears to an actor's performance (*Blood Diamond*), making a city's buildings historically accurate (*Zodiac* and *Once Upon a Time in Hollywood*), and adding fans to the stadium of a sporting event (*The Fighter*). On the other hand, developers of CGI have struggled with the "uncanny valley," especially with images of the human face. Because humans are so attentive to subtle nonverbal cues of people's faces, we are especially unnerved when faces seem weird or off. For instance, whenever films try to recreate photorealistic faces, such as in *The Polar Express* or *The Irishman*, they seem strange and alien. Even movies with giant special effects budgets have struggled to replace deceased actors with a digital version (such as *Rogue One*), for even a few minutes of screen time without entering the uncanny valley. These CGI faces look too perfect, lacking the distinctive (and imperfect) details that make each human face look unique. A bit like autotuned voices, CGI takes away the uniqueness of each individual face, which is unnerving to the viewer. For this reason, human characters in computer-animated movies from studios such as Pixar now have obviously cartoonish facial qualities, with huge eyes and massive round faces, to allow audiences to read them as cartoons and not photorealistic faces. This is also why CGI aliens, animals, or spaceships sometimes seem just a bit *too perfect* and not quite "real."

When images reference other images limitlessly (rather than physical reality) the simulated versions tend to ramp up toward greater and greater spectacle. Because imagery in popular culture is based on drawing interest to gain downloads, sell movie tickets, generate likes, etc. in a competitive economic marketplace, the simulated images tend to gravitate toward greater and greater spectacle, outrageousness, and intensity over time. In short, simulation trends toward greater and greater sensory stimulation (recall Chapter 8). As Guy Debord (1994) argued, **spectacle** is best understood as a kind of worldview immersed in commodified fragmented images (built on the practices of advertising) altering cultural expectations and social relations of everyday life. The now ubiquitous special effects in Hollywood movies clearly represent the trending toward greater sensory stimulation altering cultural expectations. For instance, from 2017 to 2022, the three highest-grossing movies of each year (e.g., *Avatar: The Way of Water, Avengers: Endgame, Jurassic World, Star Wars: The Last Jedi*, and *The Fate of the Furious*) all prominently featured spectacular visual effects. But, going back to the 1980s and 1990s, the year's top-grossing movies were sometimes special effects driven spectacles but they were also quite often romantic films (*Pretty Woman* and *The Bodyguard*), broad comedies (*Three Men and a Baby* and *Home Alone*), and earnest dramas (*Rain Man* and *Platoon*) with almost no spectacular special effects. In a generation, these relatively simple, character/story-driven movies have been pushed to margins in the film industry replaced by the franchised spectacles of the 21st century (which, as discussed in Chapter 7, are referenced endlessly, intertextually). Similarly, art forms once defined by their sparse simplicity and direct human emotions have been transformed into sensory stimulating spectacle. For instance, the stage play was historically characterized by a minimalistic focus on human experience (think of *Death of a Salesman* or *Hamlet*); today, it has been transformed into the visually stimulating effects of the highest-grossing non-musical play in Broadway history: *Harry Potter and the Cursed Child*.

The quiet contemplation of viewing paintings is transformed into crowded, noisy, multimedia art museum exhibits featuring "blockbuster" Impressionists such as Monet who are marketed like one-name iconic pop stars such as Drake, Beyoncé, or Madonna. A series of successful traveling exhibits have projected massive images of the paintings of Van Gogh, Dalí, or Da Vinci, with elaborate multimedia audio visual shows (produced by Grande Experiences). The actual physical paintings are not present, only the simulated images projected onto massive screens. Confirming Debord's assumptions, foundational aspects of cultural meaning-making, cultural symbols, and storytelling are largely expressed via the sensory stimulation of spectacle. While such twists can be explained through the media logic of digital technology, the ways that the trends seem to suffocate out other possibilities makes the concepts of simulacrum and spectacle so important.

Within the worldview of simulation and spectacle, consumers now fill their home with giant high-definition televisions with surround-sound systems. The spectacular images of contemporary movies, sporting events, and television demand technologies suited to sensory stimulation. The *average* size of televisions continues to grow each year now topping 50 inches (Chandler, 2019) with the purchase of 65-inch televisions and larger growing at the fastest rate.

Perhaps the complete embrace of the worldview of spectacle is best represented in something deeply meaningful to many people: family holiday traditions. In many neighborhoods, decorating the family home for Christmas and Halloween has evolved from a few strings of lights and a plastic snowman to a multimedia event with hundreds of lights and synchronized music (see Figure 10.2). Businesses have emerged that decorate people's homes in the latest holiday styles. People explain that these elaborate decorations help them "get into the holiday spirit" or make it "feel like the holidays." This intuitive common sense is what Debord means by a worldview that seeps into our consciousness and becomes our reality—to desire commodified spectacle is simply a "natural" feeling in the contemporary culture. For instance, performing spectacular gestures, posted onto social media, for a child's birthday party, an invitation to prom, the announcement of an *in utero* baby's sex, etc. are entirely unsurprising in the present culture. The media logic of digital media, especially social media, encourages spectacular performances to solicit likes, retweets, etc. In this regard, individual users have completely internalized the worldview of spectacle.

When spectacular reality meets business and politics

As noted in the introduction to this chapter, media consumers appear to be struggling with the pleasures and anxieties of simulation. In short, many people are uncertain how to navigate a world that prominently features

Figure 10.2 Spectacular Christmas decorations. Hannamariah/Shutterstock.

simulated realities. For instance, cultivation theory, developed by George
Gerbner, argues that media, particularly television, depicts a false reality
(Gerbner, Gross, Morgan, Signorielli, & Shanahan, 2002). So, when viewers regularly watch television, especially those who watch over four hours
a day, they falsely perceive the TV reality as the real world. In other words,
the more time someone spends in the television world, the more it becomes
their reality. Most prominently, television, with an emphasis of spectacle
(see above), depicts a world filled with violent crime. Importantly, this
isn't any specific genre, network, or streaming service; television as an in-
stitution depicts a world filled with violence. Whether someone is watching news, reality TV, nighttime dramas, true crime docuseries, sports, or
even cartoons, the world appears especially and disproportionately violent. Over time, watching a lot of TV compels viewers to genuinely believe
they are at great risk of being the victim of a violent crime (even when
statistically the risk is quite minimal). Most significantly, a wide range of
research studies confirm that over time the images and ideas we regularly
see in media become our perceived, and often false, reality. For instance,
true crime docuseries and podcasts have become incredibly popular in recent years. These series are designed to be binged, so frequently people will
consume hours in a row. How does someone's view of the world change
after watching hours of murder and rape over many, many weeks? Does
the world start to look like a dangerous place filled with violent crime?

Further, recalling the discussion of identity in Chapter 4, if viewers disproportionately see African Americans engaging in violent crime or Arab Americans associated with terrorism on television, how might this skew their perception of these cultural groups?

For Baudrillard, simulation is most dangerous when representing a false reality for life and death situations, such as war. For many Americans, recent military conflicts, such as the wars in Iraq and Afghanistan, were largely experienced via stylized images of heroism and technological sophistication created in cooperation with the defense department. For instance, the original *Top Gun* was credited with increasing recruitment to the Navy by 500% (Rose, 2022). Since *Top Gun*, military agencies now regularly cooperate with Hollywood producers to write and produce movies (e.g., the *Transformers* franchise, *Captain Marvel*) that serve as a kind of recruiting video for the armed forces. For most Americans, we prefer the heroic, sanitized versions of war in big-budget Hollywood movies to the gritty, confusing, messy, and terrifying *reality* of war. If we experience war as a glamorous and airbrushed Hollywood movie, are we less apt to protest when political leaders advocate for armed conflict? Remote drone strikes, which are depicted in popular culture as clinically precise and low-risk, clearly represent a kind of simulated warfare. In an effort to disrupt this false, sanitized image of war, artists created a giant 100 by 70 foot tarp depicting a child killed in a drone strike (the artwork is referred to as #Notabugsplat in reference to the how the victims look to remote drone operators) (Drazner Hoyt, 2014).

When reality is based on images referencing other images with no concern for the physical world, a person's reality becomes the images circulating around their phones, computers, and televisions. Specifically, politics, once the arena of debate between stuffy intellectuals and pundits, has merged with entertainment as another option to pass the time when scrolling on social media or clicking through cable television. In fact, political media is big business. Fox News is the number one cable network (Joyella, 2023) emphasizing partisan political talk of its magnetic anchors. Prior to his departure from FOX, Tucker Carlson drew more than four million viewers nightly and earned the network $108 million in ad revenue in 2020 alone (Barr, 2020). Partisan political content is frequently retweeted and shared, therefore essential to the stickiness of social media platforms (Whitaker, 2022). In fact, disinformation (i.e., conspiracy theories) is the content that attracts the most eyeballs. Disinformation thrives in this simulated world of popular culture. For this reason, spreading false information for one's political or economic gain, known as disinformation, has grown dramatically across social media and cable news. Much of this disinformation is in the form of conspiracy theories or stories that emphasize secret powerful forces ("them") with an elaborate scheme designed to destroy "our" way of life.

For instance, recent conspiracy theories have involved sinister plots to manufacture the COVID-19 pandemic by a faceless, sinister other (e.g., Chinese government) that seeks to destroy the freedom of hard-working Americans. Thinking back to Chapter 7's discussion of intertextuality, memes and other image-based iconography referencing imagined (and imaged) others are especially effective at creating fear of these dangerous others. While some of this disinformation might seem wildly implausible to outsiders, such as the conspiracy theory that Hillary Clinton ran a sex-trafficking ring from a pizza restaurant, when the sensational images reference similar sensational images endlessly, the false reality becomes all too real to the media consumer. For instance, in 2021, a poll discovered that 15% of Americans believed "levers of power are controlled by a cabal of Satan-worshiping pedophiles" (Russonello, 2021). In particular, as sensory-stimulating spectacle, conspiracy theories function as a kind of entertainment media on YouTube. Once drifting down the rabbit hole of conspiracy theories, based on Google's automated algorithms, similar videos will play endlessly on a loop continuously re-confirming the disinformation. We live in a simulated world with thousands of YouTube users believing the Earth is really flat, the United States government orchestrated the 9/11 attacks, and the genocide of the Jewish people by the Nazis was a hoax. In a clear response to the spread of disinformation, a jury decided that Alex Jones must pay the families of Sandy Hook victims nearly a billion dollars for spreading conspiracy theories about the shooting, particularly that it was staged and a hoax. For this jury, the simulation seemed to demand a disruption.

As you might imagine, the vast amounts of simulation have been associated with cynicism, meaninglessness, and polarization. The advertising practice of greenwashing represents the massive chasm between illusory simulation and physical reality. Companies who have ravaged the Earth depict themselves with images of environmentalism. Shell oil company claims to be "sustainable" (Dean, 2020). Hefty trash bags are "recyclable" (when they actually contaminate the soil), Nestlé has "sustainably sourced chocolate" (with no changes in their production process), and low-gas mileage Ford Trucks are "clean" and "environmentally friendly." More importantly, the advertising for these products feature picturesque mountains and oceans and prominently emphasize green logos with leaves/trees/earths (as an experiment, look around a grocery store and notice how many green logos on are products that often have an enormous carbon footprint). While many consumers prefer the illusion to the reality, others become disillusioned and cynical. Everything seems to be based on lies and deception, therefore people feel their world is "post-truth" and literally meaningless. In the case of the sustainability, if everyone is spreading false information about environmental issues, consumers stop believing anyone and simply choose the habits that provide the greatest convenience and pleasure.

Conclusion: Authenticity as backlash to simulation culture

In the spirit of Stuart Hall's resistant readings and critical rhetoric (discussed in Chapter 3), some media consumers are rejecting the ubiquitous simulation of contemporary popular culture. Instead of seeking meaningless stimulation, consumers appear to be seeking (and perhaps even producing) greater authenticity. This is similar to the response to MTV's spectacular hyperreal simulation in the 1980s. Grossberg (1992) described the highly successful careers of Bruce Springsteen and John Mellencamp as "authentic" rock stars (living in small towns, wearing blue jeans, writing their own songs based on personal experience, etc.) in contrast to the more stylized pop stars of the era such as Madonna and Michael Jackson. Today, in a similar trend, some consumers are drawn to the authenticity of the highly politically engaged rap of artists such as Kendrick Lamar, the Americana music of artists such as the Avett Brothers, and the nostalgia for 1960s and 1970s of artists such as Bob Dylan and, once again, Bruce Springsteen. Instead of the elaborate multimedia stage shows of contemporary pop stars such as Justin Bieber and Beyoncé, these artists have bare stages and minimalist lighting and are among the biggest concert draws over the last decade. Perhaps in response to these trends, artists such as Taylor Swift have produced more folk-inspired albums in a singer-songwriter style. Even Lady Gaga, known for her spectacular multimedia live performances, engaged in a "dive bar" tour in 2016 in which she performed on a bare stage without choreographed dancing and elaborate lighting.

Further, social media hashtags, such as #nonairbrushed me, #Iamall-woman, and #effyourbeautystandards have increasingly focused on circulating non-airbrushed images of people with diverse body types, hair textures, skin tones, etc. A number of organizations (e.g., misfits market) now collect "imperfect" fruits and vegetables discarded by supermarkets to deliver to people's homes. Increasingly, consumers are resisting ubiquitous simulation by seeking out authentic, non-simulated experience. In addition, these consumers demonstrate the power of self-reflexivity and awareness—that despite the powerful institutions of popular cultural production, ultimately consumers can powerfully influence the production and values of popular culture. Further, the very technologies that promote hyperreal simulation can also be used as a means of resistance.

Some audiences and filmmakers are now preferring "practical effects" or special effects that only use material objects and real actors over CGI techniques. The massively popular John Wick films emphasized real actors in elaborately choreographed fight scenes that feel incredibly real and physical. Further, in response to the *Star Wars* prequels which were widely criticized for their overuse of CGI that created a cartoonish quality to many of the effects, in the *Force Awakens*, JJ Abrams used more practical effects involving models and other physical objects to bring back the immediacy of the first three *Star Wars* movies. For many of these filmmakers, CGI can have a kind of unreal "weightless" quality that actually pulls the viewer out of the reality of the film.

In some respects, the growth of micro-influencers also demonstrates a desire for more grounded, real popular culture. The most popular social media influencers are so integrated with sponsorships and brand partnerships, they seem fake, or, essentially, too simulated. Micro-influencers, or social media performers with more specialized interests and smaller, but loyal audiences, can limit their sponsorships to products more directly tied to their specialized interest and not seem like a corporate shill. For instance, a YouTuber focusing on horseback riding can be sponsored by saddles, boots, or other products they actually prefer to use. More importantly, their authenticity as a credible member of a specialized community provides the currency for their loyal viewers. Micro-influencer videos are often simply produced, without the bells and whistles of the most successful "macro" influencers. It is these simple and direct qualities that provide a desired authentic alternative to the sensational spectacle of simulation.

Simulation can also compel us to aspire to a better reality, such as in the case of science fiction. Most notably, the Afrofuturism movement involves artists, academics, and activists imagining a world in which the Black community is free from oppression, especially via futuristic technology. In this tradition, *Black Panther* depicted an alternate history in which an African country had the most advanced technology and lived free of colonialism and other oppressive conditions. Afrofuturism is credited with inspiring protests against the many forms of White supremacy, especially summoning hope during times of great hopelessness and despair (Crumpton, 2020). In other words, when created by thoughtful artists, simulation can be aspirational by imagining an alternative world that we feel inspired to build.

Finally, especially during the worst of the COVID-19 pandemic, neighbors, friends, and family gathered outside in backyards for movies projected on big screens. These events were not primarily about getting lost in the simulation of the movie. These experiences were primarily communal events for authentic socializing. In fact, our kids would sit on our porch with their friends (socially distanced) playing our mobile Nintendo Switch. These simple, local events demonstrate an important facet of popular culture—it can bring people together in authentic communal experiences. We can share a collective experience with strangers at a sports bar as our local basketball team advances in the play-offs. We can dance with other families at an outdoor concert in a park in our neighborhood listening to a live, semi-professional cover band playing 1980s hits. Most significantly, during the lockdown, people had plenty of opportunities to simply drift into the simulation of popular culture. Instead, whenever it was safe and possible, people sought out genuine communal experiences that were missing when staring at the high-definition screens inside our homes.

In this chapter, we explored the role of simulation in popular culture. Today, spectacular simulated imagery is ever-present in advertising, movies, and even politics. Nonetheless, while embracing the pleasures of simulation, consumers simultaneously seem drawn to more authentic communal experiences suggesting a deep ambivalence concerning the false reality of popular culture. The groundwork of simulation prepares us to venture into the special terrain of games in popular culture in Chapter 11.

Reflecting on the simulation of pop culture in your everyday life

- Look at the media you consume every day, and identify some examples of digital perfection discussed in Chapter 10, such as photoshopped or airbrushed images, autotuned music, computer-generated special effects in film. Do you believe that digital production of pop culture "adds up" to a hyperreal simulation? Why or why not?
- Spend a moment reflecting on the most authentic, meaningful parts of your life, perhaps friendships, family, spirituality, community, the social or political causes you are passionate about, maybe even your work or hobbies. Are these parts of your life touched by hyperreal simulation in pop culture? How? How can simulation and spectacle be integrated into authentic human relationships? How might popular culture (hyperreal simulation or authentic) relate to these parts of your life?
- Does the hyperreal simulation and spectacle of popular culture reflect your core values? Why or why not? How might the idea of simulation and spectacle affect your pop culture consumption?
- View the film *The Matrix* or/and *Black Mirror* "Nosedive" (season 3, episode 1), both of which are prominent portrayals of a hyperreal spectacle in pop culture. How do these representations illustrate and deviate from the ideas presented in Chapter 10? Do you believe that representations like *The Matrix* and/or "Nosedive" represent equipment for living for us as we navigate popular culture today? Why or why not?
- How do we disrupt the thinking of people who have internalized a simulated reality with self-destructive or harmful behaviors, such as unhealthy body image standards or violence inspired by conspiracy theories?
- Do you believe that authentic popular culture is "enough" to combat the harms of hyperreal simulation, like greenwashing or conspiracy theory?

Suggested readings

Cloud, D. L. (2006). *The Matrix* and critical theory's desertion of the real. *Communication & Critical/Cultural Studies, 3*(4), 329–354. DOI: 10.1080/14791420600984243

Frentz, T. S., & Rushing, J. H. (2002). "Mother isn't quite herself:" Myth and spectacle in *The Matrix. Critical Studies in Media Communication, 19*(1), 64–87.

Kelly, C. R. (2020). *Apocalypse man: The death drive and the rhetoric of white masculine victimhood.* Ohio State University Press.

Stahl, R. (2010). *Militainment, Inc.: War, media, and popular culture.* Routledge.

Womack Y. (2013). *Afrofuturism: the world of black sci-fi and fantasy culture.* Lawrence Hill Books.

References

Appel, M., & Prietzel, F. (2022). The detection of political deepfakes. *Journal of Computer-Mediated Communication, 27*(4). https://doi.org/10.1093/jcmc/zmac008

Barr, J. (2020, August 29). Why Fox News pays a price to stick by Tucker Carlson. *Forbes.* https://www.forbes.com/sites/jonathanberr/2020/08/29/why-fox-news-pays-a-price-to-stick-by-tucker-carlson/?sh=7a5bbfa1ba9c

Baudrillard, J. (1988). Simulacra and simulations. In M. Poster (ed.), *Jean Baudrillard: Selected writings* (pp. 166–184). Stanford University Press.

Chandler, S. (2019, August 27). Why TVs are getting bigger and bigger. Forbes. https://www.forbes.com/sites/simonchandler/2019/08/27/why-TV-screens-are-getting-bigger-and-bigger/

Crumpton, T. (2020, August 24) Afrofuturism has always looked forward. *Architectural Digest.* https://www.architecturaldigest.com/story/what-is-afrofuturism

Dean, B. (2020, February 9). The five: Ads banned for greenwashing. *The Guardian.* https://www.theguardian.com/technology/2020/feb/09/the-five-ads-banned-for-greenwashing

Debord, G. (1994). *The society of the spectacle.* Zone Books.

Drazner Hoyt, K. (2014). Ethics of network subjectivity. *Technoculture, 4.* https://tcjournal.org/vol4/hoyt/

Duncum P. (2021). *Popular pleasures: An introduction to the aesthetics of popular visual culture.* Bloomsbury Visual Arts.

Gerbner, G., Gross, L., Morgan, M., Signorielli, N., & Shanahan, J. (2002). Growing up with television: Cultivation processes. In J. Bryant & D. Zillmann (eds.), *Media effects: Advances in theory and research* (pp. 43–67). Lawrence Erlbaum.

Grossberg, L. (1992). *We gotta get out of this place: Popular conservatism and postmodern culture.* Routledge.

Joyella, M. (2023). Fox News Channel's 'The Five' is the most-watched show in cable news. Forbes. https://www.forbes.com/sites/markjoyella/2023/01/24/fox-news-channels-the-five-is-most-watched-show-in-cable-news/?sh=3c704ddf4880

Kachka, B., Milzoff, R., & Reilly, D. (2016, April 3). 10 tricks that musicians and actors use in live performances. Vulture. https://www.vulture.com/2016/03/live-performance-tricks.html

Kaufman, S. (2012, March 6). The need for pretend play in child development. *Psychology Today.* https://www.psychologytoday.com/us/blog/beautiful-minds/201203/the-need-pretend-play-in-child-development

Manovich, L. (2001). *The language of new media.* The MIT Press.

Muller, R. (2021, December 2). Becoming another person through cosplay. *Psychology Today.* https://www.psychologytoday.com/us/blog/talking-about-trauma/202112/becoming-another-person-through-cosplay

Nguyen, C., and Ginovannoni, J. (2012, June 28). Why supermarket tomatoes taste like cardboard. NBC News. https://www.nbcnews.com/id/wbna48003432

Rose, S. (2022, May 26) Top Gun for hire: Why Hollywood is the US military's best wingman. *The Guardian.* https://www.theguardian.com/film/2022/may/26/top-gun-for-hire-why-hollywood-is-the-us-militarys-best-wingman

Russonello, G. (2021, May 27). QAnon now as popular in U.S. as some major religions, poll suggests. *The New York Times.* https://www.nytimes.com/2021/05/27/us/politics/qanon-republicans-trump.html

Turkle, S. (1994). Constructions and reconstructions of self in virtual reality: Playing in the MUDs. *Mind, Culture, and Activity, 1(3),* 158–167. DOI: 10.1080/10749039409524667

Tyrangiel, J. (2009, February 5). Auto-Tune: Why pop music sounds perfect. *Time.* http://content.time.com/time/subscriber/article/0,33009,1877372,00.html

Whitaker, B. (2022, November 6) Social media's role in America's polarized political climate. CBS News. https://www.cbsnews.com/news/social-media-political-polarization-60-minutes-2022-11-06/

11 The games of popular culture

Introduction

Games are more popular than ever. In many ways, we live in a culture filled with forms gaming. In November of 2022, *Call of Duty: Modern Warfare 2* sold $800 million worth of copies in three days, the largest video-game opening in history (Tassi, 2022). Further, these sales surpassed the opening weekends of two highest-grossing movies of the year, *Top Gun: Maverick* and *Doctor Strange in the Metaverse of Madness*, combined. The mobile game *Candy Crush Saga* has been downloaded over 2.7 *billion* times. Overall, video games expanded to $181 billion in revenue in 2021 (Browne, 2022) which dwarfs the revenue of the movie and music industries. In fact, two-thirds of Americans play video games (Muriel & Crawford, 2018). Board games have also grown in popularity, with billions in sales in 2021 alone. Gambling, which is largely in the form of gaming, generated $53 billion in revenue in the United States alone. While games have always been a part of human life, today, games seem to be everywhere, all the time. Even our everyday talk is sprinkled with words and phrases originally emerging from gaming: leveling up, cheat code, glitch, aggro, noob, Easter eggs, boss, etc.

In this chapter, we seek to understand why games are so popular, and why this popularity, at times, makes people uncomfortable. The academic area of game studies has exploded across many disciplines over the last two decades (see Suggested Readings), but in this chapter we focus on a few areas to help better navigate games as an ever-present form popular culture. Video games seem to have exploded because of trends we've discussed in prior chapters, including digital media logic (Chapter 1), convergence and branding (Chapter 2). But as we unpack in the first section, video games reflect the unique traits of games, including fixed rules, variable and quantifiable outcomes, and programming so player effort affects the outcome of the game or story. Indeed, though video games are one of many forms of popular culture, games as a whole are worthy of extended attention because

DOI: 10.4324/9781003372943-11

of the effects that "gamification" has had on popular culture surrounding them. As we discuss in subsequent sections, games have been used toward good and ill, just like other popular culture forms in the book. Games are engaging and immersive, and can build community; but many worry about the potential for games to inspire hyper-competitiveness, violence or become addictive. Through an extended discussion of "dangerous games," readers leave Chapter 11 with a clearer understanding of how the qualities of games influence our experience of popular culture, for better and for worse.

Games defined

Humans have played games for millennia, all over the world. The Royal Game of Ur was the first board game, played over four thousand years ago in Mesopotamia and Go, invented in China over 2,500 years ago, continues to be played today (Solly, 2020). While the definition of a game varies (incidentally, in a very stereotypically academic way, people keep debating these definitions) most academics agree that **games** have a few general characteristics: (1) fixed rules, (2) variable and quantifiable outcome, (3) player effort affects outcome (adapted from Juul, 2003).

To understand these three characteristics, consider a few turning points in the evolution of video gaming. The first publicly available games such as *Pong* involved obvious identifiable *fixed rules*, as the Atari controller allowed players to move a simple white line up and down to bounce a "ball" (circle) back and forth in a ping-pong simulation. In other words, players easily recognized the clear limitations and boundaries of the game as the choices were limited to a few simple movements. As arcade games became popular, the *variable and quantifiable outcomes* became the focus, as players competed for the "high score" in *Pac Man* or *Donkey Kong* which was prominently listed at the start of the game with the player's initials. In early arcade games, simple decisions such as moving right, left, up, or down and precisely timed jumps determined if the ghost gobbled up your Pac Man or a barrel knocked the avatar off the platform. The documentary *King of Kong* details the long-running debate about which player, Billy Mitchell or Steve Wiebe, in fact has the highest score ever on *Donkey Kong*. In fact, debates about the highest score of any video game are entirely debates about the *quantifiable outcomes* of the game.

As home gaming consoles such as Nintendo and PlayStation joined the machines developed as pay-to-play arcade games, video games became more sophisticated (as players could play for hours at a time in their homes) requiring greater *player effort*. The online game *EverQuest* emerged in the 2000s and was playfully described as "Evercrack" because player effort was so intensive that players would literally lose days in the complexities of the game. In particular, player effort affected the strength of the player's character or avatar, compelling people to continue playing the game to develop the strongest possible character. We will discuss these large-scale online role-playing games more below; but for now, it's also interesting to note that affordances like home gaming systems add to *EverQuest*'s immersive qualities, allowing people to play in their pajamas for hours on end (which was not as available through a quarter-arcade machine model of gaming). Today, after decades of trial and error, game designers perfectly calibrate the rules, variable outcomes, and necessary player effort for their targeted audience. Games can be developed for younger children to play easily (*Mario Kart*), to be played with a few minutes of effort (*Angry Birds*), or for highly skilled gamers seeking the greatest challenge (*Eldest Souls*).

Nonetheless, not all games are popular culture. If you give a group of kids a simple bouncy ball and a large flat surface, within a few minutes they can create a game with fixed rules and a way to tally points (although they may start arguing over the rules after someone wins). For most of human history, games were largely folk traditions (see Chapter 1) shared orally with rules agreed upon and handmade objects for the game-play. For instance, variations of playing cards have emerged all over the world over hundreds of years (now standardized with 52 cards including the King, Queen, etc.) (Parlett, N.D.). There are thousands of games developed from a standard deck of playing cards, many of which developed uniquely in a particular region of the world. Even today, with much greater standardization due to the Internet and mass-produced printed rules, various versions of gin rummy, euchre (our family called it buck euchre), pitch, and pinochle are played in particular geographic areas. Similarly, the game Monopoly existed decades before it was sold in stores with rules shared across local communities and household objects for game pieces. Games, already a populist form enjoyed by masses of ordinary people, become popular culture as they become commodified and mass produced. In the case of Monopoly, when Charles Darrow sold the rights to the game he "invented" (despite evidence it was originally conceived by Lizzie Magie), Parker Brothers mass produced and packaged the game board and pieces with the printed rules to be sold in toy stores (starting in 1935)—becoming popular culture. Over the decades, too, Monopoly illustrates how games work with branding and remediation, as Monopoly crossovers in McDonald's prize giveaways, and with various types of Monopoly (e.g., National Parks and *Harry Potter* Monopoly) reinvigorating the brand. The game has sold over 275 million units over time (Leopold, 2015).

Gaming as community

One of things people love about games is how they bring people together in community. As noted above, cultures all over the world play games and have played games for centuries. Games are part of cultural rituals bringing people together in public life. Some version of board games, designed to be played with others as a communal activity, existed in the ancient world in Egyptian, Russian, Scandinavian, Roman, Mayan, and Chinese cultures, to name just a few. Today, these ancient rituals continue with table-top gaming tournaments growing in popularity and cafes designed for board gaming popping up around North America (Kirtley, 2019).

At the heart of games is play and experimentation, which are two important dimensions of learning, especially for children. Cultures often use games as a way to teach children community values such as discipline and teamwork. Even other animals, such as kittens, use play to learn important skills such as hunting (Mayra, 2008). Learning a game in a community demonstrates the inherent collaborative meaning-making at the root of a lot of game play. We might give a friend a "do-over" or "practice round" while playing a new board game and bend the rules for children who do not fully understand the game's complexity. We also might reprimand an adult becoming too competitive in a game played with children or at a couple's game night intended more for socializing than intense competition (e.g., someone who exclaims, "in your face!" when correctly naming a Pictionary doodle).

Even simple mobile games are often highly communal and ritualistic. Games can be kind of binding agent for social experiences particularly as people sometimes feel a sense of disconnection from their local community. For instance, in the summer of 2016, the mobile video game *Pokémon Go* became a global sensation. In fact, "Pokémon Go soon became the most popular mobile game in U.S. history, attracting over 25 million users in the country a week after its release" (Yang & Liu 2017, p. 52). During the days after its first release, *Pokémon Go* had more users than Twitter and more engagement (i.e., time spent) than Facebook (Perez, 2016). Why was *Pokémon Go* so successful, even compared to other mobile applications? The game itself had simple graphics and not especially interesting game play qualities, although the novelty of the quasi-augmented reality interface (with the characters superimposed on the phone's screen via the camera) certainly accounted for some of the interest in the game (see Figure 11.1).

Most distinctly, as a game that used location-based data, it required players to get out of their house and travel to public spaces like parks and museums to "capture" Pokémon. The game brought people into public life and, as we noticed playing the game with our daughter, conversations with strangers looking for the same Pokémon. Somewhat unexpectedly, *Pokémon Go* helped rebuild community ties by compelling positive emotions about people's local community (Oleksy & Wnuk, 2017, p. 6).

Similarly, at the height of the COVID-19 pandemic lockdown, many people turned to video games to feel a sense of community while stuck inside their homes. For families, such as ours, a Nintendo Switch became indispensable with evenings filled with wonderful escapes into *Mario Kart* or *Overcooked*. Our son discovered *Legends of Zelda: Breath of the Wild*,

Figure 11.1 Game play of *Pókemon Go*. Wachiwit/Shutterstock.

which he would play with friends masked and socially distanced on our porch as well as participate in online gaming communities offering strategies and funny videos online (one Zelda YouTuber "Mr. A Game" has hundreds of thousands of followers). We weren't alone as many others described video gaming as a refuge from the pandemic that offered some semblance of social experiences and community life (Huertas, 2021). In particular, the game *Animal Crossing* was massively popular during the pandemic providing opportunities to reproduce social experiences via the player's avatar, especially with other players online (Huddleston, 2020). Most significantly, in *Animal Crossing*, the game play is slow and almost meditative as the characters engage in everyday activities such as collecting food, cooking, and shopping while interacting with others reproducing the rhythms of daily life.

In fact, despite stereotypes of isolated individuals as gamers, *most* video games have a strong social dimension. Most notably, massively multiplayer online role-playing games (MMORPGs), such as *World of Warcraft*, are quite popular, involving in-game collaboration in groups (guilds or clans) (Kocurek, 2014). In addition to solving problems collaboratively within the objectives of the game, MMORPGs also have significant social dimensions outside the boundaries of the game play with players staging weddings, funerals, and other events. In other words, people are clearly playing these games to meet their social needs.

Gaming is often broken into two categories: casual gamers and "hard core" gamers (Mayra, 2008). Like other fan communities, conventions gather thousands of "hard core" gamers together in community. Further, as discussed with fandom in Chapter 5, video-game communities have a kind of ranking system with clear markers of prestige and status. The currency of gaming is often the player's performance, which is precisely measured in the numerical outcomes of the game (remember *Donkey Kong*), built on the principles of interactivity.

Games as interactive

Digital technology is well suited to games as its binary code inherently involves fixed rules with numerical values. Some of the first applications of computers, beyond simple mathematical computation, dating back to the 1950s, were games (e.g., chess, computer tennis, etc.). Games, especially video games, are by design interactive requiring choices from the user (Landay, 2014). In this regard, a game's interactivity is much more engaging to many people than watching a TV show or movie, helping explain the enormous popularity of gaming. Interactivity is a kind of dialogue between the user and the computer program in which the user makes choices or selections, and the software responds. Simply, video games require effort from the players as nothing happens unless the user continues to make choices.

Today, even the most complex games with brilliant photorealistic graphics have the same basic structure of numerical representations or binary code that ultimately reduces game play to a "this or that" logic. Binary logic or "forced choice" architecture is evident in the constant choices presented in video games: should the basketball player shoot or pass, should the soldier fire her weapon or duck behind a building, should I aim my Angry Bird up or down, etc., that define interactivity. Importantly, elements of interactivity are now part of most popular culture experiences. We interact with the Spotify app to choose music (e.g., an artist or song) and create a playlist. We interact with YouTube with each selected video. As noted in Chapter 2, the algorithms of media platforms are designed to respond to the choices of individual users curating new content. Perhaps in the ultimate this or that logic, the dating app Tinder's interface reduces choosing romantic partners between swiping a profile picture either right or left.

While games tell stories—and one could imagine a spark of identification motivating someone to move Link around *Legends of Zelda*—narrative approaches really don't account for the experience of gaming (Mayra, 2008). The term ludology was coined to emphasize the experience of interactive game play, rather than storytelling, to explain why people return to games again and again. In other words, games involve "meaning making through playful action" rather than decoding messages, which is how we experience most TV and movies (Mayra, 2008, p. 19). For instance, movies are often experienced as narratives (see Chapter 6) with the viewer "decoding" the motivations of the characters or the generic characteristics (e.g., anticipating the female lead will ultimately fall in love in the romantic comedy).

On the other hand, the player of the video game is focused on the actions of the avatar, pressing the correct buttons to jump or shoot at the exact correct moment to complete the goal, through trial and error (or perhaps following a gamer on Twitch or discussing in a game forum online). Video games are essentially interactive puzzles to be solved. While stories have certainly improved for video games from the days of Atari, the details of the story told in cut scenes (a non-playable animated storytelling sequence) are quickly skipped by many players to get back to the interactive game play, especially when re-playing the game. In other words, most people play games for long periods of time not because they love the story but because they love the interactive game play. People lose track of time playing games, especially video games. Have you or someone you know spent an entire weekend playing a video game? It is hard to imagine watching TV or movies for 48 continuous hours. A couple of factors account for the pleasure of playing interactive video games for long periods of time: flow and mastery.

Flow is the experience of being totally immersed in an activity. Artists and athletes, such as painters and rock climbers, describe experiences of losing track of time while engaging in their activities of expertise. Csikszentmihalyi (1990) describes nine elements associated with flow: challenges and skills that are high and in balance, clear goals and feedback, concentration on a task, deep (but effortless) involvement, a sense of control, the loss of self-consciousness, and the sense of the duration of time is altered. Flow is most effectively achieved when goals are clear and feedback is immediate (Shernoff & Csikszentmihalyi, 2009). The feedback, clear goals, and sense of control of video gaming produces flow-like experiences for gamers. In particular, since the first arcade games such as *Pac Man* and *Donkey Kong*, game designers have made each level that is unlocked by completing some objective or goal slightly more challenging than the previous level. As each level is unlocked, the player continues to be challenged at the degree that remains within their present skills.

In video games, interactivity provides a powerful sense of control. The game prompts the player to manipulate the controller to move the player's avatar (themselves) to act, altering the outcome of the game in the feedback loop of the game's algorithms. In fact, the player seeks to "master" the game by leveling up, in the language of gaming. The convention of leveling originally emerged from video-game designers' desire to have players plug "more and more quarters in the arcade machine" with "the revelation of the new level the reward for having survived and mastered the previous environment" (Jenkins, 1998, p. 264). While video games are now mostly played on gaming consoles, laptops, and phones, the convention of leveling up remains a part of most video games. In fact, whether through the highest score or final level, video games have a kind final, perfect outcome that demonstrates complete mastery (Juul, 2003). Later in this chapter, we will explore the compulsive playing of video games as a source of worry among some. In the next section, we explore the unique prestige bestowed on e-gamers who achieve these lofty quantifiable outcomes.

Games as business

As noted above, games are *very* profitable. In fact, gaming has branched into a number of unique revenue streams, most notably esports. Esports, or watching competitive video gaming as a spectator sport, has grown in revenue to an estimated one billion dollars a year (Shapiro, 2020). Many esports events fill large stadiums with the competitive video game players treated like rock stars (see Figure 11.2). Further, fans watch their favorite gamers play video games on platforms such as Twitch, with some gamers such as PewDiePie or Markiplier gaining millions of viewers. Further, YouTube is filled with videos of gameplay with players offering real-time commentary. For other gamers, the most successful esports competitors represent the highest level of skill (not unlike Michael Jordan or Tom Brady), at the highest levels of competition.

Figure 11.2 Esports tournament. Roman Kosolapov/Shutterstock.

On the other end of the gaming spectrum are the mobile games such as *Fruit Ninja* that millions of people play on their phones every day. These simple games, usually easy enough for young children to play, are designed to be played for a few minutes at a time during moments of boredom: a barrage of bright watermelons, strawberries, oranges, limes, etc. launches into view, and the gamer must slash them at just the right time with their "sword" (their finger on the touchscreen). Watch out for the bombs! Most of us think of mobile games as silly ways to pass the time while we are waiting for a train or an appointment. These "silly" games are actually incredibly profitable. For instance, King, the company that makes the *Candy Crush* games, was sold for $5.9 billion (Handley, 2021). This is more than Disney paid for Marvel or LucasFilm. Why would the *Candy Crush* games be considered more valuable than the companies that own the *Star Wars* and *The Avengers* franchises and merchandising rights? Like social media giants, much of this revenue comes from gathering and selling users' personal information including location data (Fowler, 2022). This is especially significant as many of these games are played in large numbers by children. Mobile games, such as *Angry Birds*, collect users' behavioral information via gameplay, even predicting if the users are depressed, impulsive, or dieting based on their gaming activity. Further, these games partner with third-party advertisers tracking the users' behavior and using predatory ad targeting practices (Tiffany, 2019). In other words, the unique pleasures of gaming (e.g., community, flow, and mastery) can be monetized in unique ways.

Because of these unique qualities, game design is now spreading into some pretty unexpected domains of everyday life. **Gamification** is "the use of game design elements in non-game contexts" (Deterding, Dixon, Khaled, & Lennart, 2011, p. 22). Again, game design involves fixed rules, variable and quantifiable outcomes, and player effort. These basic qualities are now integrated into countless mobile apps. For instance, children's educational experiences now involve digital games integrated into school curriculum. In elementary school, our children used iReady, one of many web-based interactive educational platforms, in which students complete "levels" by answering questions all with a cartoonish video-game-style interface. At the end of each level, a numerical score is offered as an outcome which is used by the student's teacher for assessment. The value of gamification can be tremendous. People report losing large amounts of weight, exercising more frequently, or easily learning a new language with gamification apps. One of our kids learned to play the piano quite well in several months with an iPhone app based on gamification. Similarly, health and fitness apps use similar numerical outcomes (tracking physical activity, calories consumed, etc.) and leveling in a video-game-like design. Headspace, which has 70 million users (Anand, 2021), offers a gamified experience for, of all things, meditation. Visually, the app uses colorful cartoonish images and animation reminiscent of mobile gaming apps. The app enlists notification reminders as well as aphoristic quotations about the benefits of meditation. As a gamification process, the app provides a running total or minutes spent meditating and uses leveling within meditation packs. Most meditation packs, such as anxiety and self-esteem, have 30 sessions broken into ten daily units referred to as "levels." The user is congratulated when completing each ten pack, as though mastering a level of a video game. Further, the "run streak" (consecutive days meditating) is prominently displayed at the start each session. In the media logic of digital technology, even the ancient mindfulness practice of mediation can be gamified.

At its most dangerous, gamification is an extension of neoliberal capitalism (discussed in Chapter 9), encouraging mindless productivity and consumerism serving the interests of giant corporations (Muriel & Crawford, 2018). More and more organizations are using gamification by integrating software in a game-like design to have employees compete for rewards by tracking productivity or even healthy lifestyle choices (to reduce the organization's health insurance costs). These systems are essentially powerful surveillance tools providing real-time data concerning employee productivity and daily activities, recording and quantifying every second of the employee's workday.

Further, so called "adver-gaming" is a game developed for the sole purpose of advertising a brand (de la Hera, 2019). Advertisers have been experimenting with games as far back as the 1930s with simple board games published in magazines such as a Planters Peanuts board game. An astonishing array of companies have developed adver-games including Johnson & Johnson, Purina, Coke, Pepsi, and Dominos. Especially effective are simple online games that offer players, especially children, colorful and fun games prominently featuring Cheetos or Burger King. Research suggests adver-games create a positive brand association by linking the product with the pleasures of gaming—and, as we discussed in Chapter 2, marketing to children is considered especially effective, as it can create a longer-term positive feeling for brands. Adver-gaming is now integrated into social media apps such as McDonald's partnership with Farmville (incorporated into the Facebook platform) which offered unique rewards when players visited the McDonald's farm. Today, product placement and brand partnerships dominate the most popular games. Nike hosted a virtual live concert in the online game *Fortnite* in 2019. As noted above, "free" games for mobile phones prominently feature highly targeted ads (Sharbatian, 2020). Gatorade's brand partnerships and product placement in sports games led to a 24% increase in sales. Because players tend to play games over and over again, the brand recognition and positive associations tend to be higher than other forms of advertising (Martí-Parreño, Bermejo-Berros, & Aldás-Manzano, 2017). In short, gaming is big business, getting more profitable every year. As video games move toward greater immersiveness, the potential applications and markets seem almost limitless.

Games as immersive

Games can immerse players in another world. For the time playing the game, the player exists within the rules and logic of the game, rather than typical conditions of everyday life. In this regard, playing a game can offer the unique pleasures and psychological benefits of simulated reality described in Chapter 10. **Immersion,** which is the feeling of being completely surrounded by the game like being submerged in water, flourishes from two interrelated dimensions: psychological engagement and illusion (Therrien, 2014).

First, *psychological engagement* involves many gameplay and narrative qualities that fully absorb the player. As noted above, video games can offer the experience of flow in which the user feels lost in the experience. Further, games can involve complex characters and stories such as *The Legends of Zelda*, with a storyline and characters that extends across 29 games over almost 40 years (not including the books and online materials). In other words, the game designers build a world that is believable and authentic, from the specific details of clothing and objects to the motivations of the characters in the narrative. For instance, the classic role-playing game *Dungeons and Dragons* can be quite immersive if the dungeon master (the game organizer who creates the adventure) provides rich details to the players. These rich details so complexly engage the player psychologically they are fully immersed in the experience.

Today's console video games can involve incredibly detailed fantasy worlds (*Elden Ring*) and historical contexts (the *Call of Duty* franchise). In particular, sports games are often among the most popular console video games. These games tend to follow the principles of the first blockbuster sports video-game franchise, *Madden NFL* developed by Electronic Arts (EA). When the game developers at EA approached the former coach and popular TV announcer John Madden to be the face of their new NFL video game in 1989, he agreed only if the video game included all the complexities of a real NFL game. Before *Madden NFL*, sports games simplified football or basketball in their game play, even reducing basketball from ten players to four (*NBA Jam*) and football from 22 players to 18 (*Tecmo Bowl*). Accepting Madden's demands, EA included all the details of a real NFL game including a full playbook of defensive and offensive plays, penalties, audibles, injuries, and other elements left out of other games. Instead of an overcomplicated game that bored players, the details actually immersed players in the game play, becoming one of the most successful video-game franchises of all time generating over four billion dollars in revenue (Krum, 2022).

Second, the process of creating *illusion* produces immersion primarily through stimulating the senses, allowing a user to suspend disbelief and engage the game as though it is a real environment. As discussed in Chapter 8, video games and the televisions, stereos, speakers that accompany them can use affordances like vivid visual and sound design, 3D movements, ultra-high definition, surround sound, etc., to engage the senses and enlist the body of gamers.

Perhaps the best example of illusion through sensory immersion is virtual reality (VR). Most of us think of people flailing around in those goofy over-sized headsets when we think of VR. Virtual reality is the process of creating presence or "the perceptual illusion of nonmediation" (Riva, 2007). In other words, mere simulation crosses into true VR when the user completely forgets they are in a mediated space and is totally involved in the new environment. Using visually and aurally immersive VR technology, users can become lost in the experience. Thinking back to the discussions of sensation (Chapter 8) and simulation (Chapter 10), communication scholars believe that reality is co-constructed with others. Our reality is simply the meaning we attribute to our sensory experiences. With VR, our senses (especially sight, sound, and touch) experience an alternate reality intensifying popular cultural experiences. At this point, the chapter could turn into some wild science-fiction projections about the disruption of existence due to VR. We have been promised the virtual reality "revolution" for decades but, in truth, very few people use it regularly. Even Facebook's massive investment into their "metaverse" VR environment appears to be the latest virtual reality disappointment. In short, while it is likely that VR will continue development, no one (not even tech billionaires) seems to know when and what it will look like.

Instead of speculating about VR in the future, we will discuss it in terms of trends in popular culture moving toward more immersive experiences. Building on Chapter 10, many everyday technologies are moving in the direction of greater immersive presence. Televisions are getting larger and larger with more vivid, ultra-high definition screens offering video gaming, TV, and movie experiences far more immersive than even five years ago. Audio is increasingly experienced with rich surround-sound speakers or immersive headphones. Movies are displayed in large-screen formats (IMAX) reaching 75 feet tall and 100 feet wide. Sports stadiums have mammoth high-definition screens at live sporting events and concerts, such as the 160-foot long screen at the Dallas Cowboys stadium. Video-game designers are working tirelessly toward ever more photorealistic imagery that more closely reproduces human visual perception (Therrien, 2014). Further, many popular games, such a *Grand Theft Auto* and *The Elder Scrolls*, feature vast and detailed universes that many players enjoy simply exploring outside of the games' organized missions. The gameplay of motion-tracking games such as *Just Dance* and *Switch Sports* involve a full body experience, reading the physical movement of the player, and allowing the player to feel as though they are dancing or playing in the imagined environment animated on screen. The encouragement of games to toggle between realities, though, comes with concern, as we consider in our closing case study.

Conclusion: Games as dangerous?

Games have a kind of stigma. Perhaps it's the association with childhood, but games are often seen as trivial and silly wastes of time. Further, gamers have been marginalized through stereotypes like the nerd playing video games in their parents' basement. Academics were slow to seriously study games, and to this day, even despite the centrality of games, continue to justify their research to other academics. Of course, as noted above, games have many benefits and are played by an astonishingly diverse group of people. But video games continue to evoke public fear and dread, especially as games grow in popularity.

As prior chapters have explored, whenever a new medium or pop culture form grows in popularity, especially for children, people tend to get worried, and take that worry public. In 1954, Congressional hearings addressed the role of violent comic books on "juvenile delinquency." In 1972, the Surgeon General published a five volume report concluding that television violence has "adverse effects" on members of the society. In 1985, the PMRC hearings addressed the concerns over graphic sexual and violent pop music lyrics, especially in rap songs (Fisher, 2020). Of course, today, worries over violent video games, as well as addiction to gaming, are the subjects of great concern. Like comic books in the 1950s, TV in the 1970s, and pop music in the 1980s, kids love video games. But is there a connection between video games and violence?

This question often gets asked in a more specific form, given the epidemic of gun violence in the US (which has risen to such a level of frequency and concern that experts advocate viewing gun violence as a public health crisis, akin to the COVID-19 pandemic, which generated government measures to protect the community's health: see Ranney, 2021). Do video games inspire gun violence? Since the mass shooting at Columbine High School in Littleton, Colorado in 1999, journalists and political figures often ask if there is a causal relationship between violent video games and gun violence. Immensely popular "first-person shooter" games such as *Call of Duty* and *Halo*, in which the gameplay is from the perspective of a soldier shooting a gun, are especially under scrutiny. Because these games reward players (by leveling up) for shooting other characters, critics argue, such games encourage shooting strangers in real life.

The concerns of gun violence notwithstanding, studies have failed to find a causal relationship (Mills, 2020). From a media ecology perspective, we suggest that desires to solve gun violence through seemingly simple solutions, like banning first-person shooter video games, miss the point that we live in a deeply gamified culture. A better conversation around video games might engage questions like: when do video games best (and least) serve communities and individuals? How can we play games that enrich our lives in more meaningful ways?

With that being said, we believe that the unique combination of immersion, flow, and the compelling desire to master the next level can be a highly compulsive experience—and one which we should unpack more as a community. Compulsive gaming has many qualities of addiction, as some players are unable to control or limit their game playing which damages their personal relationships and health (Luker, 2022). A particularly toxic combination involves the ability to gamble via gamified apps such as DraftKings, which had revenue in 2021 of over a billion dollars (Yahoo Finance, 2022). Of course, merging two compulsive activities (gaming and gambling) into one app holds unique dangers for users. As more and more of our everyday life experiences become gamified, the potential for unhealthy gaming habits deserves our attention.

As people continue to process the addictive qualities of gaming, we caution against simple binaries and overgeneralizations. As this chapter demonstrates, gaming can enhance community relationships, encourage healthier everyday habits, and generate problem-solving skills, among many other benefits. At the same time, gaming can become an alienating, compulsive activity with embedded values of competitive (sometime violent) mastery and neoliberal productivity. As we assess gaming in our culture, we should always discuss the unique values and experiences associated with specific games and gaming behaviors, championing gaming practices that benefit our culture while questioning gaming that appears to promote dangerous behaviors.

One particularly concerning trend is gamifying military operations in the US military. Here, the interface of advanced military weapons, particularly remote drones, are eerily similar to video games. As one drone operator explained, drone operation "is a lot like PlayStation … Oh, it's a gamer's delight" (Pugliese, 2017). Drone operators sometimes actually switch between video games and drone operation on the same console during missions. The military routinely uses video games in their recruitment of new soldiers. The military even patterned drone operation controls after video game console controllers to more easily train soldiers raised on video games. What are the ethics of such realities, where a game interface is enacting public fears, where actual military operations are being carried out through a game design? What are the dangers of technology ending up in the hands of rogue actors? Studies also raise concerns about the psychological consequences of drone operators who engage in combat remotely, showing that they face post-traumatic stress disorder (PTSD), adjustment disorder, burnout, and other consequences like veterans who experience immediate combat (see Saini, Raju, & Chail, 2021). So as concerning as first-person shooter games can be to some, the reality of gamified war in the US military is an ethically fraught application of gaming that demands public attention.

Similarly, when considering the dangers of gaming, we suggest concerned communities look to the compulsion to master the game (versus causal connections between video games and violence). Protagonists in games still tend to be White men, heroically and violently dominating others through competition, which raises complex questions about representations of identity (see Chapter 4) as well as underlying cultural values. In contrast to gamifying toxic masculinity, some critics see real possibilities for open-ended, collaborative non-competitive gaming, referred to by Frasca (2003) as "paidia" games. These "sandbox" games, such as *Minecraft*, offer more creative outcomes and unique forms of collaboration. In other words, the variable outcome of the game is not a score ranking players in a hierarchy but rather a creative work. Such games may further blur the lines between producer and consumer, with outcomes that might one day exceed the game itself.

Reflecting on the games of pop culture in your everyday life

- How do specific games and/or types of games enrich the quality of your life? How might games inhibit your relationships or your personal well-being?
- Knowing that popular culture serves individuals and groups of people as equipment for living, how do you see games as beneficial for yourself or your community? What video games, for instance, have the potential to support your community through times of difficulty, and why?
- What specific games or types of games do you fear as dangerous? Why?
- In what ways do you see "gamification" happening in other aspects of popular culture or daily life? Do you find gamification to be effective? How so, or how not? Do you find gamification to be ethical? How so or how not?
- As games have expanded into nearly every dimension of everyday life, young people today experience much of their life (social experiences, education, music, health, etc.) in the form of gamification. What are the potential consequences of experiencing everyday life as a competitive game with clearly measured rankings of performance?
- How might the gaming experiences of flow and mastery be exploited by developers? What does it mean for corporations to profit from potentially compulsive or self-destructive behavior? What does it mean for government entities like the US military to use gaming experiences to recruit and design combat experience?

In conclusion, we've considered games as a ubiquitous, profitable, and unique form of popular culture throughout Chapter 11. Like other forms of popular culture, we considered how games help build community, and engage players through an interactive choice architecture, as well as an immersive sensory experience. As we close this chapter, we return to media ecology as offering a more complex and organic view of how humans make use of popular culture like games. Defying simple cause–effect relationships, media ecology invites us to ask how well first-person shooter games, for instance, serve the community, or even more particularly, whether they are used ethically as design features in contexts like military operations. Similarly, do gaming affordances serve the interests of community and individuals when applied to gambling? We invite readers to ask media ecology style questions as we turn to the spaces of pop culture.

Suggested readings

Cassell, J. & Jenkins, H. (Eds.) (1998). *From Barbie to Mortal Kombat: Gender and computer games* (pp. 262–297). MIT Press.

Wolf, M.J.P., & Perron, B. (Eds.). (2014). *The Routledge companion to video game studies* (1st ed.). Routledge. https://doi.org.unco.idm.oclc.org/10.4324/9780203114261

References

Anand, P. (2021, August 21). Meditation App Headspace to merge with Blackstone-backed Ginger. Bloomberg. https://www.bloomberg.com/news/articles/2021-08-25/meditation-app-headspace-acquires-blackstone-backed-ginger

Browne, R. (2022, July 7). Video game sales set to fall for first time in years as industry braces for recession. CNBC. https://www.cnbc.com/2022/07/07/video-game-industry-not-recession-proof-sales-set-to-fall-in-2022.html

Csikszentmihalyi, M. (1990). *Flow: The psychology of optimal experience.* HarperCollins.

De la Hera, T. (2019). *Digital gaming and the advertising landscape.* Amsterdam University Press.

Deterding, S., Dixon, R., Khaled, R., & Lennart, N. (2011). From game design elements to gamefulness: Defining gamification. *Proceedings of the 15th International Academic MindTrek Conference: Envisioning Future Media Environments* (pp. 9–15).

Fisher, A. (2020, September 19). 35 years ago the Senate held hearings on rock lyrics. It was a First Amendment showdown for the ages. *Business Insider.* https://www.businessinsider.com/35-years-pmrc-rock-lyrics-senate-tipper-gore-frank-zappa-2020-9

Fowler, G. (2022, June 9). Apps and kids privacy. *Washington Post.* https://www.washingtonpost.com/technology/2022/06/09/apps-kids-privacy/

Frasca, G. (2003). Simulation versus narrative: Introduction to ludology. In M. Wolf & B. Perron (Eds.), *The video game theory reader* (pp. 221–237). Routledge.

Handley, L. (2021, January 6). Riccardo Zacconi: Hitting the sweet spot. CNBC. https://www.cnbc.com/riccardo-zacconi-hitting-the-sweet-spot/

Huddleston, T. (2020, June 2) How 'Animal Crossing' and the coronavirus pandemic made the Nintendo Switch fly off shelves. CNBC. https://www.cnbc.com/2020/06/02/nintendo-switch-animal-crossing-and-coronavirus-led-to-record-sales.html

Huertas, K. (2021, June 2) The games that got us through the pandemic. *Washington Post.* https://www.washingtonpost.com/video-games/2021/06/02/video-games-covid-19-pandemic/

Jenkins, H. (1998). Complete freedom of movement: Video games as gender play spaces. In J. Cassell & H. Jenkins (Eds.), *From Barbie to Mortal Kombat: Gender and computer games* (pp. 262–297). MIT Press.

Juul, J. (2003). The game, the player, the world: Looking for a heart of gameness. Digital Games Research Association. http://www.digra.org/dl/db/05163.50560

Kirtley, D. (2019. December 21). Board games are getting really, really popular. *Wired.* https://www.wired.com/2019/12/geeks-guide-board-games/

Kocurek, C. (2014). Community. In M. J. P. Wolf & B. Perron (Eds.), *The Routledge companion to video game studies*. Routledge. https://doi.org.unco.idm.oclc.org/10.4324/9780203114261

Krum, R. (2022, July 21). 10 ways DMs can make their D&D games more immersive. CBR. https://www.cbr.com/dnd-dms-make-games-more-immersive/

Landay, L. (2014). Interactivity. In M.J.P., & Perron, B. (Eds.), *The Routledge companion to video game studies*. Routledge. https://doi.org.unco.idm.oclc.org/10.4324/9780203114261

Leopold, T. (2015, March 19). Monopoly: At 80, it just keeps Go-ing. CNN. https://www.cnn.com/2015/03/19/living/feat-monopoly-80th-anniversary/index.html).

Luker, E. (2022, July 1). Are video games, screens another addiction? Mayo Clinic. https://www.mayoclinichealthsystem.org/hometown-health/speaking-of-health/are-video-games-and-screens-another-addiction

Martí-Parreño, J., Bermejo-Berros, J., & Aldás-Manzano, J. (2017). Product placement in video games: The effect of brand familiarity and repetition on consumers' memory. *Journal of Interactive Marketing, 38*(1), 55–63. https://doi.org/10.1016/j.intmar.2016.12.001

Mayra, F. (2008). *An introduction to game studies.* Sage Publications. https://ebookcentral.proquest.com/lib/unco/detail.action?docID=448458.

Mills, K. (2020, March 3). APA reaffirms position on violent video games and violent behavior. APA. https://www.apa.org/news/press/releases/2020/03/violent-video-games-behavior

Muriel, D., & Crawford, G. (2018). *Video games as culture: Considering the role and importance of video games in contemporary society* (1st ed.). Routledge. https://doi.org.unco.idm.oclc.org/10.4324/9781315622743

Oleksy, T. and Wnuk, A. (2017). "Catch them all and increase your place attachment!" The role of location-based augmented reality games in changing people – place relations. *Computers in Human Behavior, 76*, 3–8.

Parlett, D. (n.d.). Playing cards. *Encyclopedia Britannica.* https://www.britannica.com/topic/playing-card

Pugliese, J. (2017, September 15). How drones are gamifying war in America's casino capital. https://blogs.lse.ac.uk/usappblog/2017/09/15/how-drones-are-gamifying-war-in-americas-casino-capital/

Ranney, M. (2021, March 30). We must treat gun violence as a public health crisis. *Time.* https://time.com/5951001/gun-violence-public-health-crisis/

Riva, G. (2007). Virtual reality and telepresence. *Science, 318*, 1240–1242.

Saini, R. K., V K Raju, M. S., & Chail, A. (2021). Cry in the sky: Psychological impact on drone operators. *Industrial Psychiatry Journal, 30*, S15–S19. 10.4103/0972–6748.328782

Shapiro, A. (2020, January 8). Esports posts its first billion dollar year. NPR. https://www.npr.org/2020/01/08/794704377/esports-posts-its-first-1-billion-year

Shernoff, D. J., & Csikszentmihalyi, M. (2009). Flow in schools: Cultivating engaged learners and optimal learning environments. In R. Gilman, E. S. Huebner, & M. Furlong (Eds.), *Handbook of positive psychology in schools* (pp. 131–145). Routledge.

Sharbatian, A. (2020, May 22). The power of product placements in gaming: Tapping into the virtual world. Forbes. https://www.forbes.com/sites/forbestech-council/2020/05/22/the-power-of-product-placements-in-gaming-tapping-into-the-virtual-world/?sh=6f5114b823ae

Solly, M. (2020, February 6). The best board games of the ancient world. *Smithsonian Magazine.* https://www.smithsonianmag.com/science-nature/best-board-games-ancient-world-180974094/

Tassi, P. (2022, November 1). 'Call of Duty: Modern Warfare 2' Destroys records with $800 million opening weekend. Forbes. https://www.forbes.com/sites/paultassi/2022/11/01/call-of-duty-modern-warfare-2-destroys-all-records-with-800-million-opening-weekend/?sh=4e84f5541a9a

Therrien, C. (2014). Immersion. In M. J. P. Wolf & B. Perron (Eds.), *The Routledge companion to video game studies* (1st ed.). Routledge. https://doi.org.unco.idm.oclc.org/10.4324/9780203114261

Tiffany, K. (2019, May 14) Angry Birds and the end of privacy. *Vox.* https://www.vox.com/explainers/2019/5/7/18273355/angry-birds-phone-games-data-collection-candy-crush

Yahoo Finance (2022, February 18). DraftKings reports fourth quarter revenue of $473 million. https://finance.yahoo.com/news/draftkings-reports-fourth-quarter-revenue-120000960.html

Yang, C. and Liu, D. (2017). Motives matter: Motives for playing Pokémon Go and implications for well-being', *Cyberpsychology, 20*, pp. 52–57.

12 The spaces of popular culture

Introduction

Typically, when people talk about the *meaning* of a movie, like Pixar's *Coco*, they stay within the boundaries of the screen: the story, characters, acting, music, direction, etc. without much discussion of where and when they watched the movie. But, the context (place, people present, time of day, type of device, etc.) in which you watch a movie profoundly changes the experience, and meaning, of the movie (or any other popular culture artifact). For instance, a couple might go to the local cineplex to see *Coco* on their first date, sharing a bucket of popcorn. A parent may watch the movie shoulder-to-shoulder with their child on an iPhone on an airplane trip to see a dying relative. *Coco* might be on at a family hair salon while a fidgety six-year-old gets a haircut. Maybe a family watches the movie on a giant inflatable screen at their local park with a few hundred neighbors talking and eating throughout. Finally, *Coco* might be a favorite movie to watch curled up in bed with the flu as a sort of popular culture chicken soup. Regardless, the time and place of popular culture consumption is enormously important to the experience but is too often overlooked in discussions emphasizing narrative, intertextuality, or even identity.

This chapter explores the physical context in which popular culture is experienced, and the influence of popular culture on physical environments. Media ecology suggests that media extend into new developments—so while it would seem that laptops and smartphones simply appeared, this chapter sees today's WiFi, high-definition televisions and Bluetooth speakers as extensions of television's appearance in the living room (which is an extension of the radio's appearance in homes). To better prepare ourselves to navigate the spaces of popular culture, we introduce readers first to the method that many academics use to study popular culture spaces and places: the ethnographic approach which relies on careful observation in rich, vivid detail, looking to how people experience a space (without confining themselves to a space's intended purpose). As we consider

DOI: 10.4324/9781003372943-12

throughout the chapter, ethnographic approaches recognize the communal experiencing of popular culture in both banal and remarkable occasions, preparing us to more self-reflexively engage the artifacts we choose.

We use an ethnographic approach to look at the rituals of large events experienced in public spaces, like sports arenas, to appreciate popular culture's repetitive, almost transcendent connection to our lives. We then "go small," looking at the ways domestic spaces, including their routines and norms, relate to popular culture. In almost opposition to the transcendent qualities of stadium sports and warm routines in our homes, we consider how many dynamics of business (Chapter 2) and spectacle (Chapter 7) are materially transforming environments into non-places. Shopping malls, airports, and franchise restaurants reflect generic standardization, leading to the penultimate realization of the spaces of popular culture—theme parks. As our closing case study, Black Friday shopping rituals, begs: how do we create authentic communal experiences in highly commodified, simulated places? Readers leave Chapter 12 with an appreciation for how space influences popular culture, leading to more thoughtful choices around the design and use of spaces relative to popular culture.

Introducing an ethnographic approach to popular culture

As we have mentioned, popular culture research has often emphasized social scientific approaches that use surveys and experiments to study media (e.g., uses and gratifications, cultivation theory) and critical approaches that use political and philosophical perspectives to draw attention to injustices and power imbalances associated with popular culture (e.g., ideology, hegemony, hyper-reality). Both approaches offer valuable insights, as prior chapters have shown. But both social scientific and critical approaches tend to deemphasize popular culture in its immediate, natural environment of consumption by either creating artificially controlled conditions through questionnaires and experiments (social science) or abstracting experiences into broader ideological, structural conditions (critical).

In contrast to these approaches, **ethnography** situates popular culture in everyday life, encouraging the researcher to observe and record the activities of real people in real situations. Usually, ethnographers get to know the people they are observing, even participating in all the participants' everyday cultural activities (eating, talking, laughing, dancing, etc.). Many of us are most familiar with studying "other" cultures, such as when ethnographers (often from North America and Europe) traveled around the world to rural Africa or South America and described in "loving detail" the dress, music, dance, food, and rituals of a group. In fact, ethnographers apply these same principles, the detailed recording or "thick description" (Geertz, 1983) of the way of life of a cultural group, to popular culture experiences. In other words, just as a researcher would faithfully record the musical performances of an Indigenous tribe in Australia, researchers carefully observe, record, and draw conclusions about a country music concert at a stadium in Dallas, Texas.

Along with ethnography, our look at the spaces of popular culture benefits from the critical study of physical locations, at home in such fields as rhetoric, communication, and geography. Such fields explore how the natural and designed (or human-made) environment communicates. In rhetoric, the study of public memorials like the Vietnam Veterans' Memorial (Blair, Jeppeson, & Pucci, 1991), as well as shopping malls (Dickinson, 2015), promoted an understanding of communication that wasn't only operating symbolically: seeing family members return to the memorial and do graphite rubbings of relatives' names, or place flags and other objects near the base of the black granite wall, demonstrates how communication engages us in immediate ways (see Chapter 8). Academics sometimes distinguish space from place, with space referencing a more general or abstract category, and place functioning as more particular, meaningful "setting[s] for social rootedness and landscape continuity" (Agnew, 2011, p. 317). This distinction is not as important to our purposes in Chapter 12, where we see how spaces marked as populist (versus elitist or folk) invites many people in to experience them. And, when we look to the rituals and norms of places like stadiums, homes, and theme parks, people mark, use, and experience artifacts, within them, with authenticity as well as rote consumption.

Space and popular culture ritual: Large public events

People love large-scale events all over the world. Standing amid groups of thousands or more people isn't limited to holiday celebrations and religious rituals in places like Brazil or Israel. Popular culture, notably sporting events and musical performances, routinely attract tens of thousands of people in spaces across the globe. In an era where nearly every sporting event is televised and countless concerts are available for streaming in high definition, why do people still go through the significant expense and effort to wait in traffic, stand in line, and deal with obnoxious fans at these events? In short, the ritualistic context of a massive stadium packed with spectators offers an experience quite unlike sitting at home in front of a TV.

The **ritual** approach to communication, often attributed to James Carey (1989), emphasizes observing repeated activities that are deeply tied to memory and tradition. These cycles of repetitive actions develop over time, binding people into a group with a shared sense of identity (Strate, 2007). Like sensation (Chapter 7), both ethnography and the ritual approach seek to understand embodied sensory experiences of our everyday lives. And, understanding fan culture in terms of ritual helps us appreciate why and how people invest identity in their fan communities—sports teams become an intense point of identification (see Chapters 5 and 6) through ritual.

To appreciate the immediacy of popular culture, let's look at National Football League (NFL) or major college football games as rituals. To understand the experience of a large-scale live event such as a football game, we really have to walk through the entire experience. Attending a professional or major college football game typically requires some planning. Tickets are often purchased months in advance of the event, building excitement and a sense of connection if one is attending with family or friends. Getting to the venue might involve an hour or two of travel, requiring public transportation or a ride service as parking is limited. For many people, the event requires setting aside nearly an entire Saturday or Sunday. After months of anticipation, the day finally arrives.

Approaching the stadium is something like a religious experience. In most American cities, one of the largest architectural structures is the football stadium. Particularly, in college towns such as Tuscaloosa, Alabama or Norman, Oklahoma, the football stadium dwarfs the other buildings in the city. If archaeologists thousands of years from now came across these giant structures in a dig, they would likely assume the most significant cultural rituals must have taken place inside these massive buildings. Getting to a football game is only one step of the process though, and for many fans the ritual begins with tailgating.

Tailgating is as old as football spectatorship itself, with reports of drinking and eating before the first collegiate games in the 1860s (Drenten, Peters, Leigh, & Hollenbeck, 2009). Originally, the tailgating experience was, just that, eating and drinking while sitting on the tailgate of a truck or car before the game begins. Today, while some folks keep the tailgate tradition simple (especially for high school or smaller college games), many people have expanded into tricked-out RVs with big-screen televisions, tents, stereo systems, outdoor party games (e.g., cornhole and frisbee), gas grills, and other amenities (see Figure 12.1).

Fans who tailgate often tailgate for every game, have tailgated for many years, and spend considerable time preparing food and other details before gameday. Further, starting hours before game time (often on chilly fall mornings), complete strangers will gather together to share food and drinks simply because they wear the same team's jerseys. Tailgating also evokes nostalgic memories often tied to formative high school or college experiences. Most significantly, as a patterned activity performed together, fans feel a strong sense of belonging and group identity during the tailgating ritual: fans may display banners speaking to shared identity ("Husker Nation Unite!"), join photo ops with Herbie the Husker and Lil' Red mascots, and eat bright red hot dogs to mark the occasion.

Figure 12.1 Tailgating ritual. Ruth Peterkin/Shutterstock.

Finally, the football game begins. Before kick-off, American football games usually include the singing of the national anthem, with spectators reverently standing and removing their hats, a tradition that started after World War I and expanded through World War II, due to surging patriotism during wartime. Of course, the ritual stuck and continues today at nearly all football games, not without controversy. Most memorably, in 2016, San Francisco 49ers quarterback Colin Kaepernick kneeled during the national anthem as a protest to racial injustice. A firestorm of controversy followed with strong opinions from both supporters and critics across cable news, social media, and political campaign speeches, suggesting that the ritual of the anthem is deeply tied to people's identities and meaning systems as Americans. In other words, popular culture rituals can be incredibly significant to people.

During the game itself, a wide range of ritualistic behavior can be observed. Fans wear the colors and jerseys of their preferred team, sometimes even wearing face paint and costumes such as Husker fans dressing as corn cobs and Raiders fans dressing as post-apocalyptic pirates, cheering loudly whenever their team scores. College teams have fight songs that are sung in unison by thousands of their fans. Behavior that would be deemed inappropriate or strange in most everyday contexts, such as screaming at the referees, high fiving or hugging strangers, chanting in unison with thousands of others, mercilessly taunting opposing players and fans, etc. are all perfectly normal (or, we will see shortly, normative) at a football game.

The meanings of these rituals are sometimes most noticeable during times of crisis and adversity. In the weeks after the terrorist attacks of September 11, 2001, for instance, football games were a source of much-needed normality and community, as well as some pretty jingoistic patriotism in the form of fighter jet fly-bys and impassioned renditions of anthemic songs. During the COVID-19 pandemic, postponed games left an empty place in many fans' everyday routines. In fall 2021, athletes and staff played in empty stadiums (as fans had to remain home due to social distancing protocols). Watching the eerily quiet spaces, typically at home on TV or tablet, felt a bit hollow until the full ritual of sports returned. This observation leads to a second important space for understanding popular culture's integration into peoples' everyday lives—the home.

Domestic spaces of popular culture: Norms and intimacies

The home remains the space people most frequently consume popular culture. It is where we like to watch the big game on our largest screen, where we stage a movie night with our partner or friends, where our favorite music plays while cooking dinner, where we hunker down to complete the final level of a video game, etc. In spite of much speculation over digital media domination, people in the US still watch a lot of television at home—55% of Americans, per a 2022 survey, watch TV between one and four hours per day (Fatemi, 2022). Representing the blending of media (Chapter 1), most homes in the US have high-speed Internet combined with television to facilitate regular viewing in the space: 85.5% of US households have Internet (Taylor, 2023) and homes with high-speed Internet average 2.5 televisions per house (Nissen, 2022). These two popular culture tools drive standard architecture and design of homes in the US, as new builds are designed for flat-screen televisions and wireless Internet (replacing a major selling point from some years back, speaker wiring and the number/convenience of phone jacks). When all of the rooms of a house (except, perhaps, the bathrooms) have a flat-screen mounted on a wall and/or wireless internet connectivity, it certainly suggests norms around everyday popular culture consumption.

Popular culture is intimately integrated into homelife, especially family activities. For many, family holidays are now defined, at least in part, by popular culture consumption. Families ritualistically watch movies every holiday such as *Christmas Vacation* or *A Christmas Story*. Favorite holiday pop songs are played in the home while wrapping and unwrapping presents or decorating the tree. In fact, each November and December, instead of new movies and music at the top of streaming charts (as is usually the case), streaming music and movie charts are topped by seasonal songs and movies, sometimes decades old, such as "All I Want for Christmas

Is You" by Mariah Carey (1994), "Rockin' Around the Christmas Tree" by Brenda Lee (1958), *Elf* (2003), and *Home Alone* (1990). Television networks such as Lifetime and local radio stations change their formats to exclusively play holiday content.

Popular culture not only pervades family rituals for holidays, but also the everyday routines of home life. *Norms*, or regulated patterns of communication behavior, emerge in households around a wide variety of activities such as chores, sleep, meal preparation, topics of talk around the dinner table, etc. (Carbaugh, 1982). In particular, families establish norms around popular culture consumption, notably, when, where, and how much. "Screen time" has been a hot topic in parenting in recent years, with educational and medical professionals strongly suggesting limiting children's time on tablets, phones, and laptop computers. The Mayo Clinic summarizes medical experts' reasoning, noting a connection between "too much screen time and regular exposure to poor-quality programming" and such adverse outcomes as "obesity, inadequate sleep schedules and insufficient sleep, behavior problems, delays in language and social skills development," and "attention problems" (Mayo Clinic, 2022).

How such advice is implemented (or not) in a home is the subject of norms, which can be prescribed with strict rules and enforcement (sometimes regulated with mobile apps) or more loosely negotiated based on unique factors such as if the child is feeling sick, has a friend visiting, etc. Further, children regularly compare their household screen rules with their friends and neighbors: "Peter gets to play video games whenever he wants" or "Sofia got her phone when she was twelve." A radical disruption, such as the closing of schools due to the COVID-19 pandemic, often requires a renegotiation of well-established norms. Further, as children get older, perhaps transitioning from a family iPad to a personal smartphone, new norms emerge. In short, norms regulating popular culture consumption are constantly evolving in families demanding thoughtful recalibration from parents. Perhaps most significantly, through patterned behavior, families decide when they consume popular culture alone or together in a group or pairs. Not long ago, certainly when we were kids, most families had only one or two televisions (and, of course, no mobile devices), which *required* group watching (and some bitter fights between siblings). With the rapid growth of personal smart phones and tablets since around 2010, family members can now isolate and individually watch whatever they want, whenever they want.

In particular, households today often need to explicitly establish norms surrounding binge watching television series. Binge watching involves a few characteristics, namely self-determined viewing, usually on a streaming platform, that is typically commercial free (Jenner, 2020). Binge watching is a term popularized in the past decade, but has an interesting origin dating back decades. Of course, from 1950 through the 1970s, networks completely determined the time of television viewership based on their broadcast schedule. In the 1980s, video cassette recorders (VCRs) allowed some (but only a small fraction) viewers to record a series and watch (or rewatch) it in a binge fashion. Further, box sets of VHS tapes (and later digital video discs or DVDs) of an entire season of a television show such as *The Sopranos* or *Star Trek* allowed for binge watching, but usually only by the most loyal fans.

Binge watching first truly reached the masses when Netflix, in the days of mail-ordered DVDs via their web interface, allowed subscribers to order entire seasons of discs of a television show. The high demand for seasons of shows such as *Breaking Bad* and *The Walking Dead* compelled Netflix to emphasize bingeable series (with complex, ongoing and unresolved narratives), such as *House of Cards*, when they first launched their streaming service. Of course, Netflix exploded in popularity as a streaming service and binge watching became the new norm for most households (Jenner, 2020). The affordances (see Chapter 1) of a technology's design lend themselves to differing everyday practices. The affordances of the remote control and cable television enabled viewers to "channel surf" and watch tiny bits of content across a wide range of networks. Today, essentially on the other end of the spectrum, streaming services viewed on-demand across multiple devices enable deep dives into many seasons of a single TV series in the form of binge watching.

Because binge watching allows viewers to start and stop on demand, how does a couple or family decide when to continue watching a show? Anyone absorbed in the story of a show such as *The Crown* or *Stranger Things* knows how hard it is to wait until others' busy schedules allow for group viewing. The term "Netflix cheating" emerged to describe the breach of norms around shared binge watching by watching a show without one's partner (Heritage, 2017). As a common source of relational conflict, negotiating how, when, and where to watch television shows is not a trivial enterprise.

Digital affordances have led to changes in the norms of popular culture consumption at home, but television remains a familiar, intimate medium (see Chapter 3). People continue to turn on TV (whether cable or Netflix) as background noise, with 88% of people using a "second screen" like a phone or tablet during their television viewing per Nielsen (Serwach, 2020). A National Sleep Foundation poll in 2022 found that 58% of Americans view a screen before falling asleep (National Sleep Foundation) leading to concerns over the quality and quantity of sleep that we get. The integration of popular culture into our home space makes it ever-available for routine consumption, and as we turn to our final chapter, we invite readers to question whether these habits are serving them. For now, an ethnographic approach would follow popular culture from remarkable rituals and normative routines into popular culture's transformations of public space.

Experiencing popular culture "on the road:" Non-places and tourism

The business of popular culture (Chapter 2), and particularly economic globalization (Chapter 9), have influenced the design of public spaces in some dramatic ways. For instance, movie theaters have changed significantly over the last several decades. In general, movie theaters are inherently popular cultural spaces designed for the single purpose of film spectatorship. The first movie theaters opened to the public in the early 1900s. Elaborate movie palaces with hundreds of seats were built over the next few decades with ornate paintings and wall fixtures. In the 1960s and 1970s, these palaces were replaced with standardized multiplexes featuring many uniform boxy theatres with smaller screens in a style that we are accustomed to today. The logic was simple: multiple standardized theatres housed in a single building allowed chains to efficiently screen more movies (or in the era of franchises, the same blockbuster on more screens), sell more concessions, and increase revenue (Meissner, 2022). Today, most movie theaters are these nearly identical, non-descript boxes with all of the local charm removed for purpose of more efficient commerce.

The cultural changes that affected movie theater design are everywhere. In fact, spend a moment and consider the public spaces you move through during the course of a typical week. You might shop for groceries at a giant supermarket, grab lunch at a fast-food taco chain, get your morning coffee at Starbucks, pick up some household items at Target or Walmart, etc. Most of us don't think much about these spaces as they are astonishingly unremarkable and indistinct. That is entirely by design. Referred to as **non-places**, public spaces such as shopping malls, big box stores, and franchise restaurants have no sense of local history and are erased of regional differences (Wood, 2009). Non-places are designed for quick and easy consumption (literally, in the case of fast food), therefore, they remove anything idiosyncratic to a particular geographic location (Auge, 1995). Perhaps you have had the experience of an airport layover, sitting in some non-descript TGI Fridays or Applebee's in a terminal, and completely forgetting what city you are in—is this St. Louis, or was it Atlanta?

The franchise model, sometimes referred to as McDonaldization (recall Chapter 9), with standardized menus, interior design, signage, etc. has dominated the food and retail industries over the last few decades. It is a radical shift in public spaces. Fifty years ago, local restaurants and shops were relatively regionally distinct. Cities often had specific ethnic communities from Italy, Germany, or Cuba that defined the unique cuisine and interior design of restaurants and shops. The city's public spaces fit its unique industries and functions—fish markets in Seattle, stockyards in Chicago, etc. Today, unless re-developed for tourism (which is more of a simulation of past forms, recall Chapter 10), most of these unique regional differences have been erased and turned into homogeneous chain restaurants and shops. Downtowns, such as our city of Denver, went through re-developments over the last 20 or 30 years that largely built chain restaurants and stores, often around sports stadiums (see above), such as Chili's, Panera, Nike town, Hard Rock Cafe, Hot Topic, PF Chang, and Maggiano's Little Italy.

In many ways, the design of these spaces is popular culture, built around the ritual of shopping. The interior design of the store directs consumers' movement around the space, attracting their eyes toward desired products. The lighting, décor, signage, and music are all carefully chosen to entice targeted consumers and sell products. Starbucks is one of the most successful examples of making a non-place a popular cultural consumption experience. In 2022, there were over 15,000 Starbucks locations in the US alone. You have probably noticed, as non-places, while they vary from quite small to cavernous, they are all more or less the same design (see Figure 12.2).

Figure 12.2 Interior of Starbucks. TY Lim/Shutterstock.

When customers enter a Starbucks, they are directed to a counter featuring baked goods, various fancy coffee machines (behind the counter), with a large wall-sized menu featuring simple white lettering (always "SoDo sans" font) on a green (the shade is literally called "Starbucks green") background hovering above. The menu is in a unique language essentially created by Starbucks. There are not small, medium, or large sized drinks—the customer chooses tall, grande, or venti. Before Starbucks, only a relatively small number of Americans knew the difference between lattes and cappuccinos. Of course, now these coffee drinks are as familiar as Big Macs and McRibs. Inside the Starbucks, soft music plays, vaguely associated with non-threatening folk or jazz (perhaps you may hear Norah Jones, who sold millions of albums in the 2000s with her generic "Starbucks Entertainment" style, per Stereogum, 2007).

As a ritualized experience, the private language, the curated music, etc. is part of what the consumer is purchasing with their cappuccino. As described in Chapters 3 and 5, cultural capital such as the products we consume communicates status such as being educated or wealthy. Spaces such as Starbucks are expressing a kind of cultural capital by communicating signs of upper-middle class-ness (and largely Whiteness) in the forms of differentiated products (e.g., lattes, espresso, soy milk, etc.), music, color, etc. Starbucks was originally marketed as a third place outside of home and work. In many ways, Starbucks' success can be attributed to getting the consumer out of their house, which has become a cocoon of popular culture. But as with concerns over the loss of community (see Chapter 5), one wonders if transforming spaces through the logic of popular culture consumption will effectively bring people together.

Of course, not all places are designed with the explicit purpose of business, nor are they aesthetically non-places. Our tour through the spaces of popular culture must also include tourism, where special places promise exceptional experiences, offering us a departure or break from daily routine (Urry & Larson, 2011). Tourism has become a popular culture experience on many levels. A wide variety of pop culture-oriented tourist attractions have emerged as unique meaning making locations. Walter Benjamin described *aura* as the meaning people give objects such as original paintings or architectural spaces like the Sistine Chapel. It is the sense of awe we feel in the presence of the *Mona Lisa* or a Van Gogh masterpiece. It is the perceived value of collectible objects such as the handwritten lyrics to songs by David Bowie, Bob Dylan, or Paul McCartney, or the original copy of the script of *Star Wars* written by George Lucas. A University of Kansas graduate even purchased (for $4.3 million) the original handwritten rules of basketball created by James Naismith in 1892 and donated them to the college for display at their basketball arena.

Viewing the digital images of these paintings or objects on the Internet does not produce the same awe (in fact, people play with these images irreverently, as described in Chapter 7). When art is removed from its context and mass produced, it loses its aura. Placed within an immediate, physical context, popular culture artifacts (like art) carry a unique power. Aura also extends to the sites of great tragedies, such as the sites of assassinations (President John F. Kennedy in Dallas, or the Reverend Dr. Martin Luther King, Jr., in Memphis) or terrorist attacks (as in Oklahoma City and New York City). In fact, the aura of objects and physical spaces lends itself to a tourist gaze associated with public memory as members of a culture have bestowed unique historical meaning to the events of these locations. As we have observed in visits to these spaces, visitors inhabit the physical space of historical tragedy with hushed reverence, either in silence or inaudible whispers. Children are told to show respect by remaining quiet. It is as though you can feel the presence of the moment of suffering embedded in the building or street.

A similar aura, although more playful and pleasurable, surrounds meaningful places associated with popular culture. In particular, locations where movies are filmed have become their own tourist sites, attracting visitors as these spaces have a kind of "aura" that fans desire in order to feel connected to their favorite movies (Waysdorf & Reijnders, 2018). Fans flock to the physical locations that were filmed in movies such as the houses from *Halloween* (in Pasadena, CA) and *Home Alone* (in the Chicago suburbs) and the hotel from *The Shining* (in Estes Park, CO). People travel long distances to visit the picturesque locations of the *Lord of the Rings* movies in New Zealand.

Similarly, the street where the Beatles shot the album cover for Abbey Road has become a major tourist spot in London (Atkinson, 2015). The street crossing has become a site of pilgrimage for Beatles fans; some even mark the nearby wall with graffiti. The Abbey Road photo of the Beatles is especially meaningful as representing the late "psychedelic" era of the band with shaggy hair, beards, and experimental production styles. In fact, many visitors are not so much "hard core" Beatles fans but visiting the aura of "the 60s" counterculture and authentic rock music represented in a material space. In many ways, the aura of the Abbey Road crossing is associated with a nostalgia for an idealized 1960s defined by images of hippies, free love, marijuana, etc. (recall Chapter 6). Because there is no museum and the recording studio itself is closed to the public, Abbey Road is almost entirely a space for selfies, where visitors can literally insert themselves into the iconic imagery of the 1960s.

Popular culture is ephemeral, especially in digital forms. You can't touch a streamed song or movie. For many consumers, we no longer have an album cover or DVD box to display, or share with guests as a treasured collectible. In many ways, these places give some materiality to beloved artifacts. For us, visiting Sun Studio in Memphis several years ago, the place of the original recordings of Elvis Presley, Howlin' Wolf, and Johnny Cash, offered a unique sense of aura and meaning. Nonetheless, the tourist gaze inherently involves commodified signs as the images of these spaces are nearly always for sale in one form or another. While at Sun Studios, we purchased t-shirts and other swag, commodities expressing our identities as "authentic" Americana music fans.

Of course, not all spaces for popular culture tourism have the same aura of authenticity. Theme parks are an interesting space to consider, as they represent another outlet for branding and convergence (Chapter 2), with an opportunity to envelop the visitor in an immersive, immediate experience (see Chapter 11). In academic research, theme parks have been especially harshly criticized as commodified simulation (recall the discussion of Baudrillard and his critique of Disneyland, Chapter 7). Offering multiple perspectives on popular culture, we consider what an ethnographic lens brings to theme park spaces.

Harry Potter Wizarding World at Universal Studios in Orlando, Florida opened in 2010, and has grown from 6 million annual visitors to upwards of 10 million (Sylt, 2019). Like other theme parks, The Wizarding World of Harry Potter features thrill rides (with motion simulation and 3D imagery), shows, restaurants, and shops (see Figure 12.3). While theme parks such as The Wizarding World of Harry Potter are no doubt spaces

Figure 12.3 The Wizarding World of Harry Potter. NavinTar/Shutterstock.

designed for consumption and corporate branding, the unique pleasures of theme parks are also similar to other creative works like a painting or film which invite visitors into an immersive world of narrative and characters (Waysdorf & Reijnders, 2018). In Harry Potter Wizarding World, visitors describe the experience as their favorite books/movies coming to life recreating vivid details such as shops, food, drinks, and clothing.

The park is a multi-sensory and embodied experience that feels like entering another world surrounded by screens with 3D projections, photo realistic recreations of sets from the movies, and impeccably designed costumes of the employees. Some visitors even engage in cosplay dressing as characters from books and movies, engaging in a playful sense of pretend and make-believe compelling a willing suspension of disbelief. The Wizarding World of Harry Potter is also described as a place of pilgrimage for fans who travel long distances to immerse themselves in a story that means so much to them, often as essential equipment for living during their awkward adolescent years. This experience is shared with other fans who feel similarly about the books and movies creating a powerful sense of community (Waysdorf & Reijnders, 2018). While artificial and simulated, a family "pilgrimage" to The Wizarding World of Harry Potter or Disneyland can be moving and immersive. Like the ebb and flow between the business and consumption of popular culture described across Chapters 2 and 3, we see how a commodified, simulated environment offers opportunity for authentic communal experience *and* mindless consumption. This leads us to consider how self-reflexivity may steer us toward better practices in the spaces of popular culture.

Conclusion: The authenticity and ritualized consumption of shopping

Contemporary public spaces involve complex rituals and norms with wide-ranging implications. Based on the examples above, many people long for authentic communal experiences, which compels diverse practices in everyday spaces. A unifying theme of our discussion of space revolves around commodification of everyday life: restaurants as commodified dining experience, sports as commodified ritual experience, home life as commodified normative experience, and theme parks as commodified tourist experience. An everyday routine experience shared by most people is the literal commodification of daily activities: shopping.

Shopping is ritualized activity that, for some people, is a source of stimulation and pleasure—the phrase "retail therapy" was coined in the 1980s, and one survey found one in three people in the US report shopping to alleviate stress (Gregoire, 2013). Beyond its uses and gratifications for individuals (Chapter 3), shopping involves both rituals and norms for collectives.

People wander the racks of clothing at malls, pick through bins at Sam's Club, or gawk at expensive watches in a jewelry store window. Perhaps at its most extreme, the yearly "Black Friday" event demonstrates the power of ritual in public spaces.

In the United States, on the day after Thanksgiving, shoppers line up at big box stores like Walmart and Target for special bargains on products that are popular Christmas gifts. Stories of the hysteria on Black Friday are common with shoppers reportedly lining up over ten hours before the store opens, stealing discounted products from people in wheelchairs, fist fights and shoving matches over toys and clothing, and frantically hoarding huge quantities of items in shopping carts (Dodd, 2020). The Black Friday videos are truly unbelievable (search YouTube if you are interested) often appearing like scenes from some found footage zombie apocalypse movie. Here a simple ritual, Christmas shopping in big box stores, searching for bargains, reaches an incredible emotional intensity. During Black Friday, a non-place, designed exclusively for consuming products reaches its sort of logical conclusion when shopping becomes mass hysteria. The history of the term "Black Friday" foretells the ritual that it has become in the 21st century: though marketers claim that the term emerged from struggling retailers who expected to move from the "red" to the "black" after Thanksgiving (meaning that they would earn profits), historians trace the term to the Philadelphia Police Department using the term in preparation for gridlock traffic and crowds as the downtown shopping season began (Bond, 2022).

If Black Friday is the worst of shopping rituals, how might we imagine something different? How do we create authentic communal experiences in highly commodified, simulated non-places? Returning to the example of the movie theater, fans can transform a non-descript theater into a space for complex performances and community. Screenings of "midnight movies" fill a generic movie theater with costumed weirdos, talking and singing along to movies such as *The Rocky Horror Picture Show* or *The Big Lebowski*. In fact, some movie theaters (like the Alamo Drafthouse chain) have scheduled films where fans arrive in costumes, or visit with filmmakers in open forums. While the design of non-places encourages passive consumption, with a bit of determination and collective will, people can transform these spaces into environments for unique communal experiences.

Additionally, the "buy local" movement encourages consumers to trade in Target for local hardware and specialty shops. Buying local is especially relevant for popular culture consumption as bookstores and record stores, previously pushed out of towns and cities by homogeneous chains such as Barnes & Noble and Tower Records, are now struggling due to behemoth online retailers like Amazon. April 15th is "record store day" with major musical artists staging performances at local record stores across the country, motivating music fans to return to their local music retailers. In the past decade, independent bookstores are actually thriving offering a place for community, social events, and curated book recommendations (Blanding, 2020). Believe it or not, over a decade after Blockbuster video filed for bankruptcy, there is even a movement to revive local video rental stores.

But the power struggles over the uses and meanings of public space transcends commerce. Non-places write over complex histories of their geographic locations, which may have once been farmed by migrant workers, settlers, enslaved people, and/or cared for by Indigenous People. Local artists bring these complicated histories and contemporary politics into the present moment. Street artists, for instance, paint directly onto buildings, billboards, and other public spaces, interrupting the seamless flow of consumption. Shepard Fairey is a street artist who uses pop culture iconography, such as a stencil of professional wrestler Andre the Giant, as a tag on buildings, reframing the meaning of both the wrestler and the building. Impromptu or organized murals fill many cities, often depicting iconic popular culture figures such as Marilyn Monroe, Johnny Cash, and Elvis Presley. Our family especially enjoyed a large mural of Cuban-American, and Miami-born, 1980s pop star Gloria Estefan during a visit to Miami. When former basketball star Kobe Bryant died tragically in a helicopter accident, murals spread across Los Angeles as a kind of public mourning. These are a few of many ways that ordinary people can make choices beyond ritualized consumption, as in Black Friday shopping.

Reflecting on the spaces of pop culture in your everyday life

- What types of spaces do you inhabit every day? How do you see the indelible marks of popular culture in/on these spaces?
- Have you participated in a popular culture ritual as described in this chapter, such as attending a major college or NFL football game, or shopping on Black Friday? How would you describe the experience?
- Visit a planned or impromptu memorial in your city or town. How does popular culture serve as equipment for living as people mark a space as worthy of remembering?
- What was a recent tourist experience? Did you feel like a consumer? Did you have meaningful, perhaps even authentic experiences? Explain, and consider how both were encouraged or discouraged by the design of the place you visited, and the people you visited with.

In conclusion, Chapter 12 helps us develop a greater consciousness of how space communicates power, encourages consumption, and can be reclaimed through new everyday practices and artistic expression. Through the tools of ethnography—particularly ritual and norm—we may approach the ordinary experiences of popular culture as they are performed in spaces and places. We can develop new rituals and norms. A local food truck can transform a city street into family Indian restaurant. A busker performing old pop songs with a guitar can create an impromptu space for a sing-along and authentic community interaction. Ultimately, public space is ours to do with how we desire.

Suggested readings

Brummett, B. (Ed.). (2009). *Sporting rhetoric: Performance, games, and politics.* Peter Lang.

Dickinson, G. (2009). Joe's rhetoric: Finding authenticity at Starbucks. *Rhetoric Society Quarterly, 32*(4), 5–27. https://doi.org/10.1080/02773940209391238

Jones, R. G., Jr., & Foust, C. R. (2007). Staging and enforcing consumerism in the city: The performance of othering on the 16th Street Mall. Liminalities, 4(1), 1–28. http://liminalities.net/4-1/16thstreet.htm

Raphael, J., & Lam, C. (2018). The function of hosts: Enabling fan-celebrity interactions at pop culture conventions. Continuum: Journal of Media & Cultural Studies, 32(2), 173–183. 10.1080/10304312.2017.1391177

References

Agnew, J. (2011). *Space and place.* SAGE. https://dx.doi.org/10.4135/9781446201091

Atkinson, P. (2015). Abbey Road Studios, the tourist, and Beatles Heritage. In E. Mazierska & G. Gregory (Eds.) *Relocating popular music: Pop music, culture and identity* (pp. 129–147). Palgrave Macmillan. https://doi.org/10.1057/9781137463388_7

Auge, M. (1995). *Non-places: Introduction to an anthropology of supermodernity.* Verso.

Blair, C., Jeppeson, M., & Pucci, E. (1991). Public memorializing in postmodernity: The Vietnam Veterans Memorial as prototype. *Quarterly Journal of Speech, 77*(3), 263–288. doi:10.1080/00335639109383960

Blanding, M. (2020, January 21). Lessons for retailers from the rebirth of indie bookstores. Harvard Business School. https://hbswk.hbs.edu/item/lessons-for-retailers-from-the-rebirth-of-indy-bookstores

Bond, C. (2022, November 18). Black Friday history: The dark true story behind the name. *Huffington Post.* https://www.huffpost.com/entry/black-friday-history-why-is-it-called-black-friday_l_5d951322e4b02911e1154386

Carbaugh, Donal (1982). Ethnography of communication: Cultural codes and norms. Paper presented at the Annual Meeting of the Speech Communication Association, Louisville, KY.

Carey J. W. (1989). *Communication as culture: Essays on media and society.* Unwin Hyman.

Dickinson G. (2015). *Suburban dreams: Imagining and building the good life.* University of Alabama Press.

Dodd, S. (2020, November 25). The most insane Black Friday stories ever, from 15 retail workers who are still scarred. *People.* https://people.com/home/crazy-black-friday-horror-stories/

Drenten, J., Peters, C., Leigh, T.W., & Hollenbeck, C.R. (2009). Not just a party in the parking lot: An exploratory investigation of the motives underlying the ritual commitment of football tailgaters. *Sport Marketing Quarterly, 18*(2), 92–106.

Fatemi, F. (2022, November 14). How TV viewing habits have changed. Forbes. https://www.forbes.com/sites/falonfatemi/2022/11/14/how-tv-viewing-habits-have-changed/?sh=91464d448885

Geertz, C. (1983). *Local knowledge: Further essays in interpretive anthropology.* Basic Books.

Gregoire, C. (2013, May 24). Retail therapy: One in three recently stressed Americans shops to deal with anxiety. *Huffington Post.* https://www.huffpost.com/entry/retail-therapy-shopping_n_3324972

Heritage, S. (2017, February 15). Netflix cheating is the ultimate breakdown in marital trust. *The Guardian.* https://www.theguardian.com/commentisfree/2017/feb/15/netflix-cheating-ultimate-breakdown-in-marital-trust

Jenner, M. (2020). Researching binge-watching. *Critical Studies in Television, 15*(3), 267–279. https://doi.org/10.1177/1749602020935012

Mayo Clinic (2022, February 10). Screen time and children: How to guide your child. *Mayo Clinic.* https://www.mayoclinic.org/healthy-lifestyle/childrens-health/in-depth/screen-time/art-20047952

Meissner, C. (2022). The scale of the screen: Auditorium size and number in the American movie theater. *Media Fields Journal.* http://mediafieldsjournal.org/scale-of-the-screen

National Sleep Foundation (2022). Americans can do more during the day to help their sleep at night. National Sleep Foundation. https://www.thensf.org/wp-content/uploads/2022/03/NSF-2022-Sleep-in-America-Poll-Report.pdf

Nissen, K. (2022, June 9). US TV viewing behavior largely unchanged despite proliferation of smart TVs. S&P Global. (https://www.spglobal.com/marketintelligence/en/news-insights/research/us-tv-viewing-behavior-largely-unchanged-despite-proliferation-of-smart-tvs#:~:text=The%20survey%20data%20also%20shows%20that%20the%20average%20number%20of, and%20older%20standard%2Ddefinition%20TVs

Serwach, J. (2020, December 21). We now watch TV the way we used to play music. *The Narrative.* https://medium.com/narrative/we-now-watch-tv-the-way-we-used-to-play-music-6e46cd43e948

Stereogum, (2007, January 17). Premature evaluation: Norah Jones – not too late. Stereogum. https://www.stereogum.com/4352/norah_jones_not_too_late/reviews/premature-evaluation/

Strate, L. (2007). Understanding a man in time: James W. Carey and the media ecology intellectual tradition. *Critical Studies in Media Communication, 24*(2), 177–180. DOI: 10.1080/07393180701262925

Sylt, C. (2019, June 30). The world's fastest growing theme park. Forbes. https://www.forbes.com/sites/csylt/2019/06/30/revealed-the-worlds-fastest-growing-theme-park/?sh=662490655cd9

Taylor, P. (2023, January 18). Percentage of households with internet use in the United States from 1997 to 2020. Statistica. https://www.statista.com/statistics/189349/us-households-home-internet-connection-subscription/

Urry J. & Larsen J. (2011). *The tourist gaze 3.0* (3rd ed.). Sage.

Waysdorf, A., & Reijnders, S. (2018). Immersion, authenticity and the theme park as social space: Experiencing the Wizarding World of Harry Potter. *International Journal of Cultural Studies*, 21(2), 173–188. https://doi.org/10.1177/1367877916674751

Wood, A. (2009). *City ubiquitous: Place, communication, and the rise of omnitopia*. Hampton Press.

13 Conclusion

Going "meta" with popular culture in everyday life

Introduction

Here in the final chapter, spend a moment to reflect upon the sheer scale of popular culture in today's world. While technically dating back to mass-produced print books/pamphlets and circus and stage shows in the 19th century, the systems of production and consumption of popular culture as we think about it today (corporations, advertising, mass distribution, celebrity, etc.) probably started around the 1920s with the emergence of jazz and the popularization of film and radio. This is around one hundred years of popular culture. A bit like the plastic that never decomposes, most of this popular culture is still with us in one form or another. Movies from the 1930s like *Gone with the Wind* and *The Wizard of Oz* remain in the cultural consciousness. People still listen to songs of Bing Crosby and Frank Sinatra from the 1940s. The iconic movie stars of the 1950s such as James Dean remain etched in our memory. It is hard to go a week without hearing a song from either the Beatles or Queen. In 2022, movie biopics told the stories of Elvis Presley and Marilyn Monroe, renewing interest in their decades-old work.

Now, consider the massive amounts of new popular culture being produced each year: YouTube videos, video games, pop songs, streaming TV shows, etc. All of this popular culture continues to accumulate, growing larger every year (a bit like the landfills of plastic and other trash). It stands to reason that we spend more and more time self-aware of our popular culture practices. It is a matter of survival living in a vast ocean of popular culture. It hardly seems surprising that "multiverses" are such a common theme in contemporary popular culture as popular culture itself has become a multi-layered experience with infinite choices and possible realities. Yet, with this increased awareness of popular culture invited by the tremendous *amounts* of popular culture, are we, as consumers, making choices to engage pop culture with increased awareness?

In Chapter 13, we conclude our book with a discussion of ethics. We take a deep dive into the increased presence of "meta" popular culture;

DOI: 10.4324/9781003372943-13

that is, artifacts that demonstrate a kind of self-awareness of their status as popular culture, as an invitation to engage popular culture with greater awareness. The first section helps define and illustrate meta popular culture as an outgrowth of postmodern trends that tear down authority and invite multiple interpretations of artifacts. We then consider the pleasures of meta popular culture, relative to both business logics and intertextuality (building off Chapters 2 and 7), and the promises of meta popular culture for promoting agency with and through pop culture (building off Chapter 5). Turning toward self-reflexivity as modelled by popular culture content producers, we conclude by inviting readers to recall the ways *Popular Culture in Everyday Life* has encouraged critical and reflexive choices in engaging popular culture, with potential to address issues interfacing with pop culture today.

Meta pop culture, the postmodern, and polysemy

The movie *Scream*, from 1996, told the story of a group of high-school students being randomly stabbed and killed by a masked maniac. What differentiated the movie from the countless slasher horror flicks of the 1980s and 1990s with the same basic plot was a unique knowing awareness of the characters concerning the tropes of the horror genre (discussed in Chapter 8). Characters spoke about the rules of horror movies, advising each other to never have sex, drink or do drugs; nor to say, "I'll be right back;" only to see characters break the rules and be immediately slaughtered. *Scream* was a massive hit, spawning three sequels, and in many ways perfectly capturing the cynicism, self-awareness, and irony of the 1990s. In 2022, *Scream* was predictably rebooted. In the reboot, the '90s murders of the original movie have inspired a series of "Stab" movies which are clear references to the *Scream* franchise. The teenage characters in the reboot, as surrogates for the audience, take self-awareness into entirely new dimensions. Characters are acutely aware that the trauma they are currently experiencing will certainly be represented in a horror movie in the *Stab* franchise. The characters even coin the term "requel" to describe their experiences which, in real time, appear to be both a sequel and reboot of the first film by extending the original story, but with new characters for a new generation. The characters we identify with in contemporary popular culture seem to regularly express a deep self-awareness of the conventions and expectations of their specific platform, genre, or medium.

The term "meta" has emerged as a ubiquitous buzzword of the last decade. It is commonplace for people to describe a movie like *Scream* as "so meta." Chances are, if you pressed someone making this assertion to *define* what meta means, they would likely struggle to find the right words. Meta is used a wide range of ways, but we see it most often in reference to intertextual referentiality, aka intertextuality. As we described in detail in Chapter 7, intertextuality involves a text referencing other texts or artifacts. However, in academic contexts, "meta" can refer to a "metatext" (or metacinema, metanarrative, etc.), which is when a text refers back (or "folds in") on itself (LaRocca, 2021). At its most literal, this occurs when a book describes itself as a book (such as authors inserting themselves into the story), or the images of a movie represent itself as a movie (such as *Scream* described above). Creators self-consciously refer to the *production* of popular culture in the act of performing it. Like a one-off "wink" at the camera, meta moments remind consumers that popular culture is not a seamless, simulated reality. More complex meta moments include irony or satire, which critiques generic conventions and dominant ideas in popular culture.

In theater terms, this is a "breaking of the fourth wall," where actors can literally breach the border between stage and audience, or figuratively break the pretend "glass" that exists to separate audience and performances. But with the affordances of broadcast, and especially digital media, "meta" moments can be even more pronounced. For instance, in the movie *Everything Everywhere All at Once*, the lead character is sitting in a movie theater watching herself, in another "universe" (yes, it is *another* multiverse movie), in the movie we are watching as an audience. While watching this scene, we were reminded of a childhood favorite, *The Muppet Movie*, when about halfway through, the action stops, revealing that the movie we are watching is also being watched by the characters in the movie (Kermit, Miss Piggy, etc.). These moments are memorable because they break the well-established expectations of movies and TV. Historically, the production process of movies and TV were designed to be invisible. Seeing a microphone or camera in the frame of a movie or TV show was the hallmark of unprofessional, amateurish productions and the source of ridicule. The entire point of early broadcast media was to help the audience suspend disbelief and forget this was a movie or TV show—to fully accept this new reality and get lost in the drama, comedy, or horror.

Over time, filmmakers and other artists began to play with these expectations by drawing attention to the artifice and conventions of their productions. In fact, forms of metatexuality have really existed for centuries (even sometimes in Shakespeare) but gained prominence in the 1960s and 1970s (Dunne, 1992). As discussed in Chapters 6 and 7, for instance, Western films have been subject to metatextual moments. In the 1974 comedy *Blazing Saddles*, Mel Brooks's spoof remained largely faithful to the production style of Hollywood Westerns with sweeping vistas, a rustic frontier town, and period costumes. Near the end of the film, characters move out of the frame and interact with the cameras and crew members shooting the movie (see Figure 13.1). Eventually, they ride around the back

Figure 13.1 Scene from *Blazing Saddles*.

lot of the movie studio (inserting themselves into a lavish musical that is also being filmed) breaking any illusion of the false reality of the movie. In this regard, in their broadest sense, metatexts invite the audience to be self-aware that they are consuming popular culture. Meta popular culture may compel the audience to think, "Hey, I'm watching a movie or TV show right now and this show or movie is different or similar to other shows or movies." Sometimes, metatexts reveal themselves as movies by simply us-ing ostentatious stylistic techniques, such as dazzling words on the screen, radical shifts in lighting or cinematography (e.g., going from color to black and white), or characters breaking the fourth wall by staring into the cam-era such as in movies like *Zombieland* or *Scott Pilgrim vs. the World*. In short, a meta popular culture text compels the audience to mentally step outside the boundaries of the movie, TV show, song, etc. in order to under-stand the meaning of the text *as* a movie, TV show, song, etc.

Pop music is filled with examples of metacommentary. In the 1960s, James Brown would regularly call out to his musicians changes in the section of the song he was singing such as "take them to the bridge." Pop stars like David Bowie performed in an achingly self-aware manner, commenting on the whole idea of being a pop star. Bowie would create characters with distinctive costumes and attitudes, such as Ziggy Stardust or the Thin White Duke, that both performed as pop stars and somehow were commenting and critiquing the idea of mass-produced pop idols. Since Bowie and Brown in the 1970s and 1980s, meta pop music has ex-panded. Hip-hop artists routinely describe the greatness of their rapping, while rapping, compelling the listener to think about the rapper's tech-nique (rather than simply enjoying the song). In country music, artists dat-ing back to the 1970s (Waylon Jennings) have used lyrics describing their song as "real country" inviting the listener to reflect on the steel guitar and fiddle as well as the authentic lyrics and lifestyle of the singer. David Allan Coe in 1975, in his song "You Never Even Call Me by My Name," boasted he was singing the perfect country and western song because it featured mama, trains, trucks, prison, and getting drunk. Braggadocian moments encourage us as listeners to perception check—are they really the greatest? Why?

The impulse to undermine the illusion of "respectable" art has a long and complicated history broadly associated with **postmodernism** (Harms & Dickens, 1996). The postmodern turn involved a deep skepticism toward institutions such as science, religion, and academia. There was a focus on unravelling accepted truths with a knowing awareness. Artists critiqued the very idea of "great art" such as Andy Warhol turning mass-produced images of soup cans into "masterpieces" to be displayed in stuffy museums. In one of our personal favorites, Marcel Duchamp's *L.H.O.O.Q.* or *La Joconde* merely placed a mustache on a print of the *Mona Lisa* commenting on the acclaimed masterpiece. In these cases, artists wanted viewers to reflect upon the nature of art itself, to be aware they are looking at art, think about the process of making art, and the institutions which determine what art is celebrated or what art is ignored.

In the 1960s and 1970s, this impulse extended across the culture. The Beatles, in their movies *A Hard Day's Night* and *Help!* (and *The Monkees* TV series which they inspired) seemed to constantly be winking at the camera (in a style inspired by the Marx Brothers), knowingly referencing their own celebrity and iconography. Comedians such as the satirical group Monty Python relished tearing down revered narratives, such as Arthurian legends in brilliantly silly movie *Monty Python and the Holy Grail*. In fact, sketch comedy was among the first to fully embrace a meta style, with shows such as *Saturday Night Live*, regularly going backstage or behind the scenes, showing the producer Lorne Michaels talking with cast members and writers about the show (usually disparagingly, showing the convergence of irony, sarcasm, and satire with meta moments). Similarly, David Letterman drew attention to the absurd conventions of late-night talk shows, inspiring a new generation of comedians such as Conan O'Brien and Seth Meyers to mock the very thing (talk shows, sitcoms, stand-up comedy, podcasts, etc.) they were doing. The joke is often on the audience as they are the idiots watching this terrible contrived TV show. On the other hand, if the audience is in on the joke, then they share a laugh at the expense of the conventions of television itself. Today, a lot of the comedy on YouTube has the tone of, "I can't believe people are on their phones, watching me do this right now."

In the last two decades, this self-awareness went from the margins of popular culture to the center, especially for comedy. The conventions of the situation comedy have been so savagely mocked by *Seinfeld*, *The Simpsons*, and *30 Rock*, that the multi-camera, studio audience (with piped-in laugh track) sitcom has been relegated to the margins of television—largely created for older or less "in the know" audiences without self-awareness that all of this is so outdated and uncool. Weirdly, old sitcoms like *Friends*, which meticulously follow the stylistic conventions and rhythms of the multi-camera genre, are widely popular with millennials. It is as though it is ok to like it because it was made before we knew this stuff (sitcoms with a laugh track and clearly defined punchlines to jokes) was so lame.

Superhero movies appear to be following in the tradition of the sitcom, becoming so self-aware and openly ridiculing their own conventions that they might be cannibalizing themselves. In particular, in the franchise's two movies, Marvel's *Deadpool* regularly looks into the camera, speaking with a knowing awareness and deep irreverence of other Marvel movies (never disguising that we are watching a movie), with comments such as "you're probably thinking, my boyfriend said this was a superhero movie," "the studio couldn't afford another *X-Man*," and "a fourth wall break inside a fourth wall break, that's like sixteen walls" (see Figure 13.2).

The Marvel studio is walking a tricky line, as *The Avengers* movies have a mythic, self-serious tone that is being undercut by the wildly popular *Deadpool* franchise. The waning interest in recent Marvel films such as *Black Widow* and *Eternals* suggest that audiences are increasingly inclined toward irreverently mocking superhero movies via metacommentary, rather than accepting their mythic seriousness. Can a movie feature ironic metacommentary and still have authentic emotion and a

Figure 13.2 Deadpool breaking the fourth wall.

believable engaging story? This leads to the other key feature of metatexts, which is their tendency to have an invitation for multiple interpretations, or **polysemy**.

Polysemy refers to popular culture texts with multiple meanings or interpretations by diverse audiences (Fiske, 1986). Polysemy has been associated with postmodernism because it shifts away from singular truths or meanings and invites play with meaning-making from audiences (rather than reaffirming the author's control over meaning). As a critique of the singular meaning attributed by an author or academic critic, polysemy insists that an audience's everyday experiences, informed by cultural practices and identity (see Chapter 4), or interpretations generated by fan communities (Chapter 5), will significantly inform their interpretations of a TV show, movie, or song leading to often radically different meanings. Metatexts encode features that encourage multiple interpretations.

It is, perhaps, easiest to understand the potential for polysemy to chip away at authority in metatexts that perform social satire. Like *Blazing Saddles* and other films from Mel Brooks, meta popular culture pokes fun at the received genres, expectations, conventions—really, the dominant ideas and ideologies—that we inherit. As with other ideological criticism (see Chapter 4), satire and parody demonstrate that things which appear natural, normal, and beyond question do not have to stay that way. They can change.

Metatexts often use excess as a strategy for social satire or critique, which leads to one of the major challenges with meta popular culture—not everyone reads the ideological critique in the same way, especially in today's intertextual pop culture metaverse. In the movie and television series *MacGruber* (which began as a skit on *Saturday Night Live* parodying the television show *MacGuyver* which originally aired in 1985), an inept and insecure former intelligence officer performs as a hypermasculine action star literally ripping out people's throats, among other excessive actions. Via excess, *MacGruber* comments on the action movie genre, especially from the 1980s, revealing figures like Rambo as insecure, reckless, and dangerous. Television shows such as *South Park* are also self-consciously excessive, featuring jokes, often expressed by children, about talking feces, gerbils lodged in rectums, the N-word, rape, and any other taboo topic. These jokes are frequently in service of cultural satire, critiquing political correctness, blind faith in religious institutions, and the hypocrisy of politicians and celebrities. The show is intended to create discomfort and force the audience to grapple with the inherent contradictions represented. Nonetheless, undoubtedly, a large contingency of the audience just likes to hear kids swear and tell dirty jokes. In cases such as *South Park*, can an audience have a "wrong" interpretation of a text? Dilemmas over reading parody in metatexts remind us of studies that showed political conservatives viewed *The Colbert Report* (intended as a political satire, in which comedian Stephen Colbert parodied Fox News personalities, approaches, and content) as a legitimate conservative artifact (Ben, 2009).

While it may seem poor communication practice to risk audiences missing your point, metatexts seem to embrace the instability of meaning-making. Indeed, some metatexts have contradictions built into the text itself, encouraging audiences to grapple with these inconsistencies via diverse interpretations. Most obviously, in advertising, a spokesperson will "ironically" endorse a product, creating an obvious contradiction in the audience. For instance, Eminem in a commercial for Brisk Tea angrily described why he never does commercials because he hates the products, with a series of profane words "bleeped" out. Clearly, Eminem is being paid to endorse this product and is performing in the commercial, so the audience must resolve the tension—does Eminem really hate this product? Is this product cool for getting Eminem to be in their commercial?

This leads to a common strategy for metatexts, one which illustrates the polysemy of such popular culture: having an actor play themselves in a heightened fictional universe. In sitcoms such as *Seinfeld* or the highly meta movies *Being John Malkovich* and *Unbearable Weight of Massive Talent*, actors play themselves (i.e., Nicolas Cage plays Nicolas Cage) in widely heightened situations, such as a CIA investigation of a drug kingpin. In the television show *Seinfeld*, the characters on the show are hired to produce a terrible sitcom (a show about nothing) about the characters on the show. *Curb Your Enthusiasm*, with largely improvised dialogue, mocks an aging sitcom writer (Larry David, playing himself). Many of the most popular episodes feature celebrities such as Ted Danson, Michael J. Fox, Jerry Seinfeld, Jon Hamm, and Seth Rogan playing themselves and knowingly making fun of their celebrity persona. Here, the popular culture artifact is encoded with multiple interpretations simultaneously coexisting and playing with each other, as audiences can read the musings of Larry David as a documenting of his own life and experience with other celebrities, but also as a television series—and a self-aware television series, at that.

Polysemy in meta pop culture is heightened by social media, where people gather to share interpretations and perhaps impress others with their knowledge and decoding skill. Today, metatexts are designed to instigate conversation on social media with fans offering diverse interpretations. In many respects, Easter eggs (described in Chapter 7) are carefully placed in Pixar or Marvel movies and Taylor Swift or Imagine Dragons videos as a marketing device to generate buzz about brands online. In this regard, increasingly, the meta turn in popular culture has been commodified, another corporate strategy for branding and expanding platforms, as we turn to in the next section. Yet, going meta with popular culture also has potential to build collective identities with potential to address some of the more challenging problems we face.

The pleasures of the meta: Consumption and community

Why do contemporary audiences enjoy meta forms of popular culture? Building on our discussion in Chapters 2 and 7, many audiences now extensively read about, watch YouTube clips about, and discuss popular culture *before* experiencing it. Drillable texts, Easter eggs, and even just polysemy help us feel rewarded for consuming countless hours of entertainment media. The spark of recognition is the "payment" for the labor of popular culture consumption. Metatextuality can also add layers of meaning to otherwise boring, disposable artifacts. A formulaic sitcom, or really an artifact of any genre streaming on a platform, suddenly has an injection of meaning—and, as discussed in Chapter 2, the eyeballs will "stick" to the platform.

Metatexts are at the intersection of many pleasurable dimensions of contemporary popular culture. The implausibly popular Netflix series *Cobra Kai* has built a large audience by finding a perfect balance of intertextuality, nostalgia, and meta self-awareness rewarding audiences for their appreciation of the larger *Karate Kid* franchise (including the widely derided sequels) and the earnest teen dramas of 1980s. Vampires and zombies continue to capture viewers' imaginations and are frequently the subject of metatexts. Today, TV shows like *What We Do in the Shadows*, *Legacies*, and *Interview with a Vampire* comment on the whole meaning of vampires, taking the genre meta. Vampires can become queer icons, feminist anti-heroes, or simply hot teenagers. In the process, new TV shows and movies about vampires tend to metatextually comment on *all* other representations of vampires from the past, making the audience acutely aware they are watching a TV show or movie.

A meta orientation to popular culture inherently empowers the audience by inviting multiple interpretive opportunities. This is reminiscent of participatory theatre, championed by Augusto Boal (1985), which encouraged breaking the line (or fourth wall) between the performers and the audience via experimentation in order to mutually create new understandings. A wide range of people including practitioners, activists, and academics have been using these principles for new types of performances intended to empower often marginalized communities such as prisoners. Within the realm of popular culture (which tends to lack the immediacy of theater due to channels of mass production), audiences can embrace the ideas of mutually created understandings by engaging texts with experimentation and dialogue. Throughout the book we have featured how activities such as fan fiction (see Chapter 5), redefining non-places (Chapter 12), playful unconventional intertextuality (Chapter 7), hybrid identity performances (Chapter 9), and mindful, embodied encounters with technology can break down the authority (and hegemony) of popular culture producers. In the next section, we identify how popular culture artifacts are increasingly supportive of self-reflexive experience with popular culture; but it goes without saying that nothing is ever completely safe from the production forces that will transform something creative and useful into a formula for consumption.

While generally empowering the audience, not all metacommentary deconstructs authority in the spirit of participatory theater. At their worst, metatexts can compel feelings of superiority particularly in hierarchical fan communities (see Chapter 5). Toxic fandom, built on an accumulation of cultural capital, especially an encyclopedic knowledge of franchised universes such as *Star Wars* or Marvel, can embolden trolls (who in our minds always have the voice of the Comic Book Store Guy from *The Simpsons*) to have a smug condescension, especially on social media. This helps explain the incredible hubris of some fans who feel empowered to launch elaborate (and sometimes quite cruel) campaigns against specific actors or directors who they feel, based on their unique expertise, have not been "true" to the "canon" of the franchise (see Chapter 5).

The pleasures of meta stylistic devices have obviously been recognized by Hollywood. If a producer is out of good ideas to extend or reboot a long-running franchise, the mantra seems to be "go meta." As franchises such as *Scream* continue they tend to develop greater and greater meta dimensions. *Nightmare on Elm Street*'s seventh sequel, Wes Craven's *New Nightmare* (1994), featured the actors from the first film playing themselves (not the characters from the film) and Freddy Krueger haunting the dreams of people making movies about him. Frequently, as a franchise becomes more and more meta, it seems to drift further and further from reality and the joys of the original film. By adding layers of commentary and irony, meta orientations can distance the audience from authentic experience, engagement in narrative, and emotional identification with characters and performers. *Everything* starts to feel like either a joke to be ridiculed and or a self-referential text to be researched and critiqued. Eventually, the audience is no longer simply watching a movie with a fun and compelling story or dancing and singing along with a catchy pop song. Sometimes, meta means popular culture turns into homework or something only worthy of criticism and contempt.

So how can we sort out meta popular culture that has potential for more than just keeping us "stuck" to a platform? We return to an idea that has been named often in the preceding chapters, and illustrate how pop culture creators are embedding it in their own work: self-reflexivity.

Toward a self-reflexive metaverse

As people continue to seek and make meaning in popular culture, the complexity of it all only seems to grow. In many respects, nothing is sacred. Memes, TikToks, and YouTube shorts represent political figures (like Hillary Clinton) to undermine not just their authority, but also their humanity. We not only compel audiences to think about a PR machine that fabricates a politician's image, but also to reveal frailty and stupidity. Such metatexts exceed a deconstruction of authority and encourage nihilism. Even revered historical figures, such as Abraham Lincoln, become metatexts treated with an ironic detachment in Mountain Dew or Geico commercials, poking fun at their so-called honesty and integrity (see Figure 13.3). What are the consequences to living in a culture without a meaningful history, when everything is represented as a joke to be derided as pointless? And how can we turn the power of meta popular culture more toward the good?

Across the communication discipline, the concept of **metacommunication,** which simply means communication about communication, is widely embraced as a method of competent practice in a wide range of contexts. For instance, members of small groups can communicate openly about their decision-making norms and goals. Further, in relationships, partners can express their expectations regarding privacy and self-disclosure. In both cases, by making explicit the expectations that are often left unstated, the communication can become much less uncertain and more

Figure 13.3 Abraham Lincoln in Quicken Loans commercial.

closely tied to the needs and goals of all participants. Similarly, we can more overtly define our needs and goals regarding our everyday popular culture practices.

Recall that **self-reflexivity** names the awareness of, and ability to adapt, one's communication to be more in the service of our values, more in the service of meaning-making with others. Importantly, as Calafell (2013) encourages us, reflexivity is more than "skillfully and artfully recreating the details of lived experience and one's space or implication in it" (p. 7). If we are to decenter the practices of domination of which we are all a part, self-reflexivity must necessarily include "intersectional critique, an illumination of power, and acknowledging one's relationality to all of this" (p. 7). Put differently, being mindful isn't enough—we must also locate ourselves in the intersections of social identities, so as not to replicate domination, so as to realize justice. Amid the sea of meta-pop culture, we identify examples of self-reflexive practice which encourage the following moves: Dialoguing together, performing a self-conscious critique of genre and ideology, and heeding one's internal moral compass to hold popular culture accountable.

We suspect nearly all of us have had a beloved popular cultural figure revealed to have behaved in some truly awful ways. Over the years, most of us have danced and sung along to Michael Jackson, Kanye West, and/or R Kelly. We laughed to the jokes Louis CK and Bill Cosby, started our day with Matt Lauer and Charlie Rose, or found ourselves fully absorbed in the films of Woody Allen and Roman Polanski. When heinous behavior is revealed, casual fans are left wondering how to respond. To simply ignore or stop consuming popular culture may erase a celebrity's wrongdoing, pushing it out of one's minds never to be thought of or discussed again. As an alternative, there is popular culture in the metaverse asking us to dialogue together, to grapple self-reflexively with complex ethical questions embedded within these popular culture scandals.

Recent documentary series, such as *We Have to Talk about Cosby*, offer compelling models. In the documentary, writer/director Kamau Bell interviews people ranging from comedians, victims of Cosby's abuse, rape survivor advocates, African-American community leaders, and Cosby's fans to reflect on how to proceed in the wake of the revelations of Cosby's serial sexual abuse. The documentary invites the audience to wrestle with Cosby's work, mutually creating new understandings of not just Cosby's legacy but a wide range of intersecting issues: Should we cancel celebrities who engage in shameful behavior? Can we still enjoy his previous work as an artist? What do we owe the victims? How does our unconditional love of celebrities sometimes enable violent and criminal behavior? Not offering simple answers, the docuseries compels viewers to grapple with these contradictory issues in an intentional and ethical manner.

While certainly engaging, we can understand if a four-hour documentary about a serial rapist is not your preferred genre of entertainment media. As a second suggestion for meta pop culture reflexivity, we consider Jordan Peele's work. Using intertextual reference, mystery, and social satire, filmmaker Jordan Peele invites the audience to engage his films at a meta level considering a number of dimensions outside the boundaries of the movie itself (and instigating innumerable Reddit posts). Making highly entertaining films, Peele playfully provokes the audience with a combination of horror, comedy, and biting cultural criticism. In his breakout hit *Get Out*, he invites diverse interpretations via contradictory performances of political and racial identities such as the well-intentioned White characters inadvertently sounding awkwardly racist ("I would have voted for Obama for a third term if I could"). When Black characters perform an upper-middle-class Whiteness (explained via a wild twist revealed at the end), audiences must confront the inherent intertextual references to Black characters from previous movies and TV shows and consider how the excessive horrific fantasy of the film is actually grounded in a perverse reality. Even more overtly metatextual, in 2022's *Nope* Peele comments on the history of film (and the nature of photography itself), with the characters seeking the "perfect shot" of the alien force in the sky. Why do we feel compelled to photograph things? Why do we invest so much meaning in filmed images? How do photographic images define our reality, especially in regard to our identity? Peele's self-conscious blurring of genre (recalling the cultural hybridization discussed in Chapter 9) undermines the dominant ideas received as an inheritance, inviting us to question ideologies alongside his polysemous artifacts.

A third example of self-reflexivity in the metaverse appears in the TED Talk of feminist writer Roxane Gay. Gay (2015) recalls that she did not embrace the label of "feminist"—not because she did not believe in such feminist principles as equal pay, equal ability to do with one's body what one chooses, and equality for women more generally. Gay and others do not seek to label themselves as feminist because they fear the response that they would get in doing so. Gay describes the 2014 MTV music awards, when Beyoncé performed in front of a large sign that read "FEMINIST." Following Beyoncé's performance, Gay describes, analysts "graded her feminism, instead of simply taking a grown, accomplished woman at her word." Here, we see the use of intersectional reflexivity at work in assessing the public conversation about social identities, and what it means to claim support for women. Gay continues that she, too, is less than perfect. She's a bad feminist because she's "full of contradictions," beginning with her appreciation for "thuggish rap" (namely, Yin Yang Twins' "Salt Shaker").

Refusing to perform cancel culture as a public shaming exercise, Gay describes how she listens to songs like "Salt Shaker," "even though the lyrics are degrading to women" and "offend [her] to [her] core." Gay walks listeners through her journey to "change the channel" (which, as we discussed in Chapter 4, is the original move when cancelling someone), though. Rather than publicly absolving herself of the guilt she feels—in her words, "justify[ing] bad choices"—she recognizes that she is "creating a demand for which artists are more than happy to contribute a limitless supply. These artists are not going to change how they talk about women in their songs until we demand that change by affecting their bottom line." Gay then describes a range of possible ways to reduce the demand for songs that demean women, including making "better choices" of what she listens to, refusing to publish content without a greater diversity of women, and so on. Gay hopes that such "small acts of bravery and hope ... trickle upward to the people in power—editors, movie and music producers, CEOs and lawmakers." We agree with Gay that it's better to be a bad feminist than no feminist at all, and that all of us as participants in popular culture spaces curb our demands for perfectionism—while still calling for accountability. Self-reflexivity as a mindful awareness of one's actions, one's standpoints within social identities (and the power they organize), and an ability to adapt one's behavior are important skills to put to work in navigating popular culture and everyday life.

Conclusion: Self-reflexivity and popular culture in everyday life

In many ways, this entire book has been designed to compel the reader to ask questions about habitual practices of consuming popular culture. We've invited you to consider your favorite artifacts in popular culture (even going so far as to identify yourself as a fan), recognizing that we can fill diverse needs with popular culture—including the need for comfort, familiarity, and, yes, even background noise that helps people to not feel so lonely or on edge. But we've also pointed to the ways that popular culture can serve not only you, individually. Taking yourself as the member of community/ies, we asked you to consider how popular culture serves as equipment for living, providing bits of wisdom or advice to you and your neighbors (and even those who share similar social identities as you do), as you navigate challenging situations. Each chapter closed with questions to get you thinking more about how popular culture serves you and those around you in this way, building from ethical case studies that asked you to consider whether motives to earn greater profit or attention in today's networked economy are worth the choices that creators (and the consumers who access their content) make.

Along the way, we also encouraged greater reflexivity in the form of critical thinking; that is, not accepting "common sense" or popular (widespread, perhaps "trending") wisdom as the final word of truth on a matter. Knowing that each new form of media (and sometimes popular culture) stokes fears in people, we challenged, for instance, whether horror or video gaming or EDM is actually harmful. Further, against the reputation that cancel culture has earned in much of the US, we looked to the history of the term in Black culture, and demonstrated its potential as a self-reflexive practice. Critical thinking refuses to accept received wisdom at face value, which includes the media ecology perspective we've taken throughout the preceding 12 chapters: though people typically want to view new communication technologies as utopian (TikTok is the greatest thing ever!) or dystopian (video games are ruining our society!), the media ecology perspective encourages us instead to see how people make use of technologies to serve their needs and interests. New communication technology is an organic extension of old communication technology. So while it's easy to look at something like a flip phone as "soooo outdated!" or a Walkman and cassette player as fashionably "retro," media ecology asks us to see them instead as the root systems which are part of the same grasses sprouting around us today. Likewise, though sped-up songs on TikTok or airbrushed photos on Instagram feel to old fogeys like us the most recent dystopian future, media ecology suggests that they simply emerge within the affordances available to content creators. Even if they are not serving "us," they are serving someone. But just because they are serving someone does not mean that this service is for the greater good.

How might we sort out the greater good in terms of popular culture usage? Each chapter has given us tools through which we might *talk together* about what it means for popular culture to serve the greater good. Chapter 1 sets forth the premise that popular culture can provide collectives equipment for living, while dispelling techno-utopian and dystopian ideologies with a media ecology framework. Chapters 2, 3, and 9, together, provide a multifaceted view on the business of popular culture, begging us to consider whether it's worth meeting individual *desires* (which sometimes masquerade as needs) through the "stickiness" of contemporary convergence logics, and all the overconsumption and waste that the global system normalizes. Together, Chapters 4, 5, and 11 demonstrate the potential for communities: whether communities share social identity intersections in common, share interpretive frameworks and interpretations in common, or play together (or all of the above!), communities push content creation with more than their purchasing power. Chapters 8, 10, and 12 call attention to those parts of our humanity and environment which have the potential to push (or, perhaps ground) experience beyond language, or at least beyond the spectacular realities that large corporations want to sell us: the spaces we circulate within, and the senses and embodiments we experience, may allow us to question, and then, to create worlds that do not replicate domination. Chapters 6, 7, and this chapter's discussion of "meta" help readers unpack the potential for language and symbolic meaning-making to call attention to the human act of meaning-making itself, which punctures the illusion that reality must be seamlessly consumed as it was given. Modeling self-reflexivity in our talk about popular culture (as Roxane Gay does in her TED Talk), turning to artifacts that perform a self-conscious critique of ideology (as in Jordan Peele's work), and locating (perhaps even screening together) artifacts that convene a dialogue on difficult subjects (as in *We Have to Talk about Cosby*) are three meta moves that position popular culture users as more than simply consumers.

In closing, we hope you've enjoyed this exploration of popular culture as a kind of "goldilocks" zone between "highbrow" art designed for consumption by wealthy and powerful people, and folk traditions, which were (and still are) designed to be experienced by smaller groups of people who share a geography and/or social identity. Popular culture as uniquely populist is more than mere entertainment, and more than simply a way to make money—though each of these qualities matter to how we navigate its ubiquitous, consequential presence in our daily lives. The complexity of popular culture, like the sheer amount of choices available to most consumers, can be paralyzing. But we believe media ecology, equipment for living, and self-reflexivity, along with the unique approaches from each chapter, give readers the tools they need to make their way toward a more just today and tomorrow.

Reflecting on going meta with pop culture in your everyday life

- Do you enjoy "meta" pop culture? What artifacts in particular, and what do you enjoy about them?
- Have you ever had the experience of "not getting" a metatext, like a parody or satire? What was that like? Given the potential for people to not get parody or satire, what does that say about the use of these tools to critique ideology?
- This chapter identifies three "meta" moves of self-reflexivity: convening a dialogue about difficult subjects in popular culture (like *We Have to Talk about Cosby*), self-consciously critiquing genre and ideology (like Jordan Peele), or modelling self-reflexive talk

in our talk about pop culture (like Roxane Gay). Locate other examples that perform these moves. How have these examples inspired you?

- In this book, you've read about several exigencies (or problems marked by a sense of urgency) in which popular culture plays a part. Environmental exigencies, like e-waste (Chapter 9), plastics pollution, and the climate crisis, relate to the business of pop culture as a system which seems to demand ever-newer and ever-more-spectacular equipment with which to deliver ever-more-sensational and ever-more-engaging content. As elaborated in Chapter 4, popular culture also joins practices that exclude (and perhaps even oppress) people on the basis of social identities. The "alternative facts" and conspiracy that some "pop political" figures peddle helps sustain an alternative reality (Chapter 10), threatens to erode not only the pocketbooks of people who consume it—but, arguably, the ability of democratic politics to function. Locate one piece of popular culture that responds to these exigencies and discuss it together with your class or/and family. What does this piece of pop culture do well to promote justice and an ethical social life? What could it do better?

Suggested readings

Herbig, A., Herrmann, A. F., Watson, A., Tyma, A. W., & miller, j. (2020). Critical rhetoric and collaboration: Missing principle #9 and ProfsDoPop.com. *International Journal of Communication, 14*, 885–898.

References

Ben P. (2009, April 27). Conservatives think Colbert is serious. *Mother Jones*. https://www.motherjones.com/politics/2009/04/conservatives-think-colbert-serious/

Boal, A. (1985). *Theatre of the oppressed* (C. A. & M. L. McBride, Trans.). Theatre Communications Group.

Calafell, B. M. (2013). (I)dentities: Considering accountability, reflexivity, and intersectionality in the I and the we. *Liminalities: A Journal of Performance Studies, 9*(2), 6–13. http://liminalities.net/9-2/calafell.pdf

Dunne, M. (1992). *Metapop: Self-referentiality in contemporary American popular culture*. University Press of Mississippi.

Fiske, J. (1986) Television: Polysemy and popularity. *Critical Studies in Mass Communication, 3*(4), 391–408, DOI: 10.1080/15295038609366672

Gay, R. (2015). Confessions of a bad feminist. TED Talks. https://www.ted.com/talks/roxane_gay_confessions_of_a_bad_feminist?language=en

Harms, J. & Dickens, D. (1996). Postmodern media studies: Analysis or symptom? *Critical Studies in Mass Communication, 13*(3), 210–227, DOI: 10.1080/ 15295039609366976

LaRocca, D. (2021). *Metacinema: The form and content of filmic reference and reflexivity*. Oxford University Press.

Samuel, S. (2018, May 31). Atheists are sometimes more religious than Christians. *The Atlantic*. https://www.theatlantic.com/international/archive/2018/05/ american-atheists-religious-european-christians/560936/

Index

Note: Page numbers followed by "n" refer to end notes.